The Angel's Cry

MICHEL POIZAT

The Angel's Cry

Ɑ

BEYOND THE
PLEASURE PRINCIPLE
IN OPERA

TRANSLATED BY

ARTHUR DENNER

Cornell University Press

ITHACA AND LONDON

TRANSLATION OF THIS BOOK WAS ASSISTED BY A
GRANT FROM THE FRENCH MINISTRY OF CULTURE.

Published in France as *L'Opéra, ou Le Cri de l'ange: Essai sur la jouissance de l'amateur d'opéra* by Éditions A. M. Métailié. Copyright © 1986 by Éditions A. M. Métailié, Paris.

First published 1992 by Cornell University Press.

International Standard Book Number 0–8014–2388–0 (cloth)
Library of Congress Catalog Card Number 91–55532
Printed in the United States of America
Librarians: Library of Congress cataloging information appears on the last page of the book.

⊗ The paper in this book meets the minimum requirements of the American National Standard for Information Sciences—Permanence of Paper for Printed Library Materials, ANSI Z39.48–1984.

For Rithée Cevasco
and for Alain Didier-Weill

Opera, above all, has been chosen for the task of serving the human voice and promoting its rights.

—Alban Berg, "Voice in Opera"

Denn das Schöne ist nichts als des Schrecklichen Anfang. . . .
Ein Jeder Engel ist schrecklich.

For beauty is nothing but the beginning of terror. . . .
Every angel is terrible.

—Rainer Maria Rilke, *First Duino Elegy*

Contents

Preface

This work approaches opera in much the same way we sometimes approach dreams, the kind of dreams that leave us with a persistent and enigmatic emotion and that demand to have their hidden sources deciphered. Those powerful and rare moments that every devotee of opera has nonetheless experienced will be our point of departure as we venture into the unconscious complexities of that lyric ecstasy which opera lovers so ardently seek.

For some time now, since the "rebirth" of lyric art in France, opera has been subjected to a constant and sometimes truly inquisitorial examination. That is the function of certain stagings, of every kind of analysis of this question, whether the perspective taken is historical, aesthetic, sociological, whatever. This investigation is often fruitful, because when called upon in this way, opera does speak to us—about the society that saw its birth, its development, and, some will say, its death. Opera also speaks to us of its authors, those who participated in its construction, of the ideologies they advanced or resisted, and of the griefs and joys of their lives. Yet there is another, more basic question that opera is hardly ever asked: "Opera, what desire brought you forth into the world?" What, indeed, could create the desire to engender that strange monster which issues from the sometimes acrobatic couplings of music and words?

As we try to answer this question, borrowing from the methods of psychoanalysis, it will become evident that beyond the iridescent effects—whether superficial or more profound—left by sociohistorical, ideological, or psychological contingencies, opera gives voice to a certain truth: human beings can suffer from their status as speaking subjects, and they can find an ecstatic pleasure in seeking to forget or deny their fundamental attachment to language.

Claude Lévi-Strauss writes in *The Naked Man:*

Music no doubt also speaks; but this can only be because of its negative relationship to language, and because, in separating off from language, music has retained the negative imprint of its formal structure and semiotic function: there would be no music if language had not preceded it and if music did not continue to depend on it, as it were, through a privative connection. Music is language without meaning: this being so, it is understandable that the listener, who is first and foremost a subject with the gift of speech, should feel himself irresistibly compelled to make up for the absent sense, just as someone who has lost a limb imagines that he still possesses it through the sensations present in the stump.[1]

Is it perhaps this primordial act of separation that opera speaks of, letting us know that it is paid for with suffering? And is it perhaps in the nostalgia for a paradisiacal unity of preseparation that the opera lover's ecstasy resides?

This book focuses on the voice in opera, for I believe that the answer to the question lies there. Accordingly, the other frequently analyzed aspects of opera—story, libretti, critical commentary—will enter into the discussion only to the extent that, like a slip of the tongue, a figure of speech, a dream image, they can reveal something about the stakes that underlie them. In this respect, the thoughts of an eminent commentator may find themselves considered alongside an advertising slogan, the observations of an interviewed fan, or the words of a libretto or of an ancient or modern myth. The psychoanalyst is more familiar with this kind of approach than the reader schooled in the hierarchical values and categories of academe, so I have thought it wise to forewarn the reader as to how I will proceed.

If there is a preferred reader to whom this book is addressed, it is the avid and informed opera fan. If the reader is also a psychoanalyst, he or she will, I hope, will recognize the offspring of the discipline behind the arrangement of some of my remarks, in spite of my limited use of psychoanalytic jargon. Should the reader be an academic, I ask indulgence for my occasionally casual usage of certain concepts that elsewhere have been defined with great precision, especially in the field of

[1]Claude Lévi-Strauss, *The Naked Man*, trans. John Weightman and Doreen Weightman (London: Jonathan Cape, 1981), 647.

linguistic theory. I have, for example, used as rough equivalents such terms as "speech," "word," "signifier," and "language," without dwelling on the important theoretical problems that differentiate them. This work is not an academic treatise. It is simply an arrangement of material, an indication of a possible course through a labyrinthine and luxuriant cultural edifice, an initial encounter with a group of problems, each of which may call for a deeper, more detailed, and more thoroughgoing study.

And as for the opera lovers who may read this book and are neither psychoanalysts nor academics, it is my hope that in the pages that follow they will hear an account and a few elements of analysis that will echo their own experience and their own questions about the delights or disappointments they encounter, the emotions they feel—in short, the passion they have for opera.

MICHEL POIZAT

Paris

Translator's Note

Several terms used in this translation may require some explanation. The first is *jouissance,* a word that may be unfamiliar to readers not acquainted with the work of the French psychoanalyst Jacques Lacan. Alan Sheridan writes in his Translator's Note to Lacan's *Écrits: A Selection* (New York: Norton, 1982):

There is no adequate translation in English of this word. "Enjoyment" conveys the sense, contained in *jouissance,* of enjoyment of rights, of property, etc. Unfortunately, in modern English, the word has lost the sexual connotations it still retains in French. (*Jouir* is slang for "to come.") "Pleasure," on the other hand, is pre-empted by *"plaisir"*—and Lacan uses the two terms quite differently. "Pleasure" obeys the law of homeostasis that Freud evokes in "Beyond the Pleasure Principle," whereby, through discharge, the psyche seeks the lowest possible level of tension. "Jouissance" transgresses this law, and in that respect, it is *beyond* the pleasure principle.

Occasionally I translate *jouissance* as "bliss" or "ecstasy," but because neither of these terms quite conveys the literal and metaphorical senses of orgasmic experience expressed by the term, or its transgressive aspects, usually it remains untranslated in this work.

Three other terms that deserve comment are "trans-sexual," "trans-verbal," and "trans-sensical," for the French *hors-sexe, hors-parole,* and *hors-sens,* respectively. Lacan uses them also. They can be glossed not as "asexual," "nonverbal," and "nonsensical," but rather as "beyond-sex," "beyond-speech," "beyond-sense." "Trans-sexual," "trans-verbal," and "trans-sensical" thus refer to what stands at the peripheries or in the margins of sexual difference, of words, and of meaning. The terms are hyphenated both to signal an unhabitual usage, in the case of "trans-sexual," and to emphasize the relation of tension between these categories and those to which they stand in opposition and which they in some sense exceed.

A. D.

PART ONE

"THE PURE FEELING"

Pleasure and Jouissance

Several years ago French television stations and movie houses carried a commercial that many people may still recall: an opening shot of the Avenue de l'Opéra, which then continues up the avenue and into the Palais Garnier, at that time still the home of the Paris Opéra. The camera ascends the grand staircase and cuts to a marble bust of Puccini while offscreen a diva begins to sing. Under the sway of this voice, a tear wells up in the composer's stony eye and rolls down the petrified cheek; he seems to be waking from the sleep of the dead. Displayed across the screen are the name and slogan of the brand of magnetic recording media whose quality is touted: "BASF . . . l'émotion intacte." The pure feeling.

This commercial points to the outburst of tears as the signal of the elation felt by the fan, listener, and spectator of opera in those rare and fleeting moments when the music lover is irresistibly captivated—ravished, in the root sense of the word—by a soaring voice that drives everything else away, even himself, until he becomes oblivious of the discomfort of his seat and of his end-of-the-day fatigue, until he no longer sees what is often the ugliness of the sets and the costumes or, frequently, the discrepancy between the singers' physical appearance and their roles, until ultimately he literally ceases to hear the equally frequent poverty of the libretto.

What escapes this commercial, however, what it cannot capture visually, is another signal, one that every opera lover knows: the thrill or shiver that courses through the body in those supreme moments of musical ecstasy.

Tears . . . shivers . . . Tears of joy? Is that what they are? These moments are not exactly moments of jubilation, or are so only very rarely; rather they are moments of physical thrill, of stupefaction, as the listener seems on the verge of disappearing, of losing himself, of dissolving in this voice, just as the singer on the stage seems on the verge of disappearing as a human subject to become sheer voice, sheer vocal object, all for the gratification of the fan. Are those tears, then, tears of joy, or tears that trace the painful loss, the enigmatic and unconscious grief that such moments evoke?

And those shivers: people call them shivers of pleasure. Perhaps they are. But the shivers are also the visceral expression of a feeling of dread. And is there really a fundamental difference between the thrill that comes at the climax of the love duet in Act II of *Tristan und Isolde* and the shudders of dread—experienced explicitly as such when Lulu screams her death cry under Jack the Ripper's knife—that unfailingly overcome us no matter how familiar we are with this work, no matter how prepared we may be for that rending cry?

Tears, shivers . . . Can this be what we call musical pleasure? A strange pleasure indeed that admits of all the affective signs of a bereavement and actual physical suffering, too, as the listener "chokes up" in the painful attempt to contain the surge of emotion, insofar as our cultures do insist upon the repression of tears. And though the observation that follows will take on its full resonance only as this study progresses, I should point out another aspect of these tears: men succumb to them as often as women do. Dare I say: even more? In any case, the fact remains that opera presents one of those rare situations in which our sociocultural prejudices not only allow a man to shed tears but even sanction his gratitude to the singer and the composer for having provoked a reaction that in any other circumstance might be taken for a sign of weakness, a lack of virility to be overcome or hidden at all costs. Of course, the sense of decorum ultimately prevails and tears are discreetly blotted away in the darkness of the hall before the spectator departs. Yet no man would feel ashamed of his tears or dream of ridiculing or looking down on another man so moved during the "Porgi amor" of the Countess in *Le Nozze di Figaro* or at the Transfiguration of Isolde. On the contrary, he is credited with great sensitivity and in some quarters even esteemed for expressing what is generally considered a specifically feminine quality. The rarity of this situation is enough to call our attention to it and to signal the need for some interpretation.

Musical pleasure is thus a strange pleasure indeed, and if in this study I come to speak of elation, ecstasy, or gratification—of jouissance—it is insofar as this jouissance is distinct from mere pleasure.

The distinction between pleasure and jouissance had been pointed out quite clearly in the context of opera long before psychoanalysis began formally to differentiate them: a number of passionate, often convulsive debates that have shaken the history of opera took shape around this division. The discussions that set French cultural circles astir in 1774 on the occasion of the production of Gluck's *Orfeo ed Eurydice* illustrate that distinction. Here I will draw on material from an article by François Azouri in the issue of *L'Avant-scène Opéra* devoted to that opera.[2]

This debate was marked by a rare intensity, as Marie Antoinette reports in a letter to her sister Marie Christine dated 26 April 1774: "They can speak of nothing else, every head is filled with the most extraordinary excitement you can imagine, it is incredible: the divisions, the attacks, you would think it was a religious matter." And in fact, it was a matter of religion, or in any case of morals, insofar as religion and morality have to do with the regulation of jouissance. But what was really at stake in these discussions, in these divisions? After attending a performance of *Orfeo,* Julie de Lespinasse writes: "I could listen to that aria ten times a day; it tears me apart, sends me into an ecstasy of sorrow.[3] I have lost my Eurydice. . . . That music drives me mad: it sweeps me away, my soul craves this kind of pain." It is all there in this sentence, everything properly in place: the feeling of madness, of captivation, of rapture ("it sweeps me away"), an ecstatic gratification in the lost object, the feeling of its recovery, but never without the pain of remembering its loss, never without the desire for this pain. In his *Mémoires pour servir l'histoire de la Révolution opérée dans la musique par M. le Chevalier Gluck,* G. M. Leblond writes: "The new spectacle had an extraordinary effect. We saw for the first time a tragedy in music listened to from beginning to end with uninterrupted attention and ever-growing interest, provoking tears even in the wings and cries of admiration from the entire hall." That is what Gluck's partisans had to say. Yet as Azouri notes, another wave of opinion quite violently rejected these effects, even as it acknowledged the quality of the work. The fundamental theme running through the discourse of those of this

---

[2]François Azouri, "Le Plaisir d'une révolution," *L'Avant-scène Opéra* 23: "Orphée et Euridice" (September–October 1979), 59.

[3]She had just lost her lover.

latter opinion is that "they find no *musical pleasure*"[4] in these experiences of emotional upheaval. *Cries* and convulsions, they maintain, cannot be called pleasure. So it is that the *académicien* Marmontel, one of Gluck's principal adversaries, asks, "What kind of pleasure is it that these wrenching emotions provide?" while La Harpe, another of Gluck's opponents in the Académie, denounces the composer's *Alceste* for "its monotonous and tiresome screaming." Gluck counters with irony: perhaps he should modify the score, he says, so as to make his music "regular, repetitive, enchanting, and so tender that the most vaporish little missus might hear it without the slightest nervous irritation."[5]

At the heart of this whole quarrel lies an opposition between a pleasure whose watchword is moderation, "characterized by a *limit* to the intensity of the artistic effect on its audience," and a musical emotion more in line with the aesthetics of Diderot and the Encyclopedists, an emotion that, like "a kind of seizure," in the medical sense, operates by means of the very paroxysm it reaches: this, according to Sulzer, author of the article "Aria" in the *Encyclopédie,* is the function of the aria in opera: "to alleviate the passions by giving them free rein at the moment when they reach their greatest intensity."

Thus we find two camps: one of them—a camp that has much in common with what the Querelle des Bouffons some twenty years earlier had dubbed "the King's Corner"—comprises those who espouse a limited pleasure ruled by moderation, a pleasure provided by the kind of music that Gluck, a detractor, characterized by its "regular and repetitive" form. These traits correspond (in my interpretation) to the mastery of music by speech in opera—that is, to the recitative, especially the French style of recitative, such as that developed by Rameau. In the other camp are those who accept and propound the sensory upset and emotional turmoil proffered by a music that its opponents liken systematically to the cry, to *la criaillerie* or screaming, to a tearing apart, while its defenders identify it in the aria as the privileged source of the sought-after emotion. Contemporary debates formulated this opposition in terms of philosophical, ethical, and political disputes of even longer standing. At issue ultimately are two fundamentally opposed conceptions of the social function of art.

[4]My emphasis here, and elsewhere in this work unless I indicate otherwise.
[5]Azouri, "Le Plaisir d'une révolution," 59.

One of these conceptions holds that art ultimately performs a function of social integration, or at least works to maintain a given social or psychological order. This notion of pleasure describes, in Azouri's words, "a moderate agitation, such that a given state is left unchanged: closer to rest than to movement, it approaches the Aristotelian definition." We are reminded of the modern idea of homeostasis, which sees pleasure as a sign of return to equilibrium in an organism previously destabilized by stress or tension. The other conception, by contrast, takes a more revolutionary position: it proposes that "emotive upheaval, in changing the disposition of all the parts of an organism, reveals the real position of each part and the true order of the whole. A disturbed organism is the thoroughgoing reply of a regenerated society."[6]

However passionate the philosophical aspects of this question, it seems that as far as this rift between pleasure and jouissance is concerned, the crux of the matter in fact lies elsewhere: at the very heart of the whole operatic institution, at the basis of the very instinct that drives human beings to want to "speak in song" and that in so doing leads us to seek gratification in that strange monster born of the tortured and torturous union of words and music that is opera.

While the term "rift" aptly describes the antagonism between the two positions I have just outlined, it is in fact less than helpful here in that it introduces the false notion of a twofold process or of a clear separation between two levels of a single process. It would be more accurate to speak of *tension,* a tension between, on the one hand, the pursuit of gratification in an object that lies beyond a limit of absolute transgression and, on the other hand, a mastery of this pursuit, a control that would impose its rule on the "vector" so as to keep it from exceeding the limit. A matter of degree, then, this tension would define, at its most stable or regular extreme, what the eighteenth century called pleasure; and at the other extreme, the point of greatest tension, closest to transgression, what can be defined only as the asymptotic term in a quest for the impossible, for pure and complete gratification, or, quite simply, for jouissance. This quest must indeed be impossible: how else could an institution so prodigious and costly as opera have lasted for centuries? How else to explain the endless peregrinations of those countless devotees one encounters again and again

[6]Ibid.

in London, Bayreuth, Milan, or Paris, in quest of this or that work, of this or that singer who has such absolute power over them that she is called diva? For those who have heard the call, it is indeed a matter of a Quest, with all that this implies in the way of constant itinerancy, ordeal, privation, and suffering. The following section will give us some idea of these ordeals.

On the Steps of the Palais Garnier: The Quest and Its Ordeals

The fundamental ordeal, repeated over and over again, has to do with securing a seat. Like any ordeal, this one requires both inspiration and perspiration, savvy as well as endurance. As the demand for seats has grown over the years, a system has been put in place at the Paris Opéra to administrate and apportion the unavoidable suffering that comes with this ordeal. This system is surely unparalleled in France in that it functions entirely by the consensus of its participants and excludes all recourse to any outside authority that might lend it legitimacy. The system is not officially recognized by the Opéra box office, and it is out of the question to seek its intervention in disputes over who has which place in the final queue when the box-office window opens. And yet, surprisingly enough, this system actually works; not flawlessly, of course, but still, it works.

For a closer look at how a consensual operation so foreign to the more traditional push-and-shove mentality of the French might function, let us go to the steps of the Palais Garnier on the night of 25 January 1985, on the eve of the premiere of Wagner's *Tristan und Isolde*, conducted by Marek Janowski, directed by Michael Hampe.

It is midnight. The spectators coming from the dress rehearsal have now gone their separate ways. But a small group remains, standing about on the steps. A final discussion of production details? Someone approaches the group, asks a question, receives a numbered ticket from a booklet complete with counterfoils, and joins the others. And so forms the nucleus around which, throughout the night and until 1:30 the following afternoon, when the box office opens, gather those who are ready to spend thirteen and a half hours outdoors on the steps of the opera house, in good weather or bad, to obtain two seats that fold out from the wall behind the upper-tier boxes for a performance of *Tristan.* They are relatively inexpensive seats, to be sure (around $10 in 1985), and will oblige their occupants to stand for the duration of the performance if they want to see the entire stage. For thirteen hours they will wait, pausing in their vigil only long enough for a few cups of coffee and breakfast at daybreak when the cafés around the Opéra finally open.

Not all productions make such exacting demands, of course, but when it is Wagner, and *Tristan,* and singers who warrant great expectations, this level of commitment is indispensable for those who, unable to obtain seats through "normal" channels (subscription, mail order, group reservations) but unwilling to miss the show, find themselves waiting in a queue at the box-office window for the rather small quota of seats that are set aside for this purpose.[7]

I spoke earlier of the need for a certain know-how. To calculate the best time to arrive at the box office so as to maximize the probability of getting good seats while keeping to a minimum one's time in the queue is hardly a simple matter. One has to be able to anticipate the behavior of others in the same situation, which calls not only for a fine sense of the quality of the work, the singers, the conductor, the director, but for an equally sophisticated skill at assessing the current status of their reputations—which is not necessarily the same thing, for here as in other domains, fashion wields enormous influence. All this presupposes a certain expertise, as evidenced by the degree of specificity that is the rule in conversations that spring up during the long wait: a certain performance by such-and-such singer on such-and-such stage on a particular day is praised; another performance by the same or another singer on such-and-such other occasion is deprecated. Indeed, these vigils play an impressive role in the establishment and continual readjustment of value in lyric art.

Still, what is indispensable to such ordeals is suffering, and if tickets are distributed to register order of arrival, the intent is not to let anyone avoid the pain. These tallies do, of course, reduce the requisite suffering by making it unnecessary actually to queue up upon arrival

---

[7]Two weeks before the performance a certain number of tickets go on sale at the Opéra box office. For these sales the windows open at 11:00 A.M. But the day before the performance (two days before for Monday performances), the *fond de loges* (views at an angle) are sold. In these cases, the ticket windows open at 1:30 P.M. It is this latter situation that I am considering here.

and then remain in line, just as they help prevent (but never altogether eliminate) the shoving match or even the occasional brawl when the box office opens. But do not imagine for a minute that one may take a number, go home for a good night's sleep, and then innocently show up in the morning to claim a place in line. As the vigil continues into the night, the roll is called repeatedly. Absent numbers are noted, and during the final roll call, when the actual queue is physically con-stituted in numerical order, it is up to those who were present at every roll call to decide whether or not the others, those who hold numbers that have been marked absent, may reclaim their places. What is most remarkable about this system is that it is entirely self-managed: the first to arrive know who they are. Without prior arrangements, they take it entirely upon themselves to provide a book of tickets: there is always at least one person among the first arrivals who has one. By sheer consensus, this initial nucleus appoints someone to hand out the tick-ets, provides for this person's relief, organizes the roll calls, and decides who shall conduct them. It should come as no surprise if the manage-ment of this burdensome vigil can take a variety of forms, especially where the roll call is concerned. It can be good-natured—scheduled and announced in advance so that the word can get out to the neigh-boring cafés to avoid penalizing those who are simply taking a break over a cup of coffee and a roll. Sometimes, though, a genuinely re-pressive attitude prevails, with surprise roll calls and pitiless expulsion of numbers that fail to report at muster. Such attitudinal differences are determined for the most part by the "characterological" makeup of the initial core group—of those, in other words, who are most heavily invested in the suffering. Naturally, the great temptation in such cases is to seek to exact a similar investment from everyone else. Yet beyond the inherent diversity among those familiar with the rules of the game and who agree to play by them, what is truly remarkable is the total solidarity displayed in the face of those who are unfamiliar with the system, especially those who argue its unofficial nature in an attempt to slip into the final queue and disregard the assigned numer-ical order. When this happens, the ensuing tension can turn into vio-lence, and it is not rare for the fire or police department to have to intervene. But when the box office finally opens, all thoughts of chiv-alry, courtesy, or special consideration fall by the wayside (all caution to senior citizens and pregnant women: this is not for you!). The density of the queue is absolute: no breach here in which those who have failed to submit to the ordeal might insinuate themselves. Then the goal is finally at hand when it comes time to step up to the window. Pulses quicken and chests tighten in anxiety: a rapid decision must be made in selecting from among the various seats that remain. The mood is feverish, given the agitation all around. But once the tickets are in hand, the satisfaction is immense—though not without an inevitable twinge of sadness, since the attainment of a goal always destroys the pleasure of expectation.

Once back on the steps of the Palais, however, all is forgotten: those who have bonded in groups over the course of long hours part without saying good-bye. At most, come performance night, a discreet nod of greeting will recall a now dissipated sense of having once "belonged": the bonds created that night are lost until, perhaps, the time comes for another such ordeal.

Something important must be at stake to support a system so foreign to French mores, to motivate so intense a personal effort, so collective an investment. The institution of opera is itself socialized in the extreme—once an affair of princes, it has become an affair of state. The collectivity, in its ultimate avatar, the state, helps uphold the rather monstrous cultural edifice of opera, but at arm's length. It agrees to sink enormous sums of money into opera, channeling the collective contribution of its citizens into subsidizing the jouissance of the select few. Such extensive investment in the useless—according to traditional socioeconomic standards of utility, at least—is, moreover, a clear indication that a powerful jouissance machine is at work (in Lacan's words, "Jouissance is that which is useless").[8] Symptomatic in this regard is the fact that the current period of economic crisis has seen the undertaking of one of France's grandest cultural projects—the construction of an opera house, the Opéra Populaire de la Bastille.

But before I undertake to analyze the deep motivational underpinnings, the gears and springs of this machine, the following exchange, recorded one January night among Anne, Étienne, Renaud, Claude, Guy, and the author, will, better than any abstract description, give the reader a vivid idea of what constitutes the day-to-day reality of the opera fan, who "one day discovered opera, and then discovered that I could not live without it."

---

[8]Jacques Lacan, *Le Séminaire, Livre XX: Encore* (Paris: Seuil, 1975), 10.

Conversation on the Palais Steps

The following group interview, transcribed virtually in extenso, makes no claim whatever to statistical value but is offered as an accurate representation of the motivations and attitudes of passionate opera fans. The group represents a certain social and professional homogeneity—unmarried, twenty to thirty-five years old, teachers, from modest or middle-class backgrounds—but this should not be taken to suggest that the teaching profession furnishes the body of troops who throng the box-office windows for opera tickets. Still, certain professions, by virtue of their irregular schedules and their focuses of interest, are more likely than others to sanction the sacrifice of an entire night and the following morning to the quest for a seat at the opera.

The bonds that form the group assembled on this particular night are in fact those of an initiatory chain: Guy, a teacher of French at a lycée and the Grand Initiator, initiated Claude, a student of art history, who in turn initiated Renaud. Guy has initiated Anne, too, a German teacher, and she in turn initiated Étienne, who teaches mathematics. Anne is the only woman in the group. For her this vigil is a baptism of fire, the first time she will spend the night on these steps for an opera ticket. It is the first time, too, for twenty-one-year-old Renaud.

Renaud: "Yes . . . I'm a teacher too, but I teach judo. I'm also a student, in physical education. My income is a government scholarship and the money I make giving judo lessons. I spend too much on opera. I buy what I consider—and my parents think so, too—too many records. They get after me about that at home. And it seems I bother the entire building in the complex where I live. This is the first time I've come to queue up for a ticket. Usually Claude gets it for me, but since I was free tonight, I came.

Étienne: For me it's the second time here this year. Last year I must have done this four, maybe five times.

Claude: This isn't my first time, and it certainly won't be my last.

M.P.:   How many times a year, roughly?

Claude: Well, it varies considerably, depending on what interests me. Last year the opera season was fairly unremarkable, and the year before it was worse. I only queue up for tickets when it's worth it.

M.P.:   And what makes it worth it for you—the composer, the performers . . . ?

Claude: A combination of factors. Tonight, for example, I've come primarily for Janowski, because when it comes to stage direction, I can't tell before I've seen it. . . . I decided to queue up tonight because I heard the *Walküre* that Janowski conducted at the Châtelet. I knew he conducted Wagner well, and I was interested in seeing his approach to *Tristan.* I absolutely did not want to miss it.

When *Tosca* was here, I came more for Behrens than for Pavarotti. I had to see her at all costs. So each time, it's one or a number of factors that bring me here. The ideal would be to come for all factors taken together. . . . As far as my financial investment is concerned, I'm very demanding about the quality of what I want to hear, so I won't listen to opera under what I consider unacceptable conditions. Therefore I try to set aside a considerable part of my budget exclusively, if possible, to buy audio equipment sophisticated enough to suit my ear. Which means that to buy a tape player, I'll have to save up for several months. But at this level, money isn't what's important. It loses its . . . it has no more value at this point.

Guy: With me, my income is inversely proportional to the extent to which it's eaten away by opera! What with festivals, performances, and recordings, I spend on average, say . . . 800 francs a month on opera, if I include my vacation expenses.

I come to stand in line for tickets much less than I used to before 1980. At that time, I was doing this about twice a week. Since 1980, I do it no more than about once a month . . . if that. This year I've come three times, four maybe, if you count *Tosca.* Otherwise, I try to get seats at the last minute. I still try to see each performance at least once or twice, but there are things I only see once and even some I miss altogether. Whereas five or six years ago I'd see every performance of a single production. Now, I'd say I make—if "make" is the right word—two or three, when the production is good. But inevitably I've become harder to please and much less . . . convinced by what I see nowadays in comparison with what I've seen in the past.

M.P.: And how long have you had such a passion for opera?

Guy: Since April '73, the Paris Opéra reopened under Liebermann in April '73; that's why I can date it precisely.

M.P.: Can you say how you came to have this interest, this passion for opera?

Étienne: I remember, I must have been twelve or thirteen. My father took me to see *Aïda.* It made quite an impression on me. But for a time afterward, until three years ago, I lost interest. The spark was the television broadcast of the Boulez-Chéreau *Ring*. That's what started it all.

Renaud: For me, *Faust* and *Carmen* were my lullabies for a long, long time. They were my medicine. And then, stupidly, I became disgusted with opera after my parents took me to see one. I was twelve or thirteen years old. It was *La Bohème,* and I was so bored that I amused myself by pulling out the tacks from the seats! It was horrible, horrible. I was really bored! When I was twelve or thirteen, music, as far as I was concerned, had to really move, and I completely neglected opera. Opera no longer existed, except when my father or my mother would put on a record, which I would quickly take off the turntable and replace with something loud. And then not long ago, when I got to know Claude, he invited me over to Guy's one day and he played a record. And so I said to myself, "Renaud, you're stupid, you have to stop listening to that shit, and now you're going to devote yourself just to this, because this is nice."

M.P.:   Which record was it?

Renaud: I don't remember. I didn't even pay attention, I'm just a beginner and I don't really know the names. Then I began to buy records, records, and more records. It's terrible—worse than drugs. I've listened to all of them two or three times at least—every one I own. I have about thirty or thirty-five boxed sets. That's not a great deal but . . . in three months . . . I think that's too many. Yes, too many. And then you need to constantly renew your supply of music. . . . That's how it happened to me.

M.P.:   Is your collection very diverse or does it center on a single composer?

Renaud: Since my mother listened mostly to French operas, that's what I bought at first, operas by French composers. And then, very gradually, I began to discover Mozart and then Verdi, all the Italian composers and then, finally, Wagner. I flipped over Wagner. He really blows me away.

On the other hand, I've been . . . well, disappointed by the operas I've seen here at the Palais Garnier. I still prefer recordings to live performances. I've yet to see a performance I really like, one that really moves me. Well, maybe . . . the last *Tosca. Tosca* . . . was nice.

Claude: Ah, good! I was going to strangle you!

Renaud: *Tosca,* yes. *Tosca* was nice, but I still thought it lacked that little something that makes you explode with applause . . . or at least inside. No, for the time being, I still prefer records.

Anne: Some people are very hard to please!

Renaud: Right. (*turning to Claude*) It's his fault!

Claude: My fault! I didn't do anything.

Renaud: Sure you did.

Guy: That's strange, now everyone is feeling guilty all of a sudden.

Anne: What did he do? What is he guilty of?

M.P.: Is there always an initiator?

Anne: I must have slipped through the net. I discovered *Tristan und Isolde* in a civilization course that dealt with Wagner. I bought a recording of *Tristan,* which I loved, and that same year I went to see *Parsifal* at the Opéra . . . I don't remember when it was. You can tell who isn't a true fan! Vickers and Nadine Denize sang.

Guy: Seventy-six.

Anne: It was in '76, that's right. An opera fan had taken me, so . . .

Guy: May 1976!

Anne: I remember that night: my friend made me study all the leitmotifs thoroughly beforehand, and then I remember the very particular atmosphere . . . and above all, the quality of the applause. That's what really struck me. It wasn't at all snobbish applause—it was really delirious, it shook the floorboards! No? Don't you agree?

Guy: Oh, I do.

M.P.: In your opinion, is the passion for opera more masculine than feminine?

Anne: No, I don't think so. I have two examples that occurred to me this afternoon. I remember hearing a few years ago about a girl, a single woman . . . I was going to say embittered. In other words, someone who would fit the description of old maid, and what people said about her, what they considered quite remarkable was the fact that she regularly attended all the operas: she would travel to Milan. . . . That really struck me in someone who on the surface was almost . . .

Claude: Normal!?

Anne: No! Muffled, very reserved. In the teachers' lounge—she was a teacher, too—she never opened her mouth. We never heard her say a thing, and we knew she was always on her way to the opera. This afternoon, I was also thinking about B., who fits exactly the same description . . . impenetrable existences . . . that you have to fill in for yourself . . . and completely invested in opera. The striking thing about B. is that when she goes to the opera she spends entire nights talking to people, whereas . . .

Claude: . . . elsewhere she is rather introverted.

Anne: Yes. . . . What she visibly lacks. . . is contact. She also told me once that opera had helped her through her family problems. She said to me: "That's how I was able to . . ." I think she said "save myself." We're entering religious territory here. Yes, opera was her salvation!

Claude: Soon people will be genuflecting as they pass by the Palais Garnier. And why not?

Anne: Perhaps. . . . I think she finds in the world of opera and music an intense existence that surely she has nowhere else, neither in her professional life nor in her personal life. I associate her with this teacher, the woman who traveled all alone to Milan and whom you would never have thought capable of this. That's another funny thing about it: usually one doesn't imagine those people, these women capable of such a gesture, a little crazy . . .

Claude: It's funny how often we talk about madness, while in fact, once you're inside, it doesn't seem mad at all: it's normal, it's life.

Still, what's very interesting is that you always meet up with the same audience at the Paris Opéra. It's the same one you also find in Bayreuth, at La Scala, in Vienna. And you begin to notice, as you move further into this mil . . . "milieu" isn't the right word, "world" is no good either . . . in . . .

Guy: This universe?

Claude: Right, universe, clearly; in this universe you realize that you're always meeting the same people again and again.

Guy: That's so true. It's very, very striking. I move around quite a lot among the European operas and when I'm at La Scala or the Vienna Opera, when I'm in Munich, in Paris or London, without fail I meet someone I know. Every time, no matter what the time of year.

Claude: And then the password is: "But didn't I see you at Bayreuth?"

Guy: Or else you run into people . . . you don't even say hello to each other. You see them and you know them.

Anne: A little while ago we were speaking about money. I come back to B. because clearly she really made an impression on me. She says she has constant money problems and for her the eternal conflict is "Am I going to buy this ticket or am I not going to buy this ticket?" Usually "I'm going to buy it" wins out. It's very funny. This passion for the opera, it dislodges an ordered universe: on the one hand making it bearable and on the other straining at it, especially at the financial level. There are certain financial limits that one must not go beyond and yet one does go beyond them. Finally, those are the only transgressions.

Guy: But in the end, isn't what is true for opera in B.'s case also true in the end for any other passion? Take the bibliophile, for example . . .

Anne: It's not the same kind of passion. Book collecting is an investment.

Guy: I don't agree. I have friends who are bibliophiles. They could be dying of starvation and yet still they will treat themselves to a first edition. They, too, tend to spend beyond their means. It's true that there's an emotional investment unique to opera, but we may feel that it's unique merely because it's the only one we know, I'm not sure . . .

M.P.: We say bibliophile—suffix "phile"—but for the opera lover the word is "melomaniac"—suffix "mania"—which is to say madness. That ought to indicate something.

Claude: In any case, they're fundamentally different. The pleasure experienced isn't at all the same. When you read a book, the pleasure is intellectual, but . . . I can't define it . . . when you go to the opera, when you really like something, maybe the story, that can be a source of pleasure, of sensations at least, I don't know if it's pleasure. And you can be moved quite simply by the music or you may not know why you were moved.

It happened to me at Bayreuth, I had tears running down my face, but I had no idea why. It was *Parsifal,* the end of the first act. I cried and cried and I didn't know why I was crying. It wasn't to be believed. The story wasn't really heartrending . . . but the emotion made you cry. I was surprised. I kept asking myself, "Why am I crying?" And I couldn't stop. The tears kept coming and coming. I don't know what causes that. It's really something . . . else. Music is something I can't seem to categorize. Whereas the theater . . . works on other centers. With music . . . you wonder . . . "What's happening to me?"

It can also happen that . . . for example, the last time they did the *Flying Dutchman* at Bayreuth . . . you lose your strength, you feel like— and it's the same with the *Walküre,* when really you have very, very powerful emotions—like standing up and applauding, shouting "Bravo!" And then the "Bra . . ." comes out but the "vo" won't come. You collapse into your seat and can't move, you're completely out of it, short-circuited. It's as though you've received an electric shock. You're completely incapacitated, you see other people around you all astir and you don't understand why. You're already somewhere else. It's a very odd sensation. . . . But that kind of thing is rare, very rare. And also, you never experience exactly the same sensation, you have a different reaction every time. When I went to see *Tosca*, I didn't have the same emotion. Come Monday, when I'll go to see *Tristan*, it will be something else entirely. . . . But still, that intensity is very rare.

Renaud: To add to what has just been said . . . I won't say that I won the European championship thanks to *Tannhäuser*, but almost. By the semi-finals, I was completely out of it. And then the referee stopped the fight because he'd seen that I'd raised my hand. I was sweating, I wasn't well at all . . . used up. The team doctors came. Creams, massages . . . they gave me something to drink. And then all of a sudden *Tannhäuser* came into my head, and just like that . . . tranquility . . . I didn't know why . . . and then, I don't know . . . the masseur was speaking to me, I was answering him, talking to people, and at the same time I was hearing *Tannhäuser*. We resumed the match and I won. And on the way home . . . on the bus trip back, I had brought along cassettes, and on these cassettes, which I hadn't yet listened to, incidentally, there was a passage from *Tannhäuser* I had liked and recorded. It's not one of the extraordinary passages. Just a little one I happen to like, I don't even remember from which act. I began to listen to it, and now, without fail, before every fight I put on my Walkman and play *Tannhäuser*. It's just a little violin passage, just music. There's no singing, but, I don't know, maybe it's because the music is so pure. It's very short, it lasts . . . I don't know, maybe two minutes, not more. I recorded it back to back for half an hour, which means that for half an hour I have the same two-minute passage. And now, if I don't have it before a match, I don't feel well. I say to myself, "Something's wrong. What am I going to do?" It's completely idiotic because I've enslaved myself to a passage from *Tannhäuser* before every match. A slave, that's right . . . I've become a slave.

Anne: Ah! Now that opens up a whole new range of possibilities, that does!

Claude: Before your next German class, you're going to listen to *Tannhäuser* and feel truly inspired.

Renaud: But it's not *Tannhäuser* itself that I find fantastic, it's just a little excerpt that I think is sublime. Like that moment in *The Magic Flute* I played for you at my place. (*turning to Claude*) You said you thought the singer sang badly, that she was yelling.

Claude: And she was.

Renaud: Well, for me, yelling and all, it's still sublime. Maybe she sings badly, but for me, it does . . . just what it takes to make it vibrate inside.

Anne: It's a fix, then!

Renaud: Well, yes. A fix. And why not?

M.P.: And you, Claude. You haven't told me how you acquired this passion for opera.

Claude: In fact, it was Guy who initiated me. One must acknowledge origins and not repudiate paternity in matters operatic! The curious thing is that my discovery of opera occurred while I was a musician. I played the drums in a rock band and it really surprised my musician friends that my love for opera, my beginning to love opera, in no way interfered with rock, or with my style of playing, and I still play drums and still listen . . . less perhaps . . . to rock, or to be exact, to punk rock. And it hasn't stopped me from having this passion—I'm not sure that's the right word—for opera.

The first time I went to the opera it was . . . by chance! Seats had been made available to the school and I took advantage of it to spend a night out with my friends. They were doing . . . what was it? Oh, yes! *Les Contes d'Hoffmann,* staged by Chéreau. Actually, I didn't like the music at all. Rather, it was the staging that . . . made the greatest impression on me . . . in a photographic sense. Things developed gradually. I really believe it has to do with apprenticeship. When your background is like mine—I come from poor peasant stock from Brittany—this isn't exactly in the cards. And it was by listening to opera with Guy that little by little something fell into place. And then I went to see Behrens for the first time, in *The Flying Dutchman.* I had seen it on TV and—this might sound stupid, but I found this woman extremely ugly. And so I went to the opera with preconceptions. I don't know why. She started to sing and from that moment on, I realized that on the stage, she became incredibly beautiful, physically beautiful. My first reaction when I heard her sing wasn't "She sings well" but "She's beautiful!" Strange! That was the decisive moment, the one that won me over. But let me get back to this important question of apprenticeship. Because one has to learn how to listen to this type of music and it's true that our ear isn't at all accustomed to it. In France, people haven't been taught how to listen to this type of music, even though the media are constantly, constantly drowning us in music. When you've never heard a note of classical or opera, you're simply not equipped to listen to it. To know if you're going to like it or not like it, you have to be already equipped with the means of listening to it. France is deficient in this respect, unlike Austria or even Italy, where people already have a better idea how to listen. . . . And then there's a lot of "What will people think?" For example, I know the

first time I said I was going to the opera . . . my parents' first reaction—
my brothers' too—was "Oh! So you've swung the other way? You're
going with fairies?" Because clearly opera is systematically associated
with the homosexual world. Therefore to go to the opera is to swing the
other way, really swing the other way. I'm sure there are people who
unconsciously reject or dismiss the possibility of going to the opera
because of certain taboos, and the kind of talk that goes around. Conversely, I've noticed how some people go to the opera specifically to
achieve or express their marginality.

Étienne: You think so? Given everything we have to go through just to see
an opera—it's become almost impossible.

Claude: But we're here, aren't we?

Étienne: Yes, we're here, but someone who hasn't been initiated isn't
going to queue up and put in four or five hours. . . . Still, I think some
effort has been made to present opera on television. But in fact, it's really
a double-edged sword. It's not bad on the one hand, but it conveys
absolutely no idea . . . it can even give the wrong idea. Apart from the
Boulez-Chéreau *Tetralogy,* I've rarely been able to sit through a televised
opera that I didn't already know.

M.P.:   And you, Guy, the junky in the group. How did it happen to you?

Guy: I remember, I was twelve or thirteen, this was around 1965, and I
used to listen to rebroadcasts from the Aix-en-Provence festival. I remember performances of *Così Fan Tutte* with Teresa Berganza, or Gabriel
Bacquier in *Don Giovanni.* Those are things that left their mark on me,
that I really liked. And Wagner then happened very, very quickly. I was
twenty and at that time in Paris no one was doing Wagner. And I was
interested only in Wagner. Of course, I also knew a few other operas. I
had seen my obligatory *Aïda.* And then in 1973 everything seemed to sort
of happen at once. I had a little money, the East Berlin Opera was in
town doing *Die Walküre* and at the same time the Paris Opéra, which had
just reopened, was doing *Parsifal.* And that's how it took off. At first I
couldn't imagine going to the opera if not to see Wagner. The rest didn't
tempt me. I discovered other operas very gradually. I decided to see what
a Verdi might be about, and then what a Mozart might be like, and so on.

Anne: Did someone initiate you?

M.P.:   The radio?

Guy: No, not at all. It really was a completely personal thing. Nothing
comes to mind. I even remember, in 1972, I was still in lycée and there
was a classmate of mine who had gone to see *Die Walküre* and came back

very excited. That intrigued me and I said to myself, "I'm going to have to take the plunge and go see it," but all the same, I was a little afraid. It was a kind of ordeal: would I be able to withstand it physically?

I knew quite a bit of Wagner, mostly orchestral highlights. And I saw *Die Walküre*! But there's no particular singer I associate with this memory. I remember, I was with a friend who said to me: "You know the one who sings Wotan in *Die Walküre*, Theo Adam? He's the best there is!" It's true that in '72 he was the greatest Wotan. And now that he sings so little, I'm sorry I didn't pay more attention to him at the time.

There it is, one thing led to another, almost exponentially. The first season I went three times, then I went once a month, and after awhile I told myself I should try the views at an angle to see what that was like; because it was turning out to be an expensive proposition, and then little by little, after I began to buy views at an angle or obstructed views it became astonishingly simple and has been ever since. But that happened very gradually. At first I didn't dare. It's not that I didn't have the desire to go, but I didn't dare . . . I don't know, I felt . . . afraid, perhaps. Yes. And then afterward I got over it, I mean, when I say over . . . !

Claude: Did you begin with records?

Guy: No. I'd never owned opera records. I had only orchestral highlights. The first opera recording I owned was Solti's *Parsifal*, which had just been released. But I bought it after I saw the performance. Scenically, it was, along with *Die Walküre*, an absolute discovery, and yet, in hindsight, was it bad! That ending! I found it extraordinary, extraordinary! And it was nil. Objectively, it was absolutely zero.

M.P.: From what standpoint—the staging?

Guy: The staging, yes, from what I remember and with what I know now about East Berlin. But it seemed marvelous to me, just marvelous. I wouldn't have changed a thing.

M.P.: This brings us back to what Claude was saying. The musical, really the vocal aspect of opera, eludes or rather completely transfigures everything else.

Guy: Completely. And I don't know if I could really appreciate, I had absolutely no way of judging, of critiquing what I heard in '73 or '74. . . . By '74 I had a better idea. But at first I was incapable of knowing what made a voice what a voice was supposed to be. Claude was fascinated by Behrens. As for me, I can't say whether it was the same for me, whether someone fascinated me at first. No, it was the whole experience. The music fascinated me, and that had to do with Wagner . . .

Anne: You consider yourself a Wagnerian?

Guy: . . . with Wagner because I didn't experience the same thing with other composers.

Claude: It's the vertiginous quality in Wagner that you don't find anywhere else.

Anne: Yes. That's what I was going to say.

M.P.: Yes . . . but aren't there some opera lovers, Mozartians, for instance, who reject Wagner? Don't you have the feeling that there is a kind of rift . . . ?

Guy: Absolutely. In Italy, for example, it's really striking.

Claude: And with a little experience, you begin to see it in the audience. There are people you never see except at a Wagner opera. There are people who come only for Wagner.

Guy: There are people who are completely consumed by Wagner, who live for Wagner. It's crazy.

Claude: We have this friend—he pinches pennies all year long to afford two months or a month and a half at Bayreuth, with the best seats, at top prices.

Guy: Every year he spends between twenty- and twenty-five thousand francs and he doesn't have a fantastic income: he's a music teacher. He starves himself all year long but at Bayreuth, without fail, he buys himself the best seats at six hundred or seven hundred francs, and this for every performance, along with an audio system and a Wagner record collection . . .

Claude: And not just at home. The first time I met him in Bayreuth, it so happened that I hadn't been able to get seats for *Tristan*. He said to me, "If you like, come listen to it on the radio." It was being broadcast live on the radio. We went to where he boarded . . . he took a room in a local house. I get there; we go to his room. He'd hooked up the tape recorder to a timer and set it to start recording the moment the broadcast began. This required a tuner, a state-of-the-art tape recorder, and headphones to match. "Stax."

Guy: He had two or three pairs, didn't he?

M.P.: In case one of them broke?

Guy: Right. He had three Revox, too.

Guy: In any case, he devoted his entire life to Wagner.

Claude: And he can't stand Verdi. Just the idea of playing Verdi . . . he belonged to an orchestra.

Guy: Verdi revolted him!

Claude: He breaks out in hives!

Guy: The great tragedy is that he can't play Wagner; he's not good
enough. . . . He tried to play *The Dutchman* and it was dreadful for him
because it's horribly difficult to play. But what strikes me about him is his
total lack of perspective with respect to Wagner, his life, Ludwig II.

Guy: It's his own universe, a universe within a universe. I have photos
from the *Tetralogy* on the wall in my office, I have Verdi, Wagner. But he
has Wagner in his bedroom. He has Ludwig II's bed at Linderhof with its
blue velvet bedspread. He has a whole series of things. It's quite nice,
really—very cozy. But it's a universe that he has completely . . . consecrated. The ultimate devotion . . . perfectly impregnable . . . with no
room for critical distance.

Anne: We were talking a little while ago about the rift between Mozart,
Verdi . . . Wagner, to put it schematically. I came late to opera. One of
the things that put me off at first was the stupidity of the plots. It really
shocked me at first and I'm certain this was why I didn't take to opera
more immediately. I began with Wagner. I began, and I have to say quite
easily, with *Tristan und Isolde* and *Parsifal.* I believe it's a reflection of my
familiarity with the religious dimension. I'm sure of it. For a long time I
listened only to Wagner, until I discovered, on television, *The Marriage of
Figaro.* I was captivated by its humanity. But Italian opera still somehow
escaped me. Whenever I'd read the synopses, I'd think, "What's the
point of setting this to music?" Which meant that I discovered it only
relatively recently, through Callas's recordings: *Norma* . . . highlights,
not entire operas. I've only started to be affected by it. . . . And when
I've seen an opera I've really liked—*Parsifal,* for example—I get very
enthusiastic, but I felt that way too after seeing *The Tempest* that Strehler
directed. I must be somewhat impervious to music.

Claude: Give yourself time!

Anne: Strehler's *Tempest* was miraculous. I left with the feeling that I'd
seen a miracle and that . . . it was an unsurpassable production. I felt the
same euphoria I would have felt after . . . *Parsifal,* for instance.

Claude: And the *Illusion.*[9]

Anne: The *Illusion,* exactly. Those are the momentous occasions in my
experiences with the stage, but they're not necessarily due to musical
impressions. Maybe I'm not capable of appreciating a fine voice, a good
orchestra.

---

[9]Strehler's production of Pierre Corneille's *L'Illusion comique,* which was presented in
Paris at that time.

Guy: It takes getting used to.

Anne: I agree wholeheartedly. But I was interested in what you were saying earlier, Claude, because I see how some of these things are so foreign to me. For me, the visual is very important: the magic of the image.

Claude: Sometimes you no longer need the image. It can be . . . optional. The *Walküre* we saw, the concert version—it became so fabulous that . . . the slightest gesture, the slightest glance, the flutter of an eyelid, an eyelash, or . . . the stirring of a robe . . . was enough to qualify as staging, to create something marvelous. For example, at certain moments, the back-and-forth motion of the violins behind the soloists. You're going to say I was delirious, but at one point . . . it's funny . . . I did have a kind of hallucination: there was Wotan—I mean Simon Estes and Rysanek, they were both standing—and in the movement of the violins behind them, I thought I saw a monster circle around Rysanek and this monster . . . had Wotan's head—or rather Estes's head, and all there was was his head and the rest was the dragon's body surrounding poor Brünnhilde, who happened to be there. It happened suddenly and only for an instant, but I believed it. There was no staging, but I saw this monster with arms and tentacles or feet growing around Rysanek and I was afraid for her! It worked!

We were speaking of rifts a little while ago and that term interests me because Wagner had little to do with my introduction to opera . . . even though I now see that Wagner is growing more and more important in what I listen to. For example, when I wanted to put together a cassette collection . . . it's curious . . . first I began by establishing a base of Wagner, even though I wasn't especially enamored of Wagner, no more than of Verdi, for example. From the very first, I felt the necessity, even if I hadn't begun to listen to Wagner, that it was imperative for me to have him as the basis for my collection, and now I realize how important it is for me. Because this is what happened: I noticed very quickly—this may seem a frighteningly orderly way of going about it—that I listened to Wagner in the morning, because I needed all my faculties, all my senses awake and alert to be able to tap into all the richness of the music. So every morning, without fail, I'd listen to Wagner, then around noon came Mozart, then Verdi, and in the evening, when I wanted to really throw myself into the most horrible tragedies, came Puccini or the later Verdi with all his verism. That's how it was for a long time. But now I've noticed how Wagner has managed to implant himself in every period, encroaching on the others. But I'm still convinced it was important to listen to a given piece at a given time, to listen to Wagner at a particular time of day. I would never have listened to Puccini in the morning.

Étienne: I'd rather listen to Wagner in the evening.

Claude: If I listen to Wagner in the morning, it's because emotionally I'm a clean slate . . . it's as though I were new . . . whereas at the end of the day, it's out of the question. I experience certain things and they become part of me and even if I try to push them aside, they take over, no matter what I'm listening to.

Étienne: But doesn't it speak to you? Doesn't Wagner speak to your experiences? That's my feeling: it echoes with my daily experiences.

Claude: No, it's not the same at all.

Anne: I hate listening to opera at home.

M.P.:   Is that so?

Anne: Yes! I find it takes up too much room. If I feel like listening to *Tristan und Isolde* . . .

Claude: Then all you can do is listen to it.

Étienne: Yes.

Guy: Exactly.

M.P.:   That's for sure.

Claude: It's that way with everything for me: once I begin listening to music . . . and to think that there are people who manage to read or work while they listen to music. Personally, I know I can't do that. Once I start listening to music, I become aware that I've gradually disengaged from my book, and whether I like it or not, the music has taken over.

Anne: That's precisely what I try to avoid, and I find that Wagner is too dangerous in that way. I don't want . . .

Renaud: For me it's like this: Music and only music. For me it's an evening on my bed with the turntable spinning. It's terrible because I can spend days on end shut up in my room, whenever I feel like an escape. I think: I'm making myself a movie. I play the part of the hero. I won't say that I sing, but . . . the film takes shape as the music unfolds and that can take up an entire afternoon! . . . as long as it takes to play the entire opera, given that I repeat certain sections—and some of them are long.

Claude: It's funny how here we've all been talking, and when you say "It's not that I want to sing," it reminds me that we haven't talked about the desire to sing. That would be interesting.

Renaud: But I do sing! I've seen myself explode. In dreams, I've seen myself endowed with fantastic voices—on stage, making everything tremble, the walls, the opera house. The opera is in my voice, in my power, and then when my voice stops, it's as though the opera draws back into itself: the people stay in their seats . . . they don't die, but instead they fall into a kind of inanimate state, and as soon as I start to sing again, the flame is rekindled and the world comes back to life. For a long time I had that fantasy. Now it has pretty much left me. They were rather aggressive thoughts, I think.

Anne: This relates to what you were saying earlier, when you were speaking about the dose it took to make you vibrate.

Renaud: But that's how I feel it. It seizes me here and I'm capable of committing certain acts . . . acts of madness . . . while listening to opera . . . that otherwise I couldn't do, including, I don't know . . . even the ultimate absurdity . . . kill someone to . . . *Tristan und Isolde*. Well, why not? Or to *Parsifal*.

Anne: Apocalypse now!

Renaud: Whereas normally, at any other time, without opera, it would be impossible for me. The mere fact of music . . . it makes me anxious.

Anne: And Wagner really overdoes it there. With me, if I wanted to charge myself up, I wouldn't choose Wagner. For me, Wagner is more of an opiate, and even then . . . it's too massive. For a charge, I'd take the Ninth Symphony, the end of the Ninth Symphony. To my mind, it has yet to be surpassed.

Renaud: Ah, it's the ultimate.

M.P.:   Wagner has said more or less that it was Beethoven's opera.

Anne: Yes, maybe . . . but nothing, I think, that Wagner wrote is better, purer, anyway. For me, Wagner is a rather . . . murky . . . universe.

Renaud: But doesn't it all depend on how you define purity. I think that's where the problem lies, purity is a personal thing. Take *Butterfly*, for example. I don't think it's an extraordinary opera, but when Callas sings, when she's going to kill herself, maybe it's idiotic, but I snap.

Anne: Me too!

Renaud: At that point I just fall apart, I'm down on my knees.

M.P.:   Do you think that's because you know she's going to kill herself?

Renaud: No, no, it's hearing the voice, the music, I fall to my knees, I wait and I pray for her. Anyway, its the image I have. I've never actually done it, but I know I'm capable of it. There could be ten thousand people around me, it wouldn't make any difference.

M.P.:   Have you experienced great moments like those Claude described a little while ago? Have you all felt that way?

Étienne: Not to that degree.

Anne: With Callas, anyway, I've had actual shivers down my spine.

Étienne: Yes, but not to the point of . . . I've never reached such a point of ecstasy.

Anne: For me it's a physical sensation.

Étienne: Yes, for me too, but it's not only with Callas.

Anne: But for me she's the only one.

Claude: I'd really like it if we talked about voices. I'd like to know whether hearing others sing doesn't make you want to sing. I've often noticed that after an opera, when you're leaving the hall with a group of friends, there's a tendency to mimic the stars. But there's something deeper in this mimickery. There you are imitating this soprano or the aria that some other singer has fluffed, but it seems to me it goes much deeper than that. There's a need for song, a need to feel the vibration in the ear canal, to feel it in your throat.

Guy: I often think of a situation in which I'd be on stage, singing. I don't know what I'd sing but I always feel that this would be the only time I would truly understand opera. I truly feel that that is *the* solution . . . to be . . .

Claude: There are certain melodies . . . I'm thinking of one from *Samson et Dalila:* "Mon coeur s'ouvre à ta voix." Whenever I hear it . . . arias like that one, whenever I hear them, I don't listen to them, I sing them in my head and I believe there's a difference between listening to something and singing along with it. I've noticed that I often sing along, but that's another way of saying: I'm the one who is singing, I'm singing it in my head and I hear it, you really have the illusion that you're singing and maybe that's the miracle, maybe that's why I demand so much in terms of quality in the music I listen to. But that's also the supreme self-deception! But that being said, I also feel the need—unfortunately for others—to produce sounds or simply some sort of . . . interior vibration, or else to come right out and sing, to try to sing, not in the proper tessatura, unfortunately, but in my own. And I might add, it does me good.

Anne: Yes, I love that, too. Senta's song . . .

Claude: This is your moment! Go on—"Live, from . . ."

Anne: No. But if I sing, I expose myself completely. I sing alone and I love doing it. The result is nil, but . . .

Claude: But really, who cares?

Anne: Right, who cares? I imitate Callas, *Tosca* for instance. I really like

having melodies to sing along to, it's true, whether it's orchestral music
or the music . . . of song. . . . I'm having a hard time finding the right
words.

M.P.: It's four-thirty in the morning!

Claude: Speaking of words, earlier you were saying: I'm not cultivated
enough in the field of opera. This association people make, it's strange.
Opera as a movement never was and never will be an intellectual movement. When I go to the opera or to the theater, I like to go as a virgin,
without necessarily being familiar with or knowing what I'm going to
see but with complete openness—my eyes, my ears, the pores of my skin,
completely open, my breath, everything.

Anne: And then one is usually disappointed.

Claude: But that's not important. Do you see what I'm trying to say?
And I think maybe it's wrong to say, or a false problem, or a diffidence
about speaking of culture or considering the lyric arts or opera as a
cultural phenomenon, whereas in fact it's . . . almost . . . a blind
impulse!

Anne: The concept of culture can be expanded. Culture is already there.

Claude: Then culture is life?

Anne: To be sure!

Claude: To go to the opera is . . . to listen to life?

Anne: I'm absolutely certain of that.

"To go to the opera is to listen to life?" asks Claude. Can we be so
sure? How are we then to understand the constant repetition of death
scenes on the stage, the presence of grief and of loss in the emotional
signs displayed by the opera lover overcome by the diva's singing? Isn't
it rather a fascination with death, with a certain kind of death at least?
And if we can say that to go to the opera is to listen to life, isn't it in
the sense that it is precisely when a system or institution that evokes
death, the ultimate silence, inscribes it in such forms as permit its
symbolization and authorize our mastery of it that we can say that it
helps us to live? This, among other questions, is what I will attempt to
explore throughout these pages.

PART TWO

WORDS AND MUSIC:
SENSE, THE TRANS-SENSICAL,
AND JOUISSANCE

The "Blue Note"

Claude's description of the emotion that overcame him that evening in Bayreuth perfectly expresses one of the principal characteristics of those supreme moments the opera fan devotedly seeks out: "It was *Parsifal,* the end of the first act. I cried and cried and I didn't know why I was crying. It wasn't to be believed. The story wasn't really heart-rending. . . ."

At first glance it would be tempting to explain the outburst of these tears by looking at the tragic situations often staged in opera. Our evocation of the grief and horror that attend these instants surely comes as no surprise if we recall that the normal condition of the lyric stage is to be strewn with bodies and crossed in endless procession by characters torn apart by love or hate. But such an explanation does not hold; what the dramatic situation signifies counts for nothing in the outbreak of emotion, and—as we shall see—one of the primordial preconditions for the occurrence of this emotional upheaval resides in the destruction of signification. This is what underlies Claude's statement that "music is something I can't seem to categorize. Whereas the theater . . . works on other centers. With music . . . you wonder 'What's happening to me?' "; it is what underlies Renaud's comments about *Madama Butterfly:* "When Callas sings, when she's going to kill herself, maybe it's idiotic, but I snap."[1] Question: "Do you think that's because you know she's going to kill herself?" Renaud: "No, no, it's hearing the voice, the music, I fall to my knees. . . ." In fact, as the opera fan knows at firsthand, what characterizes this emotion is

[1]Note this repeated reference to something not making sense, to something that cannot be mastered ("What's happening to me?"; "It's idiotic"), which signals a failure of the signifying order.

that far from being diffused throughout the tragic situation or scene, it occurs as an acute, irrepressible irruption linked to specific musical passages in which all that is visual and all that tends toward signification fails and falls away. In these instants pure voice alone persists. Moments devoid of tragedy or even nostalgia—certain melodies of Mozart, for example—can produce this emotion; or it can be provoked by the occurrence of a single lietmotif—indeed, the workings of lietmotif in Wagner present a striking case in point—irrespective of its dramatic context, whether of joyous exaltation at the end of the Act II love duet of *Tristan und Isolde* or of tragic rapture in Isolde's Transfiguration.

Yet to speak of a falling away, or failure, of the entire visual order may seem paradoxical, because no stage presentation draws more heavily on its visual elements than opera.[2] The various devices of mise-en-scène such as costumes and scenery, complex, mechanically driven special effects, and visual illusions such as trompe l'oeil and perspective have been fundamental in opera since its beginnings in the seventeenth century. It should not be forgotten that opera as we know it was born with the baroque period, an era with a penchant for trompe l'oeil and perspective effects, which the emergent lyric art immediately used to great scenic advantage. Joseph Losey offers a remarkable illustration of these effects in his choice of Palladio's Teatro Olimpico in Vicenza as the location for an important scene in his film version of Mozart's *Don Giovanni*: what better setting for Don Giovanni, *el burlador*, the trickster of Seville, than the trompe l'oeil masterpiece that is the backdrop of this theater?

This visual saturation and illusory re-creation of an architectural space has found the onstage staircase to be particularly useful for arranging and regulating opera's visual aspects. Indeed, the history and role of the staircase in operatic stage direction would make for a very interesting little study all by itself. It is still a favored device of visual dramaturgy in countless productions. With Patrice Chéreau's production of Alban Berg's *Lulu* (sets by Richard Peduzzi), the function of the staircase seems to have been brought to perfection: at the end of Act III Jack the Ripper slowly ascended the immense staircase connect-

---

[2]The sale or on-site rental of opera glasses is an indication of the importance of the visual in opera, even if the binoculars tended originally to be trained more often on the audience than on the stage.

ing the lower depths where the murder had just been committed to a point of utter emptiness marked by the pale eye of the moon. Similar visual effects were achieved, though in an entirely different style, through massive deployment of supernumeraries on the colossal pyramidal stairs of the set for *Aïda* in the Palais Omnisport production at Bercy in 1984 (stage direction and sets by V. Rossi): neither orchestra nor singers could be heard above the spectators' applause at Radames's triumphant entrance (a stellar moment in itself!). And a mise-en-scène can deliberately obstruct this immediacy, this "making present," through the trompe l'oeil perspective effect of a point of emptiness, a point around which the important moments of the action are organized, as yet another way of giving this point even greater presence. In Mozart's *Lucio Silla*, for example (stage direction by Patrice Chéreau, sets by Richard Peduzzi; at Nanterre, 1985), a stage wall completely obstructed the scene, destroying all depth and all perspective; yet never had the presence of emptiness been manifested so forcefully as when at key moments that wall opened to allow a glimpse of blackness, non-being, nothingness.

Here the visual aspects of opera go far beyond anecdotal elements of sets and costumes and touch on the very foundations of art. As Lacan said; "All art is characterized by a certain mode of organization around [a] void."[3] I shall not delve further into the nature of this void just yet but shall return to it later. Let it suffice for now merely to point it out.

That being said, there is something inescapably paradoxical about opera: producers spend enormous sums to produce such effects and to create sumptuous sets and costumes, only to have the spectators, in those great moments of success, close their eyes to the display the better to be ravished by the diva's singing. The collapse of the visual order in these instants, or its transfiguration under the alluring influence of voice and music, is not a secondary or accessory phenomenon of the operatic genre.[4] Quite the contrary, in a sense it is constitutive of opera. For it is the radical autonomization of the voice, its veritable transformation into a detached object that lays claim to the listener's entire receptivity, that has made possible the very apparatus that is

---

[3]Jacques Lacan, *Le Séminaire, Livre VII: L'Éthique de la psychanalyse* (Paris: Seuil, 1986), 155.

[4]Remember what Claude said about the singer whom he had thought ugly: "My first reaction when I heard her sing wasn't 'She sings well' but 'She's beautiful!' "

opera. The frequent and at times systematic incongruity of voice, role, and physical appearance in the singer—everything that we call operatic convention—is tolerable only because the spectator's perception of this incongruity dissolves in the moment when the singer's lyric flight gives rise to the spectator's jouissance. I have in mind here not only the Castafiore, who "laugh to find themselves so beautiful in this mirror," but the entire initial period of opera's history, in which concern over the fit between voice and character simply never arose: soprano voices, castrato voices for the most part, were assigned to eminently virile roles, such as Caesar and Xerxes and many other figures of masculine power. The only fit required was that the vocal power of the performer be equal to the importance of the role. The fascination that the castrato voice aroused (and arouses to this day, if the attempts that have been made to recover or approximate it are any indication) is well known. Therefore what determined the distribution of vocal parts among the characters was the scale of values associated with a particular aesthetics. This remains true, moreover, through the subsequent developments of the genre, notwithstanding the fact that ever since the end of the eighteenth century, the sexual criteria of the role have been taken into account (with certain exceptions, about which I will have more to say). The soprano voice was thus assigned to the female protagonist, the tenor voice to the male protagonist. The question remains of course as to what the governing scale of values is founded upon, and particularly why the highest voices, whether feminine (soprano) or masculine (tenor), are valued the most. I will attempt to find some answers to this question later on.

But to return to the preeminence of the vocal and musical aspects in opera, it should also be noted that this preeminence can help account both for the existence of a substantial industry devoted to opera recording and for the proliferation of opera productions in concert versions. However questionable such no-frills productions may be, especially when they deliberately go against the artistic project of the composer—as with Wagner, who conceived of opera as above all a dramaturgic form—they remain an available alternative and manage to preserve a large portion of what makes the works interesting.[5] The ease with which the Palais Garnier administration sells obstructed views is proof of the autonomy of vocal and musical dimensions of opera, as is,

[5] As Claude pointed out, the image sometimes can be "optional."

on another level, the behavior of fans who make and collect pirate recordings.

What drives the itinerant opera devotee is the desire for vocal and musical moments, never visual ones. The fan will cross the continent to hear a certain singer in a particular role, not even pausing to consider who the director of the production may be, but he will never go to such lengths to see a particular director without considering which work is being presented and which singers are scheduled to perform. And when these moments occur, the fan will seek to preserve an objective—if paltry—trace in the form of a cassette recording made on a bargain-basement tape recorder smuggled into the hall in a shopping bag. This cassette will sometimes preserve a small treasure: the night the diva transcended her role, or perhaps, much as a postage stamp endowed with a rare defect has great value for the collector, the instant when she fell in stature by tripping on her high C. This collector's attitude is a fair indication of the extent to which the voice assumes the status of object in the fan's mind. For it is insofar as the voice is indeed an object, an autonomous object detached from the body that produces it, that it can become the object of the fan's jouissance. And yet this object is fragile and evanescent. It exists only as long as it manages to elude. No tape recorder, however technologically advanced, can fully capture and reproduce it. This explains the endless repetition of the fan's reinvestment. It also explains the violence of the audience toward the singer who falters. The mission of the artist on the stage is, in a sense, to approach self-annihilation as a subject in order to offer himself or herself as pure voice. The success of this process is the condition for the dissolution of incongruity between singer and role, a dissolution that, as I have suggested, is at the foundation of the lyric arts. But when the singer fails in her mission, when she somehow reaffirms her existence not merely as a subject but as a *failing* subject, the spectator has to face that incongruity once again. Opera cannot bear up under these conditions; it becomes ridiculous. It is significant that in these circumstances the singer is cast back by the public into the position of object, but now a fallen object, a piece of refuse, to be greeted in kind with the rotten egg or ripe tomato—or, as is fortunately more common, with the vocal stand-in for refuse: booing and catcalls. This retribution for disgrace is always rather impressive, for it occurs with a violence, not to say shocking hatred, that is utterly disproportionate, if observed from the outside, to what would seem to be at stake. After all, how important can it be that a singer should bungle a note that is supposed to last no longer than a few tenths of a second in the course of a performance often more than three hours long? The singer is not an aerialist who comes crashing into a net if she finds herself a quarter of a second too late for the rendezvous with her partner. And yet the audience reaction is in some ways more fearsome for the singer than for the stumbling acrobat. It is as if the fan feels deprived of what he was awaiting with so much fervor: an instant of absolute ecstasy in the fantasy of finally possessing the inaccessible object of his quest. It is as though a fundamental encounter had been missed, and all on account of the singer, who thus becomes a scapegoat. This explains the spectator's aggression, as well as the horrendous violence that overcomes him when the fault lies with a fellow spectator sitting close by, who happens to disturb one of these supreme moments with an inopportune noise. The penalty is summary execution: the offender is shot down with dirty looks.

If one can speak of the failure, the falling away of the visual order at the supreme instants of opera, one can also speak of the falling away of the entire signifying order. Literally. Every opera lover knows at firsthand the experience of the libretto falling out of his hands: you are listening to a recording of your favorite opera, installed comfortably in an easy chair, book in hand so as to follow better the subtleties of inflection, the expressivity of the interpretation. Inevitably, if the work is beautiful and the interpretation good, certain passages will wrest your attention from the printed words: you lean back in your chair and lose yourself in listening, for all the world oblivious of the printed text. It is then that the libretto falls from your hands. Your attitude conflicts with your original project of listening attentively to the verbal exchange, as it is precisely in these powerful moments, when the singer's expressive qualities and the meaning of the words ought to come together in the deepest sense, that you should be most attentive to the literary text. Yet somehow you feel a radical antagonism between letting yourself be swept away by the emotion and applying yourself to the meaning of each word as it is sung. You must choose; and if, for example, the demands of scholarship make it essential for you to follow the text word for word, you can do so only at the expense of concentrated effort and lost bliss. It is not merely that textual intelligibility and meaningful comprehension do not contribute to the production of emotion; in fact, they ultimately limit it or even cancel it altogether.

This aspect of the experience is seen perfectly in the commercial I cited at the beginning of this work: the advertisement makes no mention of the signifying situation that motivates the singing (which, moreover, is heard as an off-camera voice); nor is it necessary to know anything at all about that situation to understand the emotion that invades the statue's lithic repose as it attacks our own composure. Only those familiar with Puccini can identify the music as Manon's: and the words of the aria, if indeed they can be understood at all—they cannot, and it will become apparent why they cannot—are not so tragic that they should move one to tears.

It is with such instants that we are concerned, instants when singing, particularly the singing of a woman, deliberately presents itself as singing, as pure music free of all ties to speech; singing that literally destroys speech in favor of a purely musical melody that develops little by little until it verges on the cry. In such instants, when language disappears and is gradually superseded by the cry, an emotion arises which can be expressed only by the eruption of the sob that signals absolute loss; finally a point is reached where the listener himself is stripped of all possibility of speech.[6] Those two musical excerpts from *Tristan,* the end of the Act II love duet and Isolde's Transfiguration, illustrate this idea most strikingly.

These momentous instants in *Tristan* are anything but isolated cases; rather they seem to exemplify the deep workings of all great operatic arias, for in these two passages one can discern in its purest and most perfect form the very project that every great aria undertakes, each in its own way—the setting in place of a point of supreme culmination. In this sense, Wagner is not so much a musical innovator as a composer who draws forth not *the* truth—for it is never unequivocal—but at least one or another of opera's multiple truths. This perhaps explains why discussions of opera inevitably turn to Wagner. Let there be no

[6]Of course, these emotional moments are not confined to moments of great lyricism: each of us, like Renaud, can cite a few measures, vocal or instrumental, that have the power to stir us to the depths of our soul every time we hear them. We must all look to our own individual historical unconscious for the roots of the specific impact of these passages. Nonetheless, what happens in the aria or in the lyrical development associated with it is so profound and generalized as to have itself constituted an art and to have determined its evolution. It is also clear that this rare and intense jouissance is never provoked by recitatives (which is why recorded opera productions sometimes dispense with them altogether).

mistake: I do not mean to say that other great composers fail to articulate this truth. Were that the case, their works would not have survived the test of time. But in Wagner—and later in Berg—a culmination, a purification occurs in which this truth is revealed. Again, let there be no mistake: the truth that can be found in Wagner derives neither from his writings nor from his theories; it comes from his music. His writings do of couse tell something of this truth, though only by protesting too much: Wagner's music often contradicts his own theories; I will have to return to these contradictions because as contradictions they are all the more significant. But let us return to *Tristan und Isolde,* to the love duet and Isolde's Transfiguration.

When we listen to these passages, something takes place in those of us who are sensitive to the music: the words, even if one understands them, even if one knows them by heart, quickly lose all meaning. The listener is swept away by the spiraling melodic ascent, by a *presentiment* (a kind of *call*) of a culmination yet to come, which eventually bursts forth as a musical cry in Isolde's Transfiguration and as sheer cry in the love duet, the cry of surprise and betrayal uttered by Brangäne, Isolde's maidservant, at the arrival of King Marke.

It is important here to develop this presentiment or anticipation a little further. It constitutes a site of particular intensity in which the desire of the composer and the desire of the listener are joined, thus forming the basis for the very existence of musical art. Alain Didier-Weill uses Chopin's term "Blue Note" for the note that crystallizes this effect:[7]

The particular way the blue note is articulated with its diachronic neighbors merits attention: if you listen, for example, to a truly inspired jazz improvisation, you cannot help being struck by the fact that the string of notes that has you enthralled leads inevitably, whatever the progression, toward a determinate point that they somehow, it can be said without exaggeration, presage or foretell: if the point where meaning explodes, the point of temporal rupture that defines the blue note, is thus in some way announced by the notes that precede it, may we not postulate—by opposition to deferred action, which Lacan finds in articulate discourse—a proleptic action specific to the discourse of music? In this sense, the blue note is not exactly what

[7]In this instance, therefore, the "blue note" is not to be confused with the blue note, or "inflected" pitch, in jazz and the blues.

ultimately gives retroactive meaning to the beginning of the musical phrase; rather, it comes as the fulfillment of the promise posited by the discourse that precedes it. The blue note is the continuation, it might be said, of the knowledge presupposed by the diachronic line.

If we were to compare musical improvisation with architecture, we might say that the improvisation is supported by a master beam that is not yet in place, that is still to come.

Everything in the improvisation[8] occurs as though the creator were reaching toward this master beam, or more precisely, as though he were called by it and merely answered its call. The attraction of this formulation is that it makes us feel that the musician must recognize the path that will lead him to the precise point of self-annihilation. This is a preexisting point, but one whose preexistence, paradoxically, the musician has himself engendered, as though, having planted the seeds of an existence yet to come, he creates in the listener a form of waiting that has all the earmarks of what can only be called hope: hope for the fulfillment of a promise to which he as a creator is passionately committed: "I recognize that, given what I am now putting before you, you have the right to expect that I will find this entity whose existence I give you reason to assume: the blue note."

. . . The blue note is not only a prelude to the jouissance that this note itself will provide; like the preliminary pleasures of amorous foreplay, it also brings us the promise of jouissance.[9]

In opera, then, everything happens as though this proleptic action were in the service of something that tends further and further, as the history of the genre unfolds, toward that supreme mark of the failure of speech and the signifying order, the cry.

[8]And by extension in any musical creation. Poised before his empty staves, what does the composer do if not improvise? The composer merely has the additional advantage of being able to revise.

[9]Alain Didier-Weill, "Quatre Temps subjectivants dans la musique," *Ornicar?* 8 (1976–1977).

Amid Speech, Cry, and Silence:
Singing in Opera

It does not seem unreasonable to look upon the history of opera as a long progression that begins with speech, sung as closely as possible to the phrasing of spoken language; covers a trajectory in which singing grows more and more detached from speech and tends more and more toward the high notes; and culminates in the pure cry. In its kinship with silence, this cry, unactualized musically, not written on the staff and thus standing outside musical discourse, intended by the composer as sheer vocal effect, represents—and we shall see how—the end point in the quest for the vocal object in which the shiver of pleasure becomes the shiver of horror, as it inevitably does at the sound of Lulu's terrible death cry at the end of Alban Berg's work. In this sense, Berg's last work marks a turning point in the genre of opera and also its point of no return.

Observant commentators have not failed to notice this historical evolution of the vocal material, an evolution at times circuitous. Their explanations of it, however, are generally unconvincing. Berlioz, for example, writes:

Since Italian audiences made it their habit to talk as loudly during performances as they would at the stock exchange, singers as well as composers gradually came to seek any possible means to capture the attention of this supposedly music-loving audience. Resonance became the only goal; to achieve it, vocal shading was eliminated, as was the mixed voice, the head voice, the lower notes of the tessatura; tenors were given only high notes to sing, in the so-called chest voice; basses became baritones . . . the highest, shrillest female voices were clearly preferred over all others. Only those tenors, those baritones, those sopranos who could hurl out their voices at the top of their lungs received any applause.[10]

However astute Berlioz's hypothesis, the fact remains that even after the disappearance of what he sees as the causal factors in the steady progression toward the high notes (audiences eventually learned to be silent as they listened to the work on the stage), the rise toward the high notes continues uninterrupted, as witness the works of Wagner, Richard Strauss, and Berg, among others.

Arthur Hoérée sees a double mechanism at work: a focusing on the upper registers and a privileging of female voices. "The deep voices," he writes, "were neglected in favor of high voices. Sacred chant hardly exceeded one octave, the range of a twelfth. The first high B (B two octaves above middle C) appeared in Legrenzi's *Eteocle* (1675). Since then, female voices with a range of two-octaves and more have reached the high F (F above high C, as in the Queen of the Night's arias in *Die Zauberflöte*), the high G . . . and now even higher." Yet several pages later, in trying to account for this evolution, Hoérée writes: ". . . transported by a *taste for extremes,* drawn to this upper register that alone permits forceful sounds, or to the low notes, dark and warm, that romanticism cherished . . . the composer renounced light singing, high notes not forceful but sweet, the former virtuosities of style."[11] This interpretation seems somehow inadequate, first because an attraction to extremes suggests a symmetrical process, a movement toward the lower as well as the higher limits of the vocal compass, which is not consistent with the facts Hoérée himself puts forward: it is the female voice that is privileged. If Bellini in the nineteenth century and Berg in the twentieth extended the upper limits of the vocal range into zones unheard of in the seventeenth century, by then, in that earlier period, in opera's earliest days, the absolute lower limit of the voice had already been found (see Charon's aria in Monteverdi's *Orfeo,* for example)—a development that is even more impressive in view of the fact that pitch was for the most part markedly lower than it is today. Parenthetically, since pitch is the issue here, now is the time to put aside the notion that this rise toward the high notes is somehow

---

[10]Hector Berlioz, *À travers chants* (Paris: Gründ, 1971).

[11]Arthur Hoérée, "La Voix et le chant," in *La Musique des origines à nos jours* (Paris: Larousse, 1946).

connected with the famous "rise" in pitch, which in any case did not take place as such: rather, what occurred was the fixing—at higher rather than lower values, it is true—of a pitch that tended to fluctuate considerably from city to city, even from orchestra to orchestra within the same city, until the proliferation of musical exchanges came to require a uniform reference. In any case, between the so-called baroque pitch of around 410 Hz and the current pitch at 440 Hz there is hardly more than a half-tone difference, which in no way can account for the difference between Donizetti's stratospheric high note and Euridice's modest plaint when Orpheus sends her back to the dead in Monteverdi's *Orfeo*.

But to return to the matter at hand, if the explanation of the attraction to extremes is fundamentally unsatisfactory, it is above all because it really explains nothing and ignores the more fundamental question: What is the basis of this fascination—not with both extremes but specifically with the upper extreme?

One of the principal properties of high-pitched singing is that it makes intelligible verbal articulation impossible. For strictly acoustical reasons, the vowel sounds become indistinguishable when they are sung above 660 Hz, or high E. "Consequently," writes Nicole Scotto di Carlo,

a singer is more likely to be understood by the audience when the greatest part of his or her tessitura (the range of frequencies that can be emitted without difficulty) falls within the zone of optimal intelligibility; in other words, below 312 Hz. The fact that it is easier to understand a bass than a soprano need not surprise us, then, considering that the entire tessitura of the bass lies within the zone of optimal intelligibility, while only one-fourth of the soprano tessitura and only a fifth of the tessitura of the coloratura soprano (the highest female voice) falls within this zone.

Compounding and interfering with the task of vowel distinction is the problem of the articulation of consonants: "The consonants result from the total or partial obstruction of the vocal passage (between and including the larynx and the buccal cavity). If one is to sing well, the passage must be completely open. It is easy to imagine the problem presented to the singer by this fundamental incompatibility between aesthetic imperatives and the demands of language." For example, during the production of the occlusives (consonants such as *p, t, k, b, d, g*), when the vocal passage is momentarily closed, the silences that result from the interruption of the melodic line introduce into the continuum of sound what might be termed "acoustical holes," which the singer instinctively attempts to bridge. How? Simply by reducing the duration and the articulatory force of the consonants; in other words, by underarticulating.[12]

The singer faces many other difficulties of this kind, and the higher she must sing, the more daunting they become. The singer thus finds herself obliged, if she wants to sing true, if she wants to sing beautifully, to resign herself to the loss of intelligibility. If she wants to elicit the emotion that arises from the musical continuity of the aria, she must resign herself to losing those silences, those breaks on which the signifying scansion of language is built. For it is the cutting apart of the continuum of vocal sound by the scalpel of silence that creates the word, or, more precisely, the verbal signifier, in much the same way as, at a secondary level of linguistic articulation, it is the flash of silence signaling the end of each word, phrase, or sentence that locks in their meaning.

Lacan remarked on this antagonism between language and singing in an incidental reference to this very issue of the function of consonants, especially the occlusives, which, as he says, "are heard precisely by not being heard." Taking his dog as a case in point, he points out mischievously that "this absence of occlusives in my dog's speech is precisely what she has in common with a speaking activity with which you are quite familiar and which is called singing. If it so happens that you often do not understand what the singer is jabbering on about, it is precisely because one cannot sing the occlusives . . . ; in short, my dog sings."[13]

Perhaps this is why (conversely) some sopranos are said to bark or yelp!

In a similar vein, Berlioz rails against *"l'école du petit chien,"* the lapdog school of singers, "whose extraordinarily high upper range allows them to emit at every turn those high E's and high F's that, for

[12]Nicole Scotto di Carlo, "Travaux de l'Institut de phonétique d'Aix-en-Provence," *La Recherche,* May 1978.

[13]Jacques Lacan, seminar on identification, 29 November 1961. For "singer" Lacan intuitively uses the female form, *la chanteuse,* not the more generic *chanteur.*

all the pleasure they offer the listener, are like the cries of a spaniel whose foot has been stepped on."[14]

It should be noted in passing that with this question of the cry and the vocal high note, the distinction between humanity and animality collapses. The prelapsarian indifferentiation of the human and the animal comes at the cost of the renunciation of speech: Orpheus communicates with animals through his singing and the angels communicate among themselves without the intermediary of the spoken word.

In short, the source of this attraction to the high notes and even to the altissimo which is so clearly manifest in the evolution of opera must be sought in its effects on language and speech.

This brings us back to the jouissance of the listener and the desire of the composer, and their relation to that element in opera which seeks to destroy the law of the word and signifying scansion—that is, singing at its absolute limit, the cry. What I have in mind here is not a rigid opposition but a constantly negotiated tension between speech and music. For if it is possible, as I have said, to speak of a progression from speech to the cry, this progression is anything but linear because it is ceaselessly caught up in the dialectic of the production of jouissance and its mastery, of attempting to transgress a limit and at the same time to reaffirm it. It is this constant tension between seeking jouissance and mastering it that in my view again and again gives impetus to what Jacques Bourgeois calls the "pendular movement" in the history of opera,[15] a swing now to the side of verbal preeminence, that of the text (*prima le parole*), now to the side of musical supremacy (*prima la musica*). For a pendular movement requires an initial push, a driving force or impulse, and it is in the tension between the poles of speech and of music that the principle of this movement fundamentally resides: speech on the one hand and music on the other; or to be more precise, on the one hand speech and its law, on the other pure voice—insofar as music and singing, as we have seen, function so that the word is separated from the voice that utters it until it literally dissolves in the jouissance that emanates from the separation.

This is not to be understood as an invitation to disregard the problems of diction in singing. Quite the contrary, for it is not in unintelligibility itself that lyric jouissance resides but in the progressive

---

[14]Berlioz, *À travers chants.*
[15]Jacques Bourgeois, *L'Opéra des origines à demain* (Paris: Julliard, 1983).

dissolution of meaning under the effect of a logic of musical composition that then escapes the logic of verbal expression. Now this effect is all the stronger, by contrast, when intelligibility is properly ensured wherever the composer has decided, consciously or not, to have it respected.

Nor must these considerations be interpreted as a call for a wholesale translation of operatic works into the language of the listener. Indeed, when we speak of intelligibility, we do not necessarily mean "comprehension." What I have in mind here is a sheer linguistic effect, what can properly be called signifying scansion, which does not require textual comprehension as such. This effect might even play upon a "false" or "nonsense" language, for example, or on a mixture of languages, of which contemporary lyric art offers many examples.

The entire history of opera, the variety of forms it has taken over time, can be analyzed as a function of this process, though naturally in a manner more complex than simply assigning preeminence first to one pole, then to the other. With each period an equilibrium point is reached, according to its own modality. Each mode of the operatic genre achieves in its own way the compromise between institutions and apparatuses that generate vocal jouissance and those that come to regulate it. That is why the problem of musical jouissance can find itself cast in moral or ethical terms. This may also be the reason for the hasty value judgments; the moral or even moralistic arguments that are heard as soon as the question of singing and opera is opened up for debate, even if the discussants are unaware of the real issue at stake in their debate and explicitly claim it to be something else. Only in this light can we understand why those debates are so violent and why religious bodies and, more generally, social regulatory bodies sometimes bring all their weight to bear in an often absurdly rigorous effort to regulate something so apparently secondary as singing and music, and specifically the relationship between music and language in singing.

In this respect we should gauge the importance—an importance that seems rather preposterous if we consider only what is more obviously at stake—of social apparatuses that control the production and diffusion of music in general and of singing in particular.

Singing: An Art under High Surveillance

In Christian Europe the Catholic church was forever legislating over anything that had to do with music and singing. From the church's earliest days until the end of the Middle Ages, an unbelievable number of edicts, bulls, and even entire church councils were devoted to these matters. I will not dwell on the profusion of ecclesiastical prohibitions, though they would make for a fascinating if complex study. I will, however, consider a few of those aspects in the field of liturgical music which clearly demonstrate the mechanisms of tension I want to delineate.

The fundamental liturgical project is plain and simple: it is concerned with transmitting and proclaiming with absolute fidelity the divine *Word,* as preserved by the sacred texts. Whatever strays from the explicit dictates of this project is therefore proscribed: instrumental music is for that reason banned from the house of God. The customary explanation for this exclusion of musical instruments (other than the organ) is that they were once associated with pagan and popular celebration. And so they were. Yet the church has consistently managed to appropriate and integrate elements of pagan tradition deeply rooted in popular practices and beliefs. Instrumental music was rejected, therefore, not only because it was pagan but because it conflicted with the original intentions of the liturgical project. But why not limit the transmission of the divine Word to reading, to pure and simple declamation? Why seek to sing the Word and thereby incur centuries of entanglement in the often literally unheard-of details that were to govern the ways it could be sung? A certain interval might be authorized, another forbidden, such as the tritone (augmented fourth, F–B, for instance), the famous *diabolus in musica.* (English Puritanism did in fact ban religious music altogether for a decade and a half during the middle of the seventeenth century, a gross error that Luther avoided; on the contrary, in fashioning his reform he systematically turned to a popularly accessible musical form: the chorale.) Thus the church recognized that singing could serve as a powerful motivation that could be integrated into the original liturgical project, but only if it could maintain complete mastery over this vocal expression. (Speaking of "mastery," it is worth pointing out that in French the same word, *maîtrise,* also used to designate a cathedral music school: one spoke of *les maîtrises des cathédrales."* This is very significant.) Here we touch on an important point to which I will have to return: the articulation between vocal jouissance and worship, between vocal jouissance and the relation of the human to the divine, between lyric and mystical ecstasy. The relation of the Catholic church to mysticism was as fraught with ambiguity as was its relation to music, and for similar reasons. Mysticism, like music, was both valued and distrusted. The fear of excess, of unleashing mystical ecstasy, is ever present, and at one time or another all the great mystics have been suspected of satanism: every mystic has had to prove the divine origin of his or her trance. The institutional triage itself, the sorting of mystics into those to burn and those to canonize, is a more obscure matter, dependent as it was on social, political, and historical considerations that had little to do with purely religious criteria; thus those criteria were anything but precise, as Joan of Arc found out.

To return to the question of singing in the liturgy, it is within this dialectical process that plainsong—so called because it must be plain, without vocal embellishment that might disturb the intelligibility of the sacred text—is structured. In plainsong, the phrasing of language determines completely the musical development, which remained un-metered and continued to be written without the scansion of the mea-sure bar even after the latter was introduced, a clear indication that the dominant consideration was something other than musical meter. A place is nonetheless set aside for nonsignifying musical development, and that place is in the vocalizations that terminate sentences or clauses, instants of musico-mystical meditation that give closure to the enunciation of the sacred text. Tradition attributes to Pope Gregory the Great (d. 604) the organization, determination, and even composi-tion of what today we call the Gregorian chant. It hardly matters here that Gregory's role was more mythical than actually historical[16] be-cause in the present context it is enlightening to note that the tradition found it necessary to relate to an embodiment of supreme authority the rule that both decrees an imperative of jouissance ("Thou shalt sing") and sets precise limits for it: "Thou shalt sing, but the Word shall be Law; pure singing shall come only after the Word, and not any which way." The subsequent history of liturgical singing was an endless series of transgressive developments and efforts to contain them, a process

---

[16]The tradition that traces the origin of plainsong to Gregory did not begin until two centuries after his death.

fraught with contradictions and leading to a paradoxical outcome in the sixteenth century—fully a thousand years later—when the quintessence of the religious spirit was distilled in a polyphonic singing in which the intermingling of voices and even of texts eventually dissolved the intelligibility of words altogether. It is as though once jouissance comes into play, regulatory mechanisms have difficulty holding their own: a dynamics is set in motion that causes the entire apparatus to shift, and then transgression seems to have the final say. The prohibition must then either be radicalized (as among the English Puritans, who simply forbade all religious music, abolished cathedral music schools, and destroyed church organs) or abandon the field and shift its operations elsewhere. In Italy, curiously, a new field of operations was found in secular music, with its return to monody and the beginnings of opera, yet here once again the regulatory spirit was to lose the upper hand, this time perhaps forever.

The regulation of singing is not the prerogative of religious authority alone. Organs of political power have cooperated fully in these regulatory endeavors and occasionally have even taken the place of the religious authorities. Nor is the regulation of singing unique to Western civilization. In ancient China, according to legend, musical creation was explicitly the province of imperial power: "At the time [around 4300 B.C.] the emperor alone had the authority to create music, an institution responsible for keeping the people on the good and moral road."[17] Here again, it matters little whether the imperial privilege was mythical or not; the important thing is that the tradition—which speaks its own truths—attributes the responsibility of guaranteeing the ethical principles of music to the emperor, the personification of supreme authority in Chinese society of the day. And what were those principles? One of them, attributed to Emperor Shun (2255 B.C.), speaks directly to our concerns: "Let the music follow the sense of the words; keep it simple and ingenuous. Vain, *empty* and *effeminate* music is to be condemned."[18] This encounter between the feminine and singing—between the feminine and pure, "empty," meaningless, or "trans-sensical" music—is a topic I shall take up later at much greater length, as it turns up again and again whenever this question arises, from Saint Paul ("Let a woman learn in *silence* with all sub-

---

[17]Ma Hiao Ts'um, "La Musique chinoise," in *La Musique des origines à nos jours.*
[18]Cited in Harry Partch, *Genesis of a Music* (New York: Da Capo, 1974), 10.

missiveness. I permit no woman to teach or to have *authority* over men; she is to keep silent.")[19] to Wagner ("Music is a woman"). To find this encounter in an edict issued by a Chinese emperor three millennia before Christ is remarkable indeed. The persistence of this association over time and across cultures is evidence that we are touching on a deep nexus, whose meaning will be explored in due course. Let it suffice for the present to point out this nexus and take note of its condemnation.

In the main, however, political power exerts control over the production and diffusion of musical art more subtly. Direct legislation by temporal authority over musical matters is the exception rather than the rule. Political power generally prefers to act by subjugating not music but those who create it, making the very conditions of their existence dependent on the power of the prince, king, or state. Yet occasionally political authority intervenes directly with explicit censorship. I have already mentioned the example of Cromwell's republic and protectorate in seventeenth-century England. Another example on the same order, much closer to our own time, brings us back to the opera stage.

In January 1936 in Moscow, an article in *Pravda* shut down the production of Dmitri Shostakovich's opera *Lady Macbeth of the Mtsensk District*. This work would not play again in the Soviet Union until twenty-five years later, retitled *Katerina Ismailova,* in a version slightly reworked by the composer, who sweetened certain passages that had offended the Stalinist critics of the opera. And it was indeed to Stalin himself that the argument developed by the *Pravda* critics, if not the authorship of the article, was attributed, along with the ensuing decision to censor the work. (Always this recourse to a figure of supreme authority to ground prohibition in musical matters, as though these problems indeed were affairs of state!) Incidentally, it seems strange that French absolute monarchy was so unconcerned with music. No doubt it is because composers had been so thoroughly subjugated by the monarchy that there was no need for the monarch to intervene personally. Under the absolute monarchy, a composer was either official or not. In those who were, from Lully to Rameau and well beyond, one finds an overwhelming fidelity to an aesthetic of verbal preeminence. The legislator had no need to intervene. This submission

[19]I Timothy 2:11–12.

of French culture to the law of the word is a constant in French operatic music up through contemporary creations (Olivier Messiaen's
Saint-François d'Assise) and even in the romantic period (Berlioz). Chal-
lenges to this aesthetic always come from abroad, particularly from
Italy.

But to return to Stalinist Russia: what are the criticisms offered by
the author of the *Pravda* article—an article headed "Musical Gibberish,"
a term that refers unambiguously to unintelligibility in discourse? I
will pass over the more obvious "moral" charges of excessive sex and
violence and dwell a little longer on an argument that is still often
heard in regard to certain types of opera, chiefly the operas of Wagner:
"The performers don't sing; they scream!" This criticism is a little
surprising because Shostakovich's opera, its moments of violence included, is, all in all, quite melodic, even if traces of the influence of
Alban Berg's *Wozzeck* can be detected in it. Like any self-respecting
Russian opera, it takes care to make room for popular melody, for
cantilena. But it ends with two terrible female death cries as Katerina,
the heroine, hurls her rival into the lake and then leaps into it herself. It
would be imputing too much to the *Pravda* article to consider that
these two cries alone were enough to justify the criticism, but it is not
unlikely that they contributed their fair share to the rather prudish
horror the author of the article displays. Nonetheless, everything about
these events suggests that it was absolutely imperative to condemn
anything in the opera that might lead to the utterance of the cry. And
when a composer takes it upon himself to transgress this implicit prohibition, the full rigor of the law, the explicit prohibition, is brought
down upon him.

The last argument developed in this famous article taxes the work
with *formalism;* that is, a certain gratuitousness in the musical composition which, by pursuing its development for its own sake, avoids *sub-
mitting* to a project, to a clear intention with a moral meaning intelligible to the spectator. Stalin's criticism is finally no different from
Emperor Shun's castigation of "vain and empty music."

Music is obviously not the only art subject to such control. All
artistic creation finds itself under the careful surveillance of social regulatory bodies. But this surveillance is generally exercised according to
a system of moral or philosophical criteria that address explicit repre-
sentations proffered by specific genres of artistic production. In paint-

ing, for example, it has been and sometimes still is forbidden to represent particular body parts or particular types of scenes. Certain cultures simply prohibit any representation of the divinity or of the human being. Yet moral or philosophical considerations of this sort are ineffectual in the domain of music, which only rarely suggests an unequivocal representation (or, for that matter, representation at all). From this standpoint, music is like mathematics; for aside from a few marginal examples of "imitative" works, music, perhaps even more than mathematics, is a game in which pure detached signifiers burdened with neither signification nor reference are combined. Mathematical games are subject to a system of regulation that is the exclusive province of the community of scientists directly concerned with these matters; yet entire religious or state apparatuses make it their business to define the basic rules of the musical game.

Now that I have underscored the importance of what is at stake ethically in a question seemingly as frivolous as the relationship between music and words, I will endeavor to show how the history of opera speaks of the persistent oscillation that determines the two extreme modalities of that relationship: on the one hand, fusion or confusion of music and speech, and on the other hand, music's antagonism toward, challenge to, and even destruction of the spoken word.

Parlar Cantando

Opera as such was born at the close of the sixteenth century in Italy, in the wake of the Florentine philosophical aesthetic debates spearheaded by Count Giovanni Bardi and then taken up by Jacopo Corsi among the circle known as the Florentine Camerata. Thoroughly imbued with Renaissance ideology, this group of artists—today we would call them intellectuals—took on the project of rediscovering the ancient roots of various modes of artistic expression, particularly the ancient ideal of Greek tragedy. Always a matter more of assumption than of actual fact, this ideal served as a call to arms against the polyphonic style of music then at its apogee (Roland de Lassus, Palestrina) and for a return to monodic singing, which alone was considered capable of restoring the word to full intelligibility. It was thus that an entire aesthetics of *parlar cantando* (Monteverdi) or *imitar col canto chi parla* (Strozzi) evolved. For it was indeed a matter of "speaking while singing," of "imitating speech through song," not the reverse. It was singing that had to bend to the inflections of "ordinary speech," to the "phrasing" of language. The preface to Marco da Gagliano's *Dafne* (1608) is quite significant in this regard; it "condemns the arbitrary use of rolls, trills, passages, and exclamations" by singers, who would do better to "scolpir la sillabe por bene intender le parole" (literally, "sculpt the syllables to make the words well understood").[20] The Florentines Emilio de' Cavalieri, Giulio Caccini, and Jacopo Peri did their best to give concrete expression to this ideal in such works as *The Representation of the Soul and the Body* (Cavalieri, 1600) and especially Peri's *Euridice,* performed in 1600 in Florence for the wedding of Maria de' Medici and Henry IV of France. But it was Claudio Monteverdi, of course, who best illustrated this ideal, first in Mantua and then in Venice; yet in so doing he also opened the door to its most radical betrayal. For Monteverdi's success derives in large part from the fact that he respects the principles of *parlar cantando,* but still allows himself to subvert its constraints in the development of chorus and arioso—or, in a word, through lyricism. If he is considered the founder of opera, it is precisely because his work is pregnant with the future developments of the genre in its theme (*Orfeo* [1607] presents the problematics of the Woman cast into Nothingness) as well as in its musical material, which can be seen either as the progenitor of the great bravura aria or as the point of reference for such composers as Gluck and Wagner, who sought to reaffirm the primacy of drama. The cry itself is already prefigured in Euridice's "Ahi" when Orpheus's gaze sends her back to the dead, though Monteverdi's musical reserve makes it more a plaint than a cry. It is in fact characteristic of Monteverdi's style that the musical line corresponds closely to the prosody of language according to a science derived from the use of various musical elements inherent in speech (inflections, intonations) in conformity with the duration and the rhythms of spoken enunciation.

[20]Federico Ghisi, "La Réforme mélodramatique," in *Histoire de la musique,* vol. 1 (Paris: Pléiade, 1960), 1438.

Prima la Voce

Very quickly, however, the ideal of fusion gave way to a radical autonomization of the musical aspect of the voice. With the apogee of the art of the castrati came a search for jouissance in the pure vocal object, at the cost of a total erosion of all concern for dramatic and textual intelligibility. In its place came the now rather unimaginable display of vocalises—high, pure, sensuous, virtuoso, and acrobatic—that over the course of a century would drive the crowds to distraction, bringing vocal ecstasy to a point of paroxysm that has not since seen its equal. (Dominique Fernandez's novel *Porporino* conveys the idea with great verve.) I will return to this strange phenomenon of the castrato voice, to its underlying significance and the fascination it held and still holds today. Here I would like simply to propose that even at this moment in the development of the operatic form in which it seems definitively to have settled its score with the spoken word, the word still managed to assert its mastery and contain its losses. It did so in two ways: by the scansion of the vocalise on the one hand and by the breaking of the work into aria and recitative on the other. The function of the scansion of the vocalise will be seen in detail when we analyze the Queen of the Night's aria in Act II of *Die Zauberflöte*. It must be noted that the division of the operatic work into aria and recitatives prepares the ground at one stroke for both the liberation of the vocal material and the division of the work into a locus of jouissance—the aria—and a locus of the mastering word—the recitative. This radical division of the work itself marks the failure of the Florentine Camerata's ideal: it is impossible to reconcile vocal jouissance with signifying organization. But it also marks the impossibility of ridding the work of its iron law: a place must be reserved for language, which henceforth will be more verbal than musical. This is the function of the recitative, which in some lyric genres returns to pure, nonmusicalized speech, as in the German singspiel or the French comic opera, or in the *Sprechgesang* of contemporary opera.

Jean-Jacques Rousseau analyzes this evolution in a particularly pertinent way in his "letter to Burney":[21]

A grand and beautiful problem to solve is how far language can be made to

---

[21]Jean-Jacques Rousseau, *Écrits sur la musique* (Paris: Stock, 1979).

sing and music to speak. The whole theory of dramatic music rests on an ultimate solution to this problem. Instinct alone has driven the Italians as far as it is possible to go in practice, and the enormous faults of their operas come not from a bad kind of music but from a good form put to poor use. The oral accent in and of itself is certainly very powerful, but only in declamation: its power is entirely independent of all music, and with this accent alone we can bring forth a good tragedy but not a good opera. As soon as music intervenes, it must deploy all its charms to conquer the heart by the ear. Unless it lavishes all its beauty, the music will be out of place, as though one were to accompany an orator with instruments; but when mixing in its riches, it must do so with great care, so as to avoid the exhaustion a long musical work inflicts on our senses.

From these principles it follows that in a drama the application of music should vary, now permitting the accent of language and poetic rhythm to dominate, now permitting the music to dominate in its turn and lavishing all the riches of melody, harmony, and musical rhythm, so as to strike the ear and touch the heart through irresistible charms. These are the reasons for the division of an opera into *recitativo secco, recitativo stromentato,* and arias.

Rousseau nonetheless shuns recourse to bare speech as a way to "prevent the exhaustion . . . to which too long a work entirely in music would lead":

The simple recitation of rapid speech calls for the declamatory accent exclusively; in the case of a stressed language, it is only a matter of making the stress apparent by setting it to musical time, by sticking faithfully to the prosody, to the poetic rhythm and passionate inflections demanded by the meaning of the speech. This is simple recitative, and *this recitative must be as close to simple speech as possible; it must stay close to the music simply because music is the language of opera* and because speaking and singing alternatively, as in the comic operas here, makes for successive expression in two different languages, and the passage from one to the other is always shocking and ridiculous; and because it is the height of absurdity that at the instant of passion we should change voices to speak a song.

Rousseau goes on to spell out the boredom (which here can be read as frustration) produced by the recitative in Italian opera. It was indeed not unusual to see Italian audiences protest violently against the return to recitative after a grand aria sung by the castrato *primo uomo* or by the soprano *prima donna* and demand that the singer proceed directly to some other aria, even though it might not come until two acts later in the opera, even though it might belong to an opera other than the one being performed that evening:[22]

The recitative casts a pall of boredom over the Italian theaters, not only because it is too long but because its singing is poor and its placement worse. Scenes that are vivid and interesting, as the scenes of an opera must always be, rendered with warmth, with truth, and sustained by natural and lively acting, cannot fail to move and to please, always favoring the illusion; but in the cold and flat recitation of the castrati, delivered like a schoolboy's lessons, they will unfailingly bore and undoubtedly be too long; *but this will not be the fault of the recitative.*

Prima le Parole?

Rousseau's reflections were occasioned by Christoph Willibald Gluck's *Alceste,* presented in Paris in 1776. The opera reflects the composer's stated desire for *reform* in response to

abuses that have arisen from the misplaced vanity of the singers or the excessive complacency of the composers and that for so long have disfigured Italian opera, turning the most splendid and most beautiful of spectacles into simply the most ridiculous and the most boring. I have striven to *limit* the music to its true function, which is to *serve* the poetry expressively while following the stages of the intrigue, but *without interrupting* the action and by trying not to smother it with quantities of superfluous *ornamentation;* I believe that the music should add to the poetry what an accurate and well-composed drawing receives from vivid colors and the harmony of light and shadow that animate the figures without altering their contours.[23]

What metaphor better formulates the way language or poetry is

---

[22]These are the famous *"arie di baule"* that each star castrato would sing upon request in the course of a performance, regardless of the opera that was being performed.

[23]"Épître dédicatoire d'*Alceste* à Léopold, duc de Toscan," in *L'Avant-scène Opéra* 73: *"Alceste"* (March 1985), 26.

supposed to function as a contour, limit, or barrier against the tendency of a colored surface—the melody—to overflow its bounds? The dedicatory letter that was written for *Alceste* reveals a constant in the history of opera: the desire to reform in the face of an overflowing force that must be contained, a deviation that must be rectified, a perversion that must be condemned. This desire dictates a course of action that demands virtue "not only in its subject . . . but—and herein lies its novelty—in its form as well."[24] It also dictates a return to the primacy of language, and—as it happens—would place itself under the aegis of one of the figures of supreme authority of the day, Leopold, grand duke of Tuscany and future emperor of Austria: "I have felt it necessary to seek support for my position in the almighty patronage of Your Royal Highness, and I have allowed myself to ask for the honor of seeing your august Name, which has so deservedly received the suffrage of an Enlightened Europe, introduce my opera."[25]

Gluck's reform, carried out principally in three works besides *Alceste* (*Armide*, *Iphigénie en Aulide*, and *Iphigénie en Tauride*)—not to mention the anticipatory *Orfeo ed Euridice*—met with enthusiastic approval from the public (including Rousseau). For, paradoxically, the musical form Gluck perfected in fleshing out his project strays from it considerably and gave rise to movements whose mechanisms are not unrelated to those set in play by Italian opera. Indeed, as Gluck[26] writes in his dedicatory preface, it was a question of "not interrupting the action." Thus he was led to "accompanied" or "melodic" recitative—in Wagner it becomes "continuous melody"—which tends to abolish the aria/recitative distinction. Now the continuous and continuously "musicalized" nature of this kind of composition, while avoiding the characteristic paroxysms of the Italian "bravura aria," also does away with the regulating effect of language, which, as we have seen, is the function of the recitative. "[Alceste's] recitatives and arias are generally quite long and call upon *all the resources of the voice* (powerful registers across the tessitura, agility in moving between them, variety of colora-

[24]Michel Noiray, "Les Éléments d'une réforme," *L'Avant-scène Opéra* 73: *"Alceste"* (March 1985), 20.

[25]The sovereignty of the Name-of-the-Father over the signifying order could not be expressed more explicitly.

[26]Or Raniero da Calzabigi, his librettist, since according to Marc Vignal, Calzabigi is the author of the dedicatory preface. See *L'Avant-scène Opéra* 73: *"Alceste"* (March 1985).

tion and timbre, clean and precise diction). From all of this there results a perpetual *tension*."[27] And this tension is sustained through the seduction, the ravishment of the listener, not, as we might expect, through the signifying elements it may comprise but through its vocal and musical elements. The effect produced is all the more intense in that a place is always set aside for displays of pure lyricism (arias, ariosos, choral interventions . . .) which in breaking with the word introduce the listener to that jouissance of the vocal object with which we are concerned here. This is what Jacques Bourgeois notes when he emphasizes that "rather curiously" *Alceste* and *Orfeo* owe their singular popularity among Gluck's operas to the fact that, unlike *Iphigénie en Tauride,* they contain not one but several genuine arias, "enclosed" and reprised, in contradiction to the principles the composer espouses.[28] Gluck thus radically liquidates the principal agent of regulation—that is, language in the form of the *recitativo secco*—and at the same time merely limits the fundamental agent of jouissance, vocal display, and does not eviscerate it. In this sense Gluck is not his own disciple, or, in the words of Berlioz, "Gluck himself did not apply his theory to his work with perfect exactitude." Federico Ghisi has said that "by a *natural* process, melody always ultimately prevails over the poetic text . . . words have never been the mistress of music but always its servant."[29] This no doubt explains the considerable emotional impact that *Alceste* had in its own day (as witness Julie de Lespinasse's or La Harpe's description) and still has today on those occasions when it is performed.

Gluck's work sparked the heated and vociferous controversy I referred to earlier, a controversy known as *la querelle des Piccinistes et des Gluckistes.* (Niccolò Piccini was one of the Italian composers imported by the proponents of Italian music.) This feud was the final chapter in some twenty-five years of fervid debate that split French intellectual and even political circles in the latter half of the eighteenth century: the famous *Querelle des Bouffons,* which took its name from "opera buffa," the term given to Giovanni Battista Pergolesi's *La Serva Padrona* (The Maid-Mistress), whose Paris production in 1752 sounded the offensive for the partisans of Italian opera against French opera, typified by Jean-

[27]Caroline Bouju, "Rosalie Levasseur, la créatrice d'Alceste à Paris," *L'Avant-scène Opéra* 73: *"Alceste"* (March 1985), 93.

[28]Bourgeois, *L'Opéra des origines à demain,* 64.

[29]Ghisi, "La Réforme mélodramatique."

Philippe Rameau. This is not the place to delve deeply into this rather mad affair, given its multiple and contradictory facets. I would simply like to show that one of the things at stake in this recurrent story is precisely the conflicting adjustment and readjustment between the search for jouissance and the insistent presence of a system to master it. Locating this conflict and the issues at stake may provide a guiding thread through the profusion of arguments and counterarguments offered up with equal violence on both sides. We will take up this thread in the ideas of Rousseau, one of the worthier of those who distinguished themselves in this astonishing squabble. His thoughts, on which I have already drawn at some length, seem to be particularly enlightening. And with all due respect to the author of *Émile*, he is called upon here as a symptom of this conflict.

The King and the Queen

It is worth beginning by observing how the two opposing camps took their respective positions under the emblematic figures of the king and the queen, according to the place in the opera house where each group would assemble. In "the King's Corner," beneath the masculine emblem of the king, gathered those who championed a French music thoroughly committed, as we have seen, to the primacy of language. In the "Queen's Corner," beneath the loge and under the feminine emblem of the queen, gathered the partisans of Italian music, proponents of lyric flight: once again, as luck would have it, the feminine meets up with the trans-sensical in opposition to the domination of the Word.

Jean-Jacques Rousseau, as might be expected, took his place in the Queen's Corner, siding with the partisans of Italian opera. So it is that he turns his pen to familiar themes that speak to the fundamental issues:

On first hearing the Italian melody, one notices only its charms; it seems fit to express only pleasant feelings. But even a minor study of its pathetic and tragic nature surprises us with the power it can achieve by the composer's artistry in the great musical works. With skillful modulation, this simple and pure harmony, these brisk and brilliant accompaniments, this divine singing can *rend the heart or ravish the soul,* sending the spectator *outside himself,* while wresting from him in his transport such *cries* as never have honored our tranquil operas.

Thus sensitive to the musical aspects of the voice, Rousseau places himself quite naturally on the side of the queen and—quite logically— launches into a devastating critique of Rameau, who, true to his position as composer to the king, composes vocal music unsurpassed in its submission to the constraints of verbal enunciation. But—and this is what is particularly salient—it is not at all this verbal tendency of Rameau's music that Rousseau stigmatizes but rather its "harmonic" tendency. For Rousseau believed that "French music is full of harmonic superfluities and complications, useless adornments designed to mask its melodic poverty."[30]

Earlier Rousseau was stifling a yawn at the recitatives of Italian opera, even as he was absolving the recitative itself of responsibility: if they tend to bore, it is because they are too long, are delivered "in the cold and flat recitation of the castrati; . . . this [is not] the fault of the recitative." For as a good French moralist—and here the paradox emerges—Rousseau "places music within the moral sphere of articulate human nature and not in the physical world of sounds."[31] Rousseau will in fact attempt the tour de force of grounding in the ethical action of language an aesthetics that in fact hinges on jouissance, which, as we know, draws its substance from the subversion of language. Here he resorts to a myth of the origins of music. He himself does not invent this myth—it can be found throughout his century, in Rameau and others, and in other centuries, too—but systematizes it, in his *Essay on the Origin of Language.* In this altogether remarkable text, with peremptory aplomb that forecloses any doubt as to the truth of his assertions, Rousseau presents the idea that language and singing come from the same womb.

With the first voices the first articulations or sounds formed according to the respective passion that dictated them. Anger produces menacing cries articulated by the tongue and the palate. But the voice of tenderness is

---

[30]C. Kintzler, preface to Rousseau, *Écrits sur la musique.*
[31]Elisabeth Guilain, "Rousseau analyste de Gluck," *L'Avant-scène Opéra* 73: *"Alceste"* (March 1985), 90.

softer; the glottis modifies it, and such a voice becomes a sound. It may occur with ordinary or unusual tones, it may be more or less sharply accented, according to the feeling to which it is joined. *Thus rhythms and sounds are born with the syllables:* passion makes all the organs speak and adorns the voice with all their splendors. *Thus verse, singing, and speech have a common origin.* . . . The first discourses were the first songs. The periodic recurrences and measures of rhythm, the melodious modulations of accent gave birth to poetry and to music together with language. . . . At first there was no other music than melody, nor any other melody than the varied sounds of speech. Accents constituted singing, quantity constituted measure, and one spoke as much by natural sounds and rhythm as by articulations and words. *To speak and to sing were formerly one and the same,* says Strabo.[32]

After this period of original mythic fusion, degeneration sets in, leading on the one hand to the autonomy of the musical component and on the other hand to the evolution of separate and diverse languages according to their geographical locations, making them more or less suitable for "natural" agreement with music.

The mythic character of this "natural" agreement of certain languages with music should be noted. It is what permitted Giustiniani, at the beginning of the seventeenth century, to write: "The French sing, the Spaniards hoot, the Germans growl, and the Italians weep."[33] It is what allowed Rousseau to claim that "if there is one European language suited to music, it is certainly Italian;" and what later allowed Wagner to write in *Opera and Drama* that "of all the modern operatic dialects, the German alone is fitted to re-enliven Art's Expression in the manner we have recognized as needful: for the very reason that it is the only one which in daily life has retained the accent on the root-syllable, whilst in those others an arbitrary convention abrogates the rule of nature, and sets the accent on syllables of 'inflection'—altogether meaningless *per se.*"[34]

But to return to Rousseau's "analysis," note that he explicitly in-

[32]Jean-Jacques Rousseau, *Essay on the Origin of Language,* trans. John H. Moran, in *On the Origin of Language* (Chicago: University of Chicago Press, 1966), 50–51.

[33]Quoted in Nella Anfuso, "Résurrection stylistique et technique vocale," *Opera International,* April 1985.

[34]Jean-Jacques Rousseau, "Lettre sur la musique française," in *Écrits sur la musique;* Richard Wagner, *Opera and Drama,* vol. 2 of *Richard Wagner's Prose Works,* trans. William Ashton Ellis (1893; rpt. St. Clair Shores, Mich.: Scholarly Press, 1972), 358.

scribes it within an ethical perspective that leads him to take a dim view of the process that separates music and language: "In dropping its oral tone and attaching itself exclusively to the establishment of harmonics, music becomes noisier to the ear and less pleasing to the heart. It has already stopped speaking, soon it will stop singing. And then, with all its accords and all its harmony, it will have no more effect upon us." The chapter headed "How Music Has Degenerated" concludes with these revealing words: "Thus we see how singing gradually became an art entirely separate from speech, from which it originates; how the harmonics of sound resulted in forgetting vocal inflections; and finally, how music, restricted to purely physical concurrences of vibrations, found itself deprived of the moral power it had yielded when it was the twofold voice of nature."[35]

Such an ethics ought logically to have steered Rousseau to the side of those like Rameau, who, on the heels of Jean-Baptiste Lully, strove to bring poetic discourse and musical discourse into strict harmony by developing, for example, what was called "French recitative." Isn't Lully said to have modeled his recitatives on the diction of La Champmeslé, the great Racinian tragedienne? But Rousseau places himself unambiguously on the other side, on the side of music, which in fact transcends or subverts language. He is thus obliged to bring his argumentation in line with his position. And given what he has just proposed, that is not a simple task. He manages it finally by introducing two ideas, just as mythical as the others: on the one hand he asserts the supposed unsuitability of the French language for music, begging the question so that he can reject Rameau without further consideration; and on the other hand, and much more interestingly, he locates the origin of language in what is the foundation of vocal jouissance itself—in the trans-verbal, in affect, or to put it in terms contemporary to Rousseau, in passion. Language, rather than being or before being a system for ordering the world or a system for regulating needs and social relations—a system for symbolizing the real, as the Lacanian discourse would put it—is for Rousseau the child of the passions:

It seems then that need dictated the first gestures, while the passions stimulated the first voices. . . . It is neither hunger nor thirst but love, hatred,

---

[35]Rousseau, *Essay On the Origin of Language*, 65, 71.

pity, anger, which drew from them the first voices. . . . But for moving a young heart, or repelling an unjust aggressor, nature dictates *accents, cries, lamentations.* Those are the oldest words, the first to be invented; that is why the earliest languages were singing and were passionate, before they became simple and methodical."[36]

Thus the cry is not the nemesis of the word: the cry is father to the word. So we come full circle and Jean-Jacques can in all good faith shore up a principle of jouissance with a moral system that ensures mastery over it.

Rousseau's approach is thus symptomatic of an attempt to resolve the conflict introduced by the fundamental tension at work, as we have seen, in the question of the voice in opera. This tension between transgressive jouissance and limit, heretofore expressed in terms of the problematics *prima la musica/prima le parole,* is reformulated by Rousseau in the opposition melody/harmony. By a cleverly if somewhat neurotically constructed reasoning, Rousseau puts the fox in charge of the henhouse. Deeply and truly drawn to the side of transgression and jouissance, Rousseau in fact aligns himself with the Italians, with pure voice, and thus against Rameau. But bending to the pressure of prohibition, he uses its logic to argue his stance and attacks Rameau not for his "regulated" aspect but for what is transgressive in Rameau's position: his symphonic elaboration in opera.[37] Rousseau applies the finishing touches to his system by placing language under the tutelage of the passions and their various affects, especially suffering and jouissance. Henceforth the quest for melody, for the voice's purely musical aspect and the jouissance that announces it, becomes a return to origins—an idea that, all things considered, is not so very different from the psychoanalytic conception of the vocal object, which will be taken up farther along.

[36]Ibid., 11–12.

[37]Which, by the way, caused a scandal twenty years earlier. Rameau's operas were in fact violently attacked by Lully's supporters for what they considered an unseemly intrusion of an overabundance of symphonic richness: "[*Hippolyte et Aricie*] has enough music in it for ten operas," André Campra said—to Rameau's partisans a supreme compliment; to his adversaries a forbidding reproach. In fact, it would be incorrect to situate Rameau categorically on the side of a lyrical music entirely dominated by the word. The tension I have been discussing runs through his work as well, though it is clearly weighted toward the other side, that of *prima le parole.*

The ramifications of this theoretical debate extend all the way to Berlioz and Wagner. What finally brought the debate to a close was not the victory of either of the contending parties' arguments but rather, with regard to its philosophical and political dimensions, the French Revolution, and with regard to its more strictly musical dimension, the work of Mozart.

Mozart: The Pasha, the Queen, and the Emperor

Like Monteverdi, Mozart does not exactly spell revolution, a change in the established rules of the game; rather, he takes the balance struck by his period to a point of perfection that will give rise to subsequent revolutions. Instead of rejecting lyric flights or even the great vocalises of the purest bel canto of his time, he inserts them into a sustained, alert, subtle, and profound dramaturgy, drawing at times on themes and texts of great literary value (Molière for *Don Giovanni*, Beaumarchais for *Le Nozze di Figaro*) and on the resources of enormously talented librettists (Lorenzo Da Ponte).

If, as it has been said, Gluck sought virtue in the form of his compositions, then it might be said of Mozart that he sought transgression in the content of his operas and not in their form. Mozart did draw upon "tainted" literary texts that risked being banned by the censors (Beaumarchais's *Marriage de Figaro*). But as far as the musical composition of his operas is concerned, he stays well within the bounds of the habitual pre-Gluckian division of aria and recitative (which most of the time is *recitativo secco*—that is, supported by the harpsichord alone—or even pure *parlando,* as in his singspiels, particularly *Die Entführung aus dem Serail* and *Die Zauberflöte*). And it is in the character of Selim Pasha in *Die Entführung aus dem Serail* that the mastering or regulatory function of language, of recitative, is literally put on display.

The Pasha, or Speech as Master

Mozart's reasons for making the part of Selim Pasha a strictly spoken one, with no aria whatever, have been the subject of much speculation. Selim Pasha is one of the central characters of the work, and contemporary conventions (what could almost be called the collective bargaining agreements governing the employment of singers) should therefore have led Mozart to compose at least one or two grand arias for him. In addressing this question Jean and Brigitte Massin begin by eliminating, with good reason, hypotheses of sheer circumstance (lack of a singer able to sing the role, trouble with the librettist, last-minute problems, etc.). They then propose an explanation in terms of Mozart's personality, the events in his life during the composition of the opera, and the meaning that the role of Selim could have taken on for Mozart, given his personality and those circumstances:

[Selim] is a pasha and therefore, however enlightened one might wish him to be, a despot. Surely Mozart was not attempting a political statement in 1781 by refusing to let a benevolent despot sing. But perhaps, hard on the heels of the violent psychological shock of having broken with his patron, deeply enraged at having been thrown out on his ear by Count Arco, Mozart felt absolutely incapable of bringing forth suitable music for a slavemaster, however benevolent or even "enlightened" this one might be in the exercise of his rule. This benevolence and enlightenment may have been just the problem: because for an Osmin—stupid, coarse, and wicked— Mozart's palette was willing and ready.[38]

This hypothesis seems particularly resonant within the context of our problematics. As a personification of absolute authority, Selim Pasha stands squarely on the side of speech and law. He *is* sentence, first condemning, then pardoning; he *is* therefore the spoken word itself. What is striking, moreover, is the fact that composers quite often give characters who might be said to represent this agency of the superego the kind of musical material that draws their singing in the direction of speech. In Gluck's *Alceste,* for example, the oracle who pronounces Admète's death sentence and the condition on which it may be avoided "speaks but does not sing: below *his single note,* the orchestra provides minimal support, the trombones kept down to the pianissimo. . . ."[39] *Recto tono* or quasi–*recto tono* singing is a veritable stereotype of these characters. It occurs again in Mozart's *Idomeneo* when "The Voice," the oracle of Neptune, announces Idomeneo's pardon and what it will

[38]Jean Massin and Brigitte Massin; *Wolfgang Amadeus Mozart* (Paris: Fayard, 1970).

[39]Michel Noiray, in *L'Avant-scène Opéra* 73: *"Alceste"* (March 1985), 43 (textual and musical commentary).

cost him. It occurs yet again, in its most striking form, in the voice of the Commendatore, a voice of condemnation, which, as the intrusion of the dimension of fixity into the realm of singing, the presence of a gaze both petrified and petrifying,[40] the support of an absolute verbal principle, can be answered only by the silence of resignation or the cry of revolt. Mozart and Don Giovanni answer with the cry.

Thus there appeared, no doubt for the first time in the history of opera, the sheer, unmodulated cry, the supreme vocal manifestation that, once carefully avoided, now was deliberately chosen by the composer. Its advent, however, had been prepared for by higher and ever higher flights of free vocalise. The castrati built their fortunes on the transports—in the root sense of the word—into which their vocalises would send the spectators, and Mozart, unlike Gluck, does not hesitate to draw widely on the resources of vocalise in his grand soprano arias, even if at times he takes the scansion of these vocalises to such extremes that the listener's jouissance is thwarted.

The Queen and the Emperor

The scansion of the vocalise is, as we have seen, a way of mastering an invasive and unbridled emotion that surges forth in those instants when the voice frees itself from the spoken word, and as it rises higher materializes, as it were, as pure vocal object, finally to crystallize in something resembling the cry. The lineamental emergence of the vocal object in the baroque vocalise is something that Patrice Chéreau grasped perfectly in his staging of Mozart's *Lucio Silla:* every time a grand aria with vocalises is about to be sung, Chéreau has the character proceed from the stage down a ramp to the level of the orchestra pit, thus emphasizing the thoroughly instrumental character of the voice part at these moments, and hence its trans-sensical and transscenic position.

If this mastering effect can be attributed to the scansion of the vocalise, it is because this scansion seems to draw the vocalise back in the direction of speaking, which, as I have said, is on one level simply the sectioning of a continuum of sound by intervals of silence. Perhaps the most striking example of this effect occurs in the grand aria of the Queen of the Night in Act II of *Die Zauberflöte* ("Der Hölle

---

[40]Leporello: "How terrible the looks he casts at us. . . . He is looking at us still" (*Don Giovanni*, II.ii).

Rache . . ."). Its words are charged with dramatic intensity: a mother is inciting her daughter to murder! It is hard to imagine a situation more extreme. And yet this tragic aria is the occasion for "acrobatic vocalises and staccato arpeggios that, as Jacques Chailley has said, could lead to its being mistaken, at least by today's audiences who do not understand the words, for Lakmé's 'Bell Song.' "[41] All emotion, all jouissance other than pleasure in and admiration for the vocal acrobatics—in the event that they are successfully accomplished—has been expelled from this aria. Consequently, any suffering on the part of the listener during this aria results not from the tragedy it expresses but from the listener's identification with the singer and with the difficulties she faces, often all too apparent. A consequence of the perils of this vocal scansion is the reintroduction of the singer as an explicit presence. By her not infrequent failure she becomes a screen interposed between the listener and the lineamental appearance of the vocal object in such jouissance as does arise. In the worst of cases, a missed note will reduce this object to outcast status, to the status of refuse, and arouse the aggression of the frustrated listener. This consequence of the musical composition of this opera is entirely secondary, for there is every reason to think that Mozart's singers were well trained in these vocal exercises, and that in any case the singers of the day wielded such power that they would never have bowed to a composer so audacious as to impose on them the kind of vocal trials that could expose them to the risk of public failure.

The reasons for this aria's "emotional deficit" are not to be sought in changing audience sensibilities, as Henri Barraud proposes. The emotional impact of so many others of Mozart's arias is patent; it is hard to understand why present-day sensibilities should be deadened for this aria alone or for those similar in form. The Queen of the Night's aria is prefigured by other grand arias by Mozart with long vocalises, notably Elektra's aria of imprecations in the last act of *Idomeneo*, "D'Oreste, d'Ajace . . .": the theme is quite similar (murderous/suicidal fury), and its vocalic scansion is similarly thwarting as rapidly descending cascades of notes eventually break the tension they induce. It is as if Mozart flinched before the intensity of the emotive charge he was manipulating; as if, as a moment of exceptional jouis-

---

[41]Henri Barraud, in *L'Avant-scène Opéra* 1: *"La Flute Enchantée"* (January–February 1976) (textual and musical commentary).

sance approached, he sought to strengthen his defenses against it. The staccato notes are Mozart's way of giving the aria the discontinuity of those microsilences that, as we have seen, are one of the foundations of language systems whose medium is sound. It is in this sense that I propose that this kind of composition, by introducing the discontinuous into the vocalise, reinscribes it under the tutelage of language. The jouissance that arises when the voice is freed from this tutelage has now been mastered by it. The inevitable evocation of the pure cry in the Queen of the Night's high G is reinserted into a system that abolishes its untenable emotional force: now the Queen of the Night's song of murder is ready to serve as musical background in a television commercial promoting a brand of packaged rice.[42] Moreover, this kind of rhythmic hyperscansion often causes Mozart's music to be characterized in terms of the accretion of notes or musical signifiers that it entails.

"Too many notes, my dear Mozart." This famous remark by Emperor Joseph II after hearing *Die Entführung aus dem Serail* is considered one of those great blunders of which the Great Men of this world are capable when they meddle in artistic matters. Now Joseph II was a particularly cultivated man who happened to know quite a lot about music. Men of enlightenment, especially when they are also despots, can and do of course say stupid things, yet perhaps they might be given some credit and not be summarily cast into the dustbins of art history. Perhaps it is not exactly this "too many notes" in itself that Joseph II was aiming at but rather an excessive mastery of emotion produced by the accretion of those notes (remember Campra's remark about Rameau's *Hippolyte et Aricie:* "Here is enough music for ten operas"). Mozart, who flirted endlessly with transgression, saves himself by shoring up his defenses against it.

But here as elsewhere, excessive defenses are a sign of their weakness: in *Don Giovanni,* the walls finally crumble with the four cries that punctuate the Commendatore's scene, "original" cries, in a configuration not to be heard again in operatic history. For not only are they

---

[42]The fundamental difference between this commercial, an advertisement for the Taureau Ailé (Winged Bull) brand of rice, and the spot I cited earlier, which used Manon's aria from Puccini's *Manon Lescaut,* is apparent: in the latter case, the commercial made explicit use of the aria's emotional power, which thus itself became the subject of the advertisement. In the rice commercial, the Queen of the Night's aria functioned simply as background music.

heard here for the first time, they are integrated, in their fourfold structure, into the musical fabric of the work, are prepared by the pulsing chromatic ascent in the orchestration for Elvira's and Leporello's screams of terror. Mozart of course immediately feels the need, or rather feels obliged, to return once again in the opera's final scene to a tightly scanned composition so as not to leave the spectator in a state of shock at the double scream of Don Giovanni/Leporello after the earth has opened to swallow up the libertine. Mozart immediately resituates the work within the sphere of moral order, in content as well as in musical form. He undertakes this moral reaffirmation more or less reluctantly, since he removed this scene from the Vienna production in 1788, a year after the production in Prague. Far from being "obtuse,"[43] nineteenth-century directors—Mahler notable among them—were actually quite perceptive in understanding the superficial character of this rehabilitation and in continuing the tradition of the Vienna production by generally omitting the final scene. For during the nineteenth century, decisive steps would be taken along the path from speech to the cry and in the relationship with lyric jouissance, which therefore was to be modified yet again.

Romantic Bel Canto

The golden age of the castrati died away with the eighteenth century, succumbing to the blows of a progressive ideology that decried the practice of castration as well as the gratuitousness and vanity of the castrati's vocal superfluities. The Gluckist reform must have taken its toll, too, since it deprived the castrati of all opportunity to show off their vocal treasure, even if Gluck himself occasionally did not scorn to make use of their artistry. The Italian opera, which had built its fortunes on the trans-sensical voice of the castrato, now reinvested its appetite for vocal jouissance in the double, sexually divided figure of the soprano and the tenor, the soprano voice carving out the lion's

---

[43]J. Victor Hocquard, in *L'Avant-scène Opéra* 24: *"Don Giovanni"* (November–December, 1979), 124: "During the obtuse nineteenth century, this final scene was so widely condemned that it was usually not included in performances" (textual and musical commentary).

share here, as though it were somehow felt that for want of the castrato, the soprano voice might constitute the privileged site where
music lovers were most likely to find what they were after. Soon one
could hear those great soprano and, to a lesser degree, tenor arias by
such composers as Bellini and Donizetti, which more and more clearly
began to prepare for a true melodic cry at the apogee of a vocalic ascent
now stripped of the trills, roulades, and scansions with which it had
been burdened. Of course, the continued sectioning of the work into
aria and recitative ensured the regulatory function I spoke of earlier,
even as the recitative was becoming more and more "orchestrated" and
musicalized. And as might be expected, this preeminence of voice and
music gave rise to a new desire to reform, one that Richard Wagner
would carry out in the composition and "theorization" of his "music
dramas."

Wagnerian Music Drama

Wagner sets forth his theoretical ideas principally in two works:
Opera and Drama, written in 1850, and *The Art-work of the Future,* written the year before. I will not attempt the impossible and try to summarize the profusion of ideas and analyses that characterize these two
works. I will limit myself to drawing out the driving ideas behind
Wagner's theoretical reflections.

Wagner begins by denouncing what he calls a "fundamental error":
"I declare aloud that the error in the art-genre of Opera consists herein:
*that a Means of expression (Music) has been made the end, while the End
of expression (the Drama) has been made a means."* Wagner will thus
endeavor to retrace the history of this error in the evolution of the
relationship between the poet and the composer. For Wagner, Gluck's
reform consisted primarily in the composer's reassertion of control
over the *singers* and had to do more with operatic production and
performance than with a genuine transformation of the operatic form
itself. He observes, however, that it was the fact that Gluck expressed
"with consciousness and firm conviction the fitness and necessity of an
expression answering to the text-substratum, in Aria and Recitative
. . . that makes [this composer] the departure-point of an at any rate
thorough change in the quondam situation of the artistic factors of

Opera toward one another." Gluck, "consciously concerned to reproduce as faithfully as possible by his Musical Expression the emotion indicated in the 'text,' and above all to never sacrifice the purely declamatory accent of the verse in favor of this musical expression . . . took pains to speak correctly and intelligibly in his music." But Wagner—and this is the important point—finds that in Gluck, the respective positions of poet and composer have not changed in the least: "rather had the Composer grown more dictatorial, since, with his declared consciousness of a higher mission—made good against the virtuoso Singer—he set to work with more deliberate zeal at the arrangement of the opera's framework." The great Wagnerian project resides in the radical recasting of the relationship between poet and composer, in their close collaboration, in their fusion even. Wagner sees this fusion in Mozart, but describes it as merely fortuitous, unconscious and unintended. "There is nothing more characteristic of Mozart, in his career of opera-composer, than the unconcernedness wherewith he went to work: it was so far from occurring to him to weigh the pros and cons of the aesthetic problem involved in Opera, that he rather engaged with utmost unconstraint in setting any and every libretto offered him, almost heedless whether it were a thankful or a thankless task for him as pure musician." But

the noble, straightforward simplicity of his purely musical instinct, i.e. his intuitive penetration into the arcana of his art, made it well-nigh impossible for him to bring forth magical effects, as Composer, where the Poem was flat and meaningless. How little did this richest-gifted of all musicians understand our modern music-makers' trick of building guard towers of music upon a hollow, valueless foundation, and playing the rapt and the inspired where all the poetaster's botch is void and flimsy, the better to show that the Musician is the jack in office and can go any length he pleases, even to making something out of nothing—the same as the good God! Oh how doubly dear and above all honor is Mozart to me, that it was not possible to him to invent music for *Tito* like that of *Don Giovanni,* for *Così fan tutte* like that of *Figaro!* How shamefully would it have desecrated Music!

Music Mozart always made, but *beautiful* music he could never write excepting when he was inspired.[44]

---

[44]Wagner, *Opera and Drama,* 17, 27, 81, 27–28, 36, 37, 82; Wagner's emphasis.

This evaluation of *Così Fan Tutte* is debatable, to say the least. Today Wagner would probably reconsider his position, not the thesis itself but his judgment of the dramatic depth in *Così Fan Tutte* which certain interpretations, insightful commentaries, and stagings have helped to reveal. Without recanting, Wagner might grant *Così Fan Tutte* its absolute musical beauty.

Wagner of course then comments regretfully on the evolution of Italian opera after Mozart: "But the amazingly lucky relationship between Poet and Composer, that we have found in Mozart's master-work, we see completely vanishing again in the further evolution of Opera; until, as we have already noticed, Rossini quite abolished it, making absolute Melody the only authentic factor of Opera, to which all other interests, and above all the cooperation of the Poet, had wholly to subordinate themselves." But the key position in his theoretical construct Wagner assigns to Beethoven rather than to Mozart. This might seem odd, considering that Beethoven composed only one opera, *Fidelio*, which Wagner fails even to mention, either in *Opera and Drama* or in *The Art-work of the Future*. Yet proceeding from the idea that "down to the present, everything which has had a real and determinant influence upon the shaping of Opera has issued simply from the domain of Absolute Music,"[45] Wagner embarks on a particularly original analysis of Beethoven. He begins by denouncing "Beethoven's primordial and puissant error: wanting somehow to make of instrumental music a genuine language. . . . In long, connected tracts of sound, as in larger, smaller, or even smallest fragments, ["harmonic melody"] turned beneath the Master's poet hand to vowels, syllables, and words and phrases of a speech in which a message hitherto unheard, and never spoken yet, could promulgate itself."[46] "The greater portion of Beethoven's works of this [second] period must be regarded as instinctive efforts to frame a speech to voice his longings." But these attempts meet with failure because "in the works of the second half of his artistic life, Beethoven is un-understandable—or rather mis-understandable—mostly just where he desires to express a specific, individual Content in the most intelligible way."[47] (Here

---

[45]Ibid., 82, 69.

[46]Richard Wagner, *The Art-Work of the Future*, vol. 1 of *Richard Wagner's Prose Works*, trans. William Ashton Ellis (1893; rpt. St. Clair Shores, Mich.: Scholarly Press, 1972), 121.

[47]Wagner, *Opera and Drama*, 72. Jean and Brigitte Massin offer an interesting analysis of this idea in *Beethoven* (Fayard).

Wagner is referring to Beethoven's last sonatas and last quartets, which were particularly ill received by his contemporaries.) This contradiction, according to Wagner, will be overcome only when "he sets off . . . to measure out the ocean's bounds, and . . . casts his anchor on the new-found shore; . . . and this anchor was the Word."[48]

There is a close resemblance, by the way, between this metaphor and the one Gluck used in his letter dedicating *Alceste:* both speak of music as a surface, a color, or an ocean that must be contained by a limit, a contour, or a shore—the Word—to which one must make fast. But

the word which Beethoven set as crown upon the forehead of his composition, this word was: *"Freude!"* ["Rejoice"!]. With this word he cries to men: "Breast to breast, ye mortal millions! This one kiss to all the world!" And this Word will be the language of the Art-work of the Future.—The *Last Symphony* of Beethoven is the redemption of Music from out her own peculiar element into the realm of universal art. It is the *human* Evangel of the art of the Future. Beyond it no forward step is possible; for upon it the perfect Art-work of the Future alone can follow, the universal Drama to which Beethoven has forged for us the key."[49]

The Ninth Symphony embodies the Wagnerian model of the poet/composer relationship because

even his *"Freude"*-melody does not as yet appear invented for, or through, the Poet's verse, but merely conceived with an eye to Schiller's poem after an incitation by its general contents. First where, in the progress of this poem, Beethoven is worked-up by its contents into a dramatic directness, do we see his melodic combinations spring ever more definitely from the diction also; so that at last the unprecedented many-sidedness of his music's Expression answers to the highest sense, at any rate, both of the poem and its wording; and with such directness, that the music, once divorced from the poem, would appear to us no longer thinkable or comprehensible.

But his most decisive message, at last given us by the master in his *magnum opus,* is the necessity he felt as Musician to throw himself into the

---

[48]Wagner, *Art-Work of the Future,* 125–26.
[49]Ibid., 126; emphasis Wagner's.

arms of the Poet, in order to compass the act of begetting the true, the unfailingly real and redeeming Melody. To become a human being, Beethoven perforce must become an entire, i.e. a social being, subjected to the generic conditionments of the manly and the womanly.[50]

The groundwork is thus laid for the fundamental metaphor of the Wagnerian thesis: "Music is a woman"[51] and the poet is the man who must come to her in Love and make her fruitful.

It will come as no surprise, then, to find ethical judgments that by now have become familiar: "Someone has very appropriately called the modern Italian opera a wanton"; or "We have seen the frivolous Opera-melody—i.e. that robbed of any real connexion with the poem's text."[52] In the face of the decadence of the Italian Prostitute, it is up to Wagner to accomplish the procreative redemption of the Mother: German music drama. Here again is the ideal of a fusion of Word and Music, but one that will radically transcend the ideal of the Florentine Camerata. For Wagner would go beyond formal equality of the poetic and musical discourses; his goal is to harmonize the deep or even unconscious truths of these two discourses, at the level of the organizing drama itself. For him it is not enough that music respect the formal intelligibility of the text; it must respect its underlying and unconscious meaning. That is what the leitmotif principle strives to accomplish in voicing the truth of an utterance—whatever the utterance may be—every time this truth has a function in the development and deep understanding of the work.

But—and this is the question Wagner ponders in a letter to Liszt of 25 November 1850—"If I show that music, the woman, becomes co-parent with the poet, the man, I must take care that this splendid woman is not given over to the first comer who desires her, but only to the man who longs for woman with true, irresistible love."[53] And for Wagner, "only from the Greek world-view, has the genuine Artwork of Drama been able as yet to blossom forth. But this drama's stuff was the Myth."[54] Here the ideal claimant to the nuptial bed is designated:

[50]Wagner, *Opera and Drama*, 110, 107.

[51]Ibid., 111.

[52]Ibid., 112, 91.

[53]In *Correspondence of Wagner and Liszt*, vol. 1, trans. Francis Hueffer (1897; rpt. Westport, Conn.: Greenwood, 1969).

[54]Wagner, *Opera and Drama*, 153.

the mythic drama—in the German language, because in German the stress and thus the point of musical coupling is a function of the root of the word and consequently of its meaning, not of "arbitrary" syllabication.

"*La Folie-Tristan*" and Continuous Melody

The preeminence of meaning in dramatic representation led to the development of a musical form that in effect accomplishes what Gluck's reform had set out to achieve: discontinuity between aria and recitative has vanished, along with the recitative and the aria themselves, in "continuous melody." "In contrast to the traditional conception of opera based on thematic opposition, on the alternation of aria and recitative, Wagner introduces the notion of melodic continuity, a kind of dynamism that escapes the constraints of the recitative and is modeled after the continuity of life, on the duration of consciousness, calling into question the role of repetition."[55] I emphasize this notion of the continuous in Wagnerian composition because it seems to be at the very heart of the emotional power of his music, a power that many listeners reject for fear of drowning in it. Remember the rift between "Wagnerians" and the rest (mostly "Mozartians" and "Verdians") pointed out in the interview on the steps of the Palais Garnier. Remember, too, what Guy said repeatedly: "I felt . . . afraid, perhaps." Such notions as "vertigo," "madness," and "excess" always loom when it comes to Wagner. He himself was aware of this. While he was composing *Tristan* he wrote to Mathilde Wesendonck: "Tristan is becoming a *terrible* thing.[56] That final act! I am afraid that my opera will be banned, unless bad performances turn it into parody. These alone will save its life, because if they were perfectly good, people would go mad. . . ."

The Mozart/Wagner rift embraces the distinction between pleasure and jouissance sketched out earlier. This may appear completely paradoxical at first glance. For that distinction (in opera, at least) was described as hinging on the relationship of language and music, with jouissance identified as an effect of the destruction or dissolution of

55D. Bosseur, "Richard Wagner," in *Histoire de la musique occidentale,* ed. Jean Massin and Brigitte Massin (Paris: Messidor/Temps Actuel, 1983).
56Cf. Rilke, in the epigraph to this book.

language by music. Wagner's whole theory seems to keep Music tightly coupled with the Word. Where, then, does the emotional impact of his work come from? It seems to come precisely from the continuity at all levels of Wagner's musical construction. Unlike Mozart, who attenuated possible emotional "excess" by introducing discontinuity into the vocalise or the lyrical development, Wagner introduces melodic continuity into the domain of the spoken word.[57] The tempo of the Wagnerian musical discourse usually has little to do with the tempo of the "natural" verbal utterance, which conventional recitative by and large respects. It can thus be said that the melodic continuity of Wagnerian singing tends to corrode or erode the signifying scansion of language, less radically than the aria, perhaps, but seamlessly from beginning to end, without interruption and without permitting a return to language by way of the usual recitative. We find this continuity not only in the absence of the aria/recitative rupture but at the level of the musical material itself, with the frequent long-held note. *Parsifal* is an extreme example—so extreme, in fact, that, depending on the tempo the conductor adopts for these long notes, the length of a performance can vary considerably from one interpretation to the next: Toscanini's, for example, was a full hour longer than Richard Strauss's (Bayreuth 1931 and 1933). And neither of these interpretations can be said to have deliberately betrayed the musical score. The work is certainly long in itself (more than four hours on average). But the fact remains that only a composition with an abundance of long values could permit such differences in performance time. Later it will become apparent why this intrusion of the continuous might tend to produce the sustained seduction so characteristic of the Wagnerian musical universe; for the moment I will merely situate it in its opposition to the discontinuity of signifying discourse, and thus on the side of what vies with language. But as with Gluck, the tension thus induced is brought to a head by the magnitude of the pure lyrical developments that remain omnipresent, ready to surge forth at any moment as the action may require, and are often very brief—the space of a phrase or a word—as they are perpetually prepared by this ever-fertile ground of the Wagnerian melodic continuum.

And if this continuum so frequently yields lyric flights that verge on the cry, if it is so frequently rent by the sheer nonmusical cry, this is no

---

[57]Note that with Wagner, one speaks of continuous *melody*, not continuous recitative.

accident, as we shall soon see: the continuous and the cry are often strangely related.

In Wagner, the pure cry or its close relation, the stratospheric high note, is raised to the status of primordial vocal element, as the composer fully intended.

It would be appropriate now to specify exactly what I mean by "cry" for it is a word that in musical commentary is used rather haphazardly, most often metaphorically, as in Henri Barraud's commentary on Monteverdi's *Orfeo*, in which he speaks of Orpheus's cry as "almost a howl"[58]—a howl that culminates, musically speaking, on a quite modest F, which takes nothing away from the emotionally expressive intensity of the passage. But whenever I speak of a *pure* or sheer cry, I mean specifically a paroxysmal vocal emission beyond the range of music and out of reach of the word. This cry is therefore not supported by the musical notation, nor can it be accommodated on the staff; and it is not supported by direct verbal notation in the text (at most, it is indicated by an "Ah!" in the libretto, though usually it is given in a stage direction such as "screams with horror" or "cries out in terror"). It is in this dual sense that the cry is literally unsupportable, unbearable, and untenable. Lulu makes us feel the horror of the cry that no human symbolic system can accommodate, and this is why the cry is so often called "inhuman."

The pure cry must be intended by the composer, precisely situated in the musical and dramatic development of the work, and may be prepared for by the orchestral or vocal musical material that immediately precedes it, and it will completely determine (how we shall soon see) the musical or vocal content that immediately follows it.

In this work I also speak of the "musicalized" or "melodic" cry to designate another point of stratospheric vocal paroxysm, but one that remains within the musical and/or verbal discourse, whether it comes as the climax of a pure vocalise independent of all verbal support or as the highest point of lyric flight on the syllable of a word, whose intelligibility is thereby destroyed. Though Marie's cry in Alban Berg's *Wozzeck* prefigures Lulu's cry in every aspect, it still falls into this second category because it is noted on the staff by a B on the first

[58]Barraud, in *L'Avant-scène Opéra* 5: *"Orfeo"* (September–October 1976), 55 (textual and musical commentary).

syllable of "Hilfe"; and this word is literally obliterated at the tonal height at which it is sung.

I will not, however, classify as a cry what is merely plaint, exclamation, or call, when it is supported by a word or by a name that remains intelligible. Thus, though Rodolfo's "Mimi!" at the end of *La Bohème* is evocative of the cry in many respects, it preserves an intelligible signifying presence and so should not be classified as a musicalized cry, any more than Scarpia's call of "Aiuto!" in *Tosca*, and for the same reasons.

"The Cry of Pain Preceded All Speech"[59]

In Wagner, then, the cry achieves the status of a thoroughly distinct component of the vocal palette, and though Wagner may not have been the "inventor" of the cry,[60] he is its theoretician. Here is what he writes in his 1870 essay on Beethoven, referring to the thought of Schopenhauer:

As the dream-organ cannot be roused into action by outer impressions, against which the brain is now fast locked, this must take place through happenings in the inner organism that our waking consciousness merely feels as vague sensations. But it is this inner life through which we are directly allied with the whole of nature, and thus are brought into a relation with the Essence of things that eludes the forms of outer knowledge, time and Space; whereby Schopenhauer so convincingly explains the genesis of prophetic or telepathic fatidical dreams, or even, in rare and extreme cases the occurrence of somnambulistic clairvoyance. From the most terrifying of such dreams we wake with a *cry*, the immediate expression of the anguished will, which thus makes definite entrance into the Sound-world first of all, to manifest itself without. Now if we take the Cry in all the diminutions of its vehemence, down to the gentler plaint of longing, as the root-element of every human message to the ear; and if we cannot but find it in the most immediate utterance of the will, through which the latter turns the swiftest

---

[59]Flamand (Music) in Richard Strauss's *Capriccio*.

[60]It is equally beside the point whether Mozart was or was not really the first to use it; what is important is that *Don Giovanni* is the first work of major consequence in operatic history to integrate it into its design in such an elaborate way.

and the surest toward Without, then we have less cause to wonder at its immediate intelligibility than at an *art* arising from this element.[61]

To summarize very schematically, without entering into an analysis of Schopenhauer's philosophical concept of "will" (which has little to do with the everyday meaning of the word), we might say that the cry is somehow the most *immediate* manifestation—in other words, the manifestation most unmediated by any system of representation whatsoever—through which "the essence of things" offers itself to knowledge or at the very least gives a sign of its presence.[62] The cries, plaints, and moans of Kundry in Act II of *Parsifal,* when she awakens to her condition as seductress under the sway of the magician Klingsor, are Wagner's "theoretical" or even "metaphysical" cry made stunningly concrete: "Kundry's shape arises in the blueish light. She seems asleep. Gradually however she moves like one awakening. Finally she utters a terrible scream. Kundry utters a loud wail that subsides to a frightened whimper. . . . [Kundry speaks] hoarsely and brokenly as if striving to regain speech."[63] These are Wagner's own stage directions for Kundry's awakening in Act II of *Parsifal.*

Wagner's theoretical trajectory is thus curiously evocative of what I have sought to retrace in Jean-Jacques Rousseau: at the limits or in the margins of a construct that strives to ground an aesthetics of opera in the fusion of music and language, anchoring the trans-sensical in meaning, there inevitably appears, as original myth, the primacy of the trans-sensical absolute in its brute vocal expression: the cry.

Sprechgesang

With Wagner and after him in Germany and in Austria, the tension between music and language increases as the voice draws closer and

---

[61]Richard Wagner, *Beethoven,* vol. 5 of *Richard Wagner's Prose Works,* trans. William Ashton Ellis (1896; rpt. St. Clair Shores, Mich.: Scholarly Press, 1972), 68–69.

[62]This notion brings to mind an analogous one in Lacan, who construes the cry as the mark of the "encounter" with a point of the Real (in the Lacanian sense of the term) that escapes symbolization (is unnameable).

[63]Richard Wagner, *Parsifal,* libretto trans. Lionel Salter, in Deutsche Grammophon 2530 162–6, Pierre Boulez, conductor (Bayreuth 1970).

closer to the edge of the cry. A shattering of the form is on the horizon and will be achieved by Arnold Schoenberg and by Alban Berg, who, after throwing out the tonal system, develop a new formula of spoken declamation to musical accompaniment. "Intermediary between recitative and what is called 'melodrama,' . . . it consists of asking the singers to 'speak notes'—in other words, to emit true notes without the vibrato characteristic of singing."[64] Opera now becomes a locus where a multiplicity of modalities and compromises between language and music cohabit, commingle and vie with each other whenever the composer's expressive intentions so dictate, the pure cry calling forth pure speech as if in response, as in the final duet of Lulu and Jack the Ripper, which gives the impression of a dialogue between a man speaking and a woman who answers with a long modulated musical cry, culminating in her terrifying death cry.

Sprechgesang marks a kind of culmination point where the distinction between speech and music becomes so tenuous that conventional musical notation proves incapable of transcribing it unequivocally. Thus Berg, for example, comes to use three types of notation in *Lulu* to convey the lyric effect he seeks. Apart from the indication "spoken" for passages whose delivery is a matter of pure and simple declamation (without melodic vocal support), they are as follows: "rhythmic declamation," accompanied only by the note stems and their groupings with no indication of pitch; note stems terminating in a cross for "melodies tending toward the spoken"; and finally, for passages that are more "spoken than sung," stems terminating in an oblique line— subtleties that make the singers' task difficult and fuel endless discussions among commentators and critics.

"Der Arie ihr Recht"[65]

In the meantime Italy, which had applauded Verdi, now acclaimed Puccini.

Verdi brought marked changes to the established equilibrium of romantic bel canto, but without upsetting it fundamentally and with-

---

[64]Bourgeois, *L'Opéra des origines à demain*, 356.
[65]"Give the aria its due"; La Roche, in Richard Strauss, *Capriccio*, scene 9.

out developing these changes into a system. With Verdi the aria tends to abandon structural symmetry and lose its characteristic detachment from the rest of the action as it flows more and more into the dramatic fabric that surrounds it. In his last works, particularly *Otello*, this formal development makes itself felt further, aiming, as in Wagner, to establish a more marked continuity between the musical and the vocal discourses. But this evolution is perhaps even clearer on a strictly vocal level. As Jacques Bourgeois has noted, "whereas the upper reaches of the register serve only an ornamental purpose in the traditional bel canto, Verdi discovers the dramatic impact of bold use of the upper register." But unlike Wagner, Verdi almost never goes beyond the melodic cry: the pure cry is a rarity in his work. It is also rare in the work of Puccini, which from a formal standpoint is not very different from Verdi's: while the vocal dialogues are interwoven with a musical orchestration of sustained richness, the fundamental energies of the opera remain quite localized in the aria. As Bourgeois has emphasized, "the Italians could never bring themselves to forgo this convention, however unrealistic it seemed."[66]

Capriccio: Prima la Musica o Prima le Parole?

These, then, are some of the high points of this love/hate story of music and language, a story that runs through every development in opera through the three centuries of its existence. A subject such as this was bound sooner or later to become itself an operatic theme, much as in a dream a buried desire sometimes throws off the disguises that have masked it and finally comes to light. This is what happens with *Capriccio*, which Richard Strauss composed in 1942.

Some 150 years earlier, on 7 February 1786, Mozart presented his one-act singspiel, *Der Schauspieldirektor* ("The Impresario"), at the Schoenbrunn Palace. The principal entertainment of the evening, however, was another one-act piece, this one by Antonio Salieri, titled *Prima la musica, e poi le parole* (First the music and then the words), with a libretto by Giambattista Casti. Salieri, good Italian that he was, was

[66]Bourgeois, *L'Opéra des origines à demain.*

resolute. Mozart had his doubts: in 1778 he wrote: "I do not know if the words of an opera ought to be the obedient daughter of music."[67] Mozart had also, as we know, been particularly impressed by the new genre of "melodrama," as he was given to understand it by Georg Benda's *Medea*, presented at Mannheim in 1778. "You know, of course," he wrote to his father, "that there is no singing in it, only recitation, to which the music is like a sort of obbligato accompaniment to a recitative. Now and then words are spoken while the music goes on, and this produces the finest effect."[68] Mozart even undertook to compose his own "declaimed opera," an unfinished *Semiramis*, the manuscript of which is now lost. But Mozart, as we have seen, solved this problem in another way.

Richard Strauss, then, takes up Casti's idea and stages the famous question "First the music or first the words?" He enacts it through the love rivalry that pits a poet, Olivier, against a composer, Flamand, both suitors to the same woman, the Countess. Beyond the finesse and the intelligence of the dialogues with which I have punctuated my inquiry up to this point, it is interesting to note that Strauss comes up with an original musical form he calls *ein Konversationsstück*, a conversation piece, profoundly altering the balance struck by Wagner. In *Der Rosenkavalier* and *Intermezzo*, most notably, Strauss had already elaborated this style: in contrast to Wagnerian composition, it preserves the natural tempo of spoken dialogue and in this sense belongs to traditional recitative; yet it is much more "musicalized" and is not interrupted by arias in the strict sense, and thus it can be said to maintain a certain kinship with Wagnerian "continuous melody." Strauss was nonetheless aware that this style of composition risked monotony, so he left room at key moments for particularly lyrical displays, as in the work's finale, a genuine aria that calls into play all the mechanisms whose effect on the listener I have described: it organizes a melodic trajectory that rises in pitch until it culminates in a note that fulfills the melomane's expectation. For while the question "Prima la musica o prima le parole?" has no answer (the Countess divides her attentions between poet and composer without according preference to either one), the

[67]See Heinz Becker, Introduction to brochure notes for Richard Strauss, *Capriccio*, Deutsche Grammophon 2550 202–204.

[68]Wolfgang Amadeus Mozart to Leopold Mozart, 12 November 1778, in *The Letters of Mozart and His Family*, trans. and ed. Emily Anderson (London: Macmillan, 1985), 339.

entire trajectory of the history of opera in its own roundabout way seems to install as its blue note—as its answer to the listener's hopes and quest—the highest sound that the voice can produce, a sound heard with a thrill of pleasure and then, once the prohibition of the cry is finally transgressed, with shudders of dread.

The *Diabolus* in Opera

"The interval between Wozzeck's last word (*nicht*) and Marie's final cry is the prophetic F–B. Like the B, the diminished fifth F–B had been prepared for from the beginning of the opera."[69] This "prophetic" interval is the one that medieval harmony considered the most perilous of dissonances: the tritone, the *diabolus in musica*. It is quite striking that *Wozzeck*'s atonal composition gives a privileged place to the major prohibition of medieval composition and that the transgression of this prohibition is directly associated with the rending cry. In Berg, the tritone of course no longer functions as diabolical dissonance: I am merely pointing out the seemingly fortuitous conjunction of what once bore the devil's brand and Marie's cry. This is not to exclude the possibility that Berg makes this association deliberately— not with a wink and a nod but by one of those implicit or even unconscious references with which his work swarms.

Later we shall see that this coming together of the devil and the cry in Act III of Berg's *Wozzeck* is not an isolated event. Similar associations are found in the Commendatore's scene in Mozart's *Don Giovanni*, where Elvira's and Leporello's cries are preceded by a chromatic rise in the orchestra, and in *Tristan*, where Brangäne's cry in Act II, like the musical cry at the climax of Isolde's Transfiguration in Act III, becomes the keystone in a *chromatic* structure. Chromaticism was another suspect mode of musical composition for legislators of medieval religious music, and we know that "exacerbated" chromaticism, as in *Tristan*, will, by dissolving the perception of tonality, open the way to atonality and its systematization by Arnold Schoenberg. Therefore the conjunction of these three elements—chromaticism, disso-

[69]Stéphane Goldet, in *L'Avant-scène Opéra* 36: *"Wozzeck"* (September–October 1981), 75 (textual and musical commentary).

nance, and the cry, which is completely liberated when the tonal system disappears—comes as no surprise.

But if the rules of musical composition set forth no explicit or formal prohibition of the cry, it is doubtless because the composing subject—or what Alain Didier-Weill has called the "musicmaking" subject (*le sujet musiquant*)—has internalized the prohibition, as all subjects do. There is no need, then, for an explicit musical rule to suppress the cry. If indeed one doubts the power of the system set up to prevent its emergence, one need only observe how the cry is avoided by or repressed in the child, how in the adult it is considered a kind of obscenity. We have already seen this system at work on various occasions, with the moral judgments, the reformist tendencies that appear as soon as singing approaches that satanic limit at which all speech fails. Note how directors and singers hesitate to transgress this limit, how they attenuate it or muffle it in spite of the composer's specific directions. And note especially that as soon as the cry is uttered, it is covered by a *tutti* from the orchestra, forte or fortissimo, as if unconsciously the composer had felt that Pandora's box had been opened and all available musical resources had to be rallied in an effort to close it, to efface or repress what should not have been given voice. These triple fortes of orchestral overlapping of the sheer cry are genuine stereotypes of musical composition (they are almost identical in Wagner, Richard Strauss, Shostakovich, and Berg).[70] Yet they are no longer so ubiquitous at the "melodic" cry, as if the fact of remaining inscribed within the musical discourse made the cry more bearable, more susceptible to symbolization by the listener.

Perhaps such terms as "resistance" and "avoidance" in the face of a universe that threatens to overflow its edges, to break through its boundaries, can be applied to the attitude of a Richard Strauss, who, having brought the voice to a point of paroxysm in *Salome* and *Elektra*, retreats with *Der Rosenkavalier* to a music more subservient—I commented on this in connection with *Capriccio*—to the constraints of text and tonality.

---

[70]One need only listen to be convinced: Alberich's cry (*Das Rheingold*), Brangäne's (*Tristan*), Brünnhilde's (*Götterdämmerung*), Katerina's (*Lady Macbeth of the Mzensk District*), Lulu's (*Lulu*), Marie's (*Wozzeck*): the orchestral treatment of Marie's cry is unique, for the orchestral covering is staggered through time, and something akin to silence immediately follows the cry; the covering comes afterward, through a fantastic crescendo that emerges from this silence and is twice reprised.

But it was inevitable that one day someone would draw the lesson of *Tristan,* would go through the looking glass to which Wagner had led opera. This passage was not without its difficulties, and it took two to bring it about: first Arnold Schoenberg and then Alban Berg. Schoenberg, aware of his historic mission to bring about "the emancipation of dissonance," just as Moses led his people from Egypt to the Promised Land, was not to complete the only major opera he undertook (*Moses und Aron*).[71] Alban Berg's second opera, *Lulu,* was to remain unfinished as well. I will take up these two unfinished works in greater detail; they are unfinished in a way that paradoxically speaks of a kind of success—we shall see how—and that at the same time is symptomatic of the obstacles one encounters when one seeks to open certain doors.

The strange story of Berg's widow's determined opposition to the completion of the last act of *Lulu* may perhaps be seen as something other than the sacred respect due the work of the deceased. We know, in fact, that all that remained to be done was the orchestration. Schoenberg was approached about taking on the project, but he refused, citing the anti-Semitism of a line in the work. Thereafter, until her death in 1976, Helene Berg refused to authorize the completion of the work; she agreed to it on several occasions but then immediately revoked her consent.[72] It may not be farfetched to see Lulu's death cry as the death cry of Woman, a kind of "black hole" whose gravitational pull keeps the opera galaxy spiraling, and to interpret Mrs. Berg's refusal as an unconscious and desperate attempt to keep it from being screamed out to the world.

Cry and Silence

I began this chapter by evoking the relationship between the cry and silence and have just examined how the tension between music and

---

[71] Arnold Schoenberg to René Leibowitz, 15 March 1948, in *Arnold Schoenberg's Letters,* ed. Erwin Stein, trans. Eikthne Wickins and Ernst Kaiser (London: Faber & Faber, 1958). His "small" operas—*Erwartung, Die Glückliche Hand,* and *Von Heute auf Morgen*—cannot be considered major works.

[72] The complete work was not heard until 1979.

language which underlies the pendular movement of opera history, perhaps driving the spiraling movement I have just evoked, finally reveals the force that sustains it: the always resisted attraction of an absolute boundary to which the cry draws ever closer. It is at this boundary that cry and silence intertwine.

The mathematician P. Soury has said that silence is to music what space is to architecture. I would say: what emptiness is to architecture. Here the "spatial" emptiness whose outlines I have tried to trace in the context of perspective effects in set design encounters another emptiness, in this case a phonic emptiness, an emptiness that the cry makes perceptible, or rather conceivable, much as converging lines of perspective give only an idea of the vanishing point, the point at infinity where they meet.

Just as the empty socket in the skull is what best makes immediate, or "makes present," what Lacan called the seeing object, so the silence we are given to hear by the cry—the cry that by "rending the silence" also lets it be heard—is what best gives presence to the vocal object, paradoxical though this may seem. Music and singing are in fact always revolving around this object, this determinate point, constantly evoking it but constantly avoiding it too. The relationship between music and silence has always invited philosophical speculation. I will confine myself to Vladimir Jankélevitch's thoughts in *La Musique et l'ineffable* as they seem to synthesize ideas on the subject particularly well.[73]

Jankélevitch observes that there are several ways to view the link between music and silence. The first is to consider that "music stands out sharply against silence"; that,

born of silence, music withdraws into silence. In this case, it is the world of noises and sounds that comes as a bracketing against a background of silence, that emerges into the ocean of silence like a ray of light illuminating for a few minutes the black emptiness of the "Xora" and homogeneous space. [But at the same time, music] needs this silence as life needs death. . . . Life, quite like a work of art, is an animate and finite construction that is defined against the infinitude of death; and music, quite like life, is a melodious construction, an enchanted moment, a very ephemeral adventure, a

[73]Vladimir Jankélevitch, *La Musique et l'ineffable* (Paris: Seuil, 1983).

brief encounter that stands alone between beginning and end in the immensity of nonbeing. In this regard, one can distinguish an antecedent silence and a consequent silence.

But there is another, opposite way of conceiving the relationship between music and silence. Silence now becomes "a discontinuous pause in the continuity of incessant sound effects." "A moment ago, living diversity broke through the uniform oceanography of ennui—that is, troubled a preexistent and underlying continuum: silence was the resonant backdrop beneath being: and now noise is the resonant backdrop that stretches beneath silence." In this sense, music is itself "a way of silence," "a melodious silence": "music that itself makes so much noise is the silence of all the other noises—because when it lifts its voice, it affirms its solitude, asserts that it alone occupies vibrant space." In this sense, Jankélevitch clearly situates silence, this silence, in the "silence of words." "If it is true that the *loquela,* as the religious teachers say, is the human noise par excellence, then the mutism that supresses this noise will be a privileged silence. Music is the silence of words, just as poetry is the silence of prose." The terms with which Jankélevitch continues are cast in a remarkable light by the present context: "Music in this way lightens the weight of the logos, eases the crushing hegemony of language; it prevents the human from being identified with the spoken. Here she is, 'the composer of silence' of whom the poet speaks."[74]

This comes quite close to what I have formulated in terms of a "contesting" or "subversion" of language. Thus it is not surprising to find in Jankélevitch associations or metaphors with a now familiar structure: "the lake, silent island, clears a soundless space in the midst of the uproar." Always this insistent image of a moving, almost overflowing surface bounded by a shore, a contour. And with Jankélevitch's reflections in mind, I believe it would not run counter to his thoughts if we translated his "uproar" as "the weight of the logos." But if music is thus a disposition or arrangement of silence, Jankélevitch notices too that music itself is infiltrated by pure silence. "And so it is that the intramusical silences and rests—numbered, chronometered, minuted—aerate the mass of discourse according to an

[74]Stéphane Mallarmé, *Sainte.*

exact metronomy: for music can breathe only in the oxygen of silence." To return to the perspective of the present work, we can now
distinguish two radically opposed silences.

The Silence That Speaks

This first silence, akin to the silence of which Jankélevitch speaks, is
a silence we have already encountered, a silence whose presence in a
continuum of vocal sound articulates the signifying scansion of language. Introduced into the musical universe, it creates rhythm and
phrasing. It also establishes scansion, which in opera is organized
together with the scansion of the text according to modalities sketched
out above. This silence can even be written in musical notation, it *is a
signifier,* is in fact called "silence" (or "pause" or "rest," with its duration specified), and in the early days of musical notation, in the
thirteenth century, was symbolized by a horizontal bar, a mark of
severance if ever there was one. It is this silence that produces the
alternation, or beat, of presence/absence in which all symbolizing processes originate; it is this silence that, when introduced as syncopation,
is an invitation to dance. And if singing is the locus of contention for
language where the tension, the objective of jouissance is fueled, it is
partly because it arranges these silences or these breaks according to
different constraints and a different desire from those that govern verbal intelligibility. When taken to the limit, the rearrangement is self-
canceling because its end point, the cry, "lacks implosion, explosion,
and separation,"[75] three acoustical traits necessary to the existence of
any human language.

The Silence That Screams, the Other Silence

But when the verbal, the articulate, is cast back into nothingness,
another silence is evoked, a silence that results from that destruction, a
deadly silence, the unsevered and *absolute presence* of the pulsing of
presence and absence. This silence, too, brings out the dimension of
fixity. Music perpetually plays with that horizon, often approaching it,
always missing it. It is through the disappearance of all rhythm,

[75]Alain Juranville, *Lacan et la philosophie* (Paris: Presses Universitaires de France,
1984), 231.

through the steadiest, most continuous and fullest of sounds, through a sound without silences that this other silence is most perfectly evoked. An extraordinary instance occurs in the orchestral prelude to Wagner's *Das Rheingold*, in which a single chord, held by the double basses for 137 measures, calls forth the primordial silence of mythic times. As André Boucourechliev writes:

The first 137 measures of the work are famous above all for their scandalous harmonic immobility within a musical universe based precisely on the dynamics of harmonic relations: they are reduced to a single chord, E-flat major. To approach them through this exclusive criterion would be to approach nothingness. . . . [The sonorous form] begins at the edge of silence, impalpable in its density and mass, and destitute of rhythm, drowned in excessive durations. The "zero degree" or rather the "minimum degree" is circumscribed here with the greatest precision.[76]

This example, though extreme, is not unique. Jankélevitch illustrates his own reflections with many others. "This fantastic pedal point, as hypnotic as a lullaby, is the pedal of static and panic silence"; and again, "this haunting horizontal of the dominant pedal dies out in gray uniformity."[77] The pedal, originally the long-held note from the pedal of the organ—whence its name—which supports the discourse of the keyboards, is in fact the privileged mode of musical writing whenever the composer wishes to evoke nothingness, the silence of infinite space, the silence in which the encounter with God is to take place. From pedal comes the term "pedal point," a veritable metonymy of silence: the long steady note that immediately precedes the "consequent" silence, the silence that must be inhabited by God, that in religious music and for the mystic *is* God. In secular music, it is the silence that must be broken by applause. Because this silence, unless infused with the divine, is unbearable and must be destroyed: that is the function of applause. The prohibition against applauding in a church, a prohibition that has existed until recently and is still very much alive in many places, may be understood by this logic. To destroy the divine silence created by the pedal point goes beyond disturbing a

[76]André Boucourechliev, in *L'Avant-scène Opéra* 6/7: *L'Or du Rhin"* (November–December 1976), 62 (textual and musical commentary).
[77]Jankélevitch, *La Musique et l'ineffable*, 171, 165.

meditation; it is to destroy God himself. It is in this context that the considerable resistance of audiences to refraining from applauding should be considered. Richard Wagner, impressed by the contemplative silence that spontaneously fell at the first performance of *Parsifal,* later insisted that no one applaud at this opera, even if ultimately Wagner himself gave the signal for applause out of consideration for the singers. This pseudo-tradition was finally codified in 1968 in a circular by Wolfgang Wagner, the current festival director, specifically requesting the audience to hold its applause at the end of the first act, in view of the sacred atmosphere that draws it to a close. Nevertheless, this traditional prohibition tends to be transgressed at each performance: almost without fail applause breaks out, and is immediately quelled of course by the indignant *sh's* of neighboring spectators. A refusal to perpetuate a rite considered passé and meaningless? Perhaps. Perhaps also habit, the necessity of rushing into the frenzy of applause while the last notes still hang in the air. Notice, too, that when this silence occurs within the work itself, it is almost inevitably broken by a spectator's cough, even in the middle of summer. Have you never noticed that no one ever coughs during the orchestra's fortissimi, only during the pianissimi? For many spectators, coughing is not due to some chance conjuncture between a moment of silence and a tickling in the throat; more often than not, the larynx begins to tickle *because* there is silence.

If continuous, nonrhythmic sound is frequently used as a way of approximating this at once attractive and distressing silence (one need look no further than its now hackneyed use for "soaring" or "floating" effects in films or images of desert, intergalactic space, or ocean depths), there is another form of music that appears to be intimately related to silence, "repetitive" music. This kind of music seems to be the opposite of silence, consisting as it does of the repetition ad infinitum of a rhythmic microcell. The scintillating character of this cell appears to make it fall on the other side of silence, on the side of Mozartian scansion, for example. And yet the endless repetition of that cell also gives rise to the fixed, the steady, the lethal, as though this side of a certain threshold rhythm shares in the nature of the continuous, in something akin to the way pointillism becomes a uniform surface at a certain distance from the eye.

Something somewhat similar happens with Indian music. The tambura player who supports the sitarist's improvisation with untiring repetition of the same arpeggio thus seems to be a figure of silence, a silence that does not function as a background against which the music stands out as much as it dissolves and resolves itself in the music that arises beneath the fingers of the improviser.

But this section is headed "The Silence That Screams." This rarefaction in the extreme, this "minimum degree" of the sonorous material (Webern, too, should be listened to in this regard) are quite far, it seems, from the phonic paroxysm of the scream. And yet as Lacan says, "the cry is not at first a call, but it elicits silence. Not that the cry is supported by it, silence being the background—it is the opposite. The cry is the abyss for silence to rush into." He then speaks of "the knot that silence forms between something that is, an instant before it is effaced, and the Other thing in which speech can fail: it is this knot that resonates when the cry empties it."[78] This paradox disappears if silence is seen as something opposed not to sound but to speech. If the terms "silence," "cry," "singing," and "speech" are arranged in that order on the axis below, it is not only because there is nothing further from speech than silence, but also because the cry, being the vocal manifestation furthest from verbal articulation, finds itself quite logically closest to silence. Singing consequently occupies all the intermediate space according to the diverse modalities of its relation to speech:

Silence, cry	Singing	Speech, signifying linguistic message

By the same logic, it is normal to find silence and the sound continuum associated, because as we have seen, discontinuity is a fundamental feature of all linguistic systems.

Under these conditions it is not surprising that Richard Wagner, the composer of silence, of the Other silence (notwithstanding the detractors who, knowing only his "Ride of the Valkyries," find him "hackneyed"), is also the composer of the cry, before Alban Berg brought it to its ultimate expression.

The problematics schematized above can in fact be found in its entirety, including the pole of speech, in the Wagnerian operatic edifice (certain passages, particularly Wotan's monologue in Die Walküre, II.i,

---

[78]Juranville, Lacan et la philosophie, 231.

nearly announce the *Sprechgesang*). As for the cry, no work goes further than Wagner's in presenting it in all its variation, in its "musical" as well as its "pure" mode: from Brünnhilde's "cry of joy" (*Die Walküre*, II.ii) to the "horrible cry" of Alberich when Wotan tears the ring from his finger (*Das Rheingold*, scene 3) to Brünnhilde's cry when Siegfried-Gunther seizes the ring from her (*Götterdämmerung*, I.iii), by way of the chorus's cry (the Nibelungen's screams in *Das Rheingold*, scene 2) or the sorrowful cries of the chorus of the Knights of the Grail (*Parsifal*, Act III). This choral orchestration of the cry has a very brief resonance in operatic history; it finds its paroxysmal expression in the finale of Bernd Alois Zimmermann's *Die Soldaten*. There is an important reason for this: choral singing is mastered singing, it is the singing of mastery par excellence. To place the cry here is to install the devil in the convent. The finale of *Die Soldaten* offers quite a remarkable illustration of this relationship between silence and cry, for here the chorus of cries is immediately followed by a long chord on the strings, held in dimminuendo until the final silence.

But if I could choose only one example, I would look no further than Act II of *Parsifal;* its musical intensity is unequaled in the history of opera. The entire problematics of the cry is condensed here, from one end of Kundry's vocal score to the other, in a literally unheard-of paroxysm that leaves the listener no option but flight, refusal, or the emotional collapse that signals the onset of jouissance. For Wagner takes the quest for the object to hitherto unexplored reaches where the fantasy of possessing it is intensified (whence the magnitude of the Wagnerian's investment) but where at the same time its truth is approached: the truth of the object is nothingness; the truth of the vocal object, this beyond or this hither of speech and even of the cry, is silence, the fixed point around which the trajectory of the quest that structures opera ceaselessly revolves, the abyss in which the fantasy dissolves like Klingsor's castle and enchanted garden, like Kundry herself after she has hurled her final cry, leaving the listener gasping in the face of the "discovery" of this emptiness. "I cried and cried," said Claude, "and I didn't know why I was crying."

Silence is what effaces and brings about the failure of the word. But it is also what brings about upheaval and apparition. It is somehow a call for a voice to be raised, it is "invocatory."[79] Thus in the prelude to

---

[79]Lacan calls the drive whose object is the voice the "invocatory drive."

Das Rheingold, a voice emerges from the inaugural continuum of silence, the voice of Woglinde, one of the Rhine Maidens, who is pure voice: she begins to sing not words but a vocalise, "Weiaa . . ."— "half-words, almost onomatopoeias . . . a kind of preverbal language."[80] Exactly like Kundry, who, with her cry of awakening, speaks "brokenly as if striving to regain speech."

This double movement allows me to define further these two silences that I have distinguished, or more exactly these *two effects* of silence. There is the silence that cuts the phonic continuum with its presence, that, through repetition, rhythmic pulsation, sets off the scansion of presence and absence and brings forth the signifier, the Word. But it may also cease to work away at the sonorous material; it may cease to beat, may yield its place entirely to the sonorous real in all its continuity without cutting it apart. This drive to effacement, this death instinct—for it is indeed a matter of the death instinct—will itself disappear and become silent—the silence of the drives—abandoning the field, after experiencing the emptiness of its object, to the continuous "real," which, escaping all symbolizing processes as well as all naming, is cast out forever into absolute, deadly silence, supreme fascination and horror.

And that, undoubtedly, is the function of music, particularly in opera, because there it comes face to face with the spoken work: to insert that unnamable silence into a system that makes it acceptable, that signifies its call but denies it even as it recognizes it, in the nostalgic yearning to dissolve into it and disappear.

[80]Boucourechliev, in *L'Avant-scène Opéra*, 6/7 (November–December 1976), 64.

The Objectified Voice
and the Vocal Object

To speak of jouissance is to speak of the enjoyment of a good, of an object (the legal usage of the term should be kept in mind),[81] and when one speaks of a quest, the idea of a search for a lost object is understood. It is now time to try to understand how the voice can transform itself into this object in which jouissance is sought and how this object is constructed as lost, thereby sustaining the errant quest for its recovery.

Many expressions in everyday language, many literary, mythical, and artistic examples, directly refer to this object-like consistency that the voice can assume, particularly in its singular propensity to be lost, stolen, or broken. By objectifying the voice in this way, the human imaginary has constructed an entity that evokes very specific features of the vocal object in the strict sense of the word, as psychoanalysis endeavors to conceptualize it.

The Lost Voice

The voice, by definition, is something that is lost: it may be lost in the distance, in an uproar. Everyone loses it under the impact of emotion, in moments of amazement ("I was dumbstruck"), particularly when emotion is aroused by the voice of the Other. Remember what

---

[81] In legal discourse, the French *jouissance* and English "enjoyment" are precise equivalents, in such expressions as *avoir la propriété et la jouissance des biens et droits,* "to have the ownership and enjoyment of properties and rights." [Translator's note]

Claude said about moments of great emotion: "You want to shout 'Bravo.' And then the 'Bra . . .' comes out but the 'vo' won't come." The singer can also lose her voice. This is her most haunting obsession.

"There are no great voices these days," runs the oft-heard complaint. Nothing in opera criticism is more commonplace than the reference to vanished, irreplaceable voices. Judgments affirming the decline of the art of singing are heard just as often:

If so many singers were not convinced that they had no further need to study, we would not have so few good artists and so many bad ones.

What a wonderful century this is, in which many singers are paid dearly to sing so badly.

It seems that there is at present such a scarcity of good examples in Italy . . . who help to keep the tottering profession from falling from its present decadence into complete ruin.

[The great singers of the past] will tell you frankly and convincingly . . . that today, no one sings well.

To contemplate the decline of an art is to be filled with great sadness.

Contemporary reflections? Aside from the last quotation, which dates from 1874, the source of all these comments is Pierfrancesco Tosi's *Opinioni de' cantori antichi e moderni, o siano osservazioni sopra il canto figurato*, written in 1723—in other words, at a time we now think of as the heyday of baroque bel canto.[82] Today opera criticism laments the Flagstads, the Melchiors, the Thills and Lubins. Perhaps in a few decades it will be the Caballés, Joneses, Pavarottis, and Domingos who will be missed, since there are no great voices, no great singers, except those of the past, as if a voice needed to have been lost to acquire an idealization that imbues it with the nostalgia of a golden age gone forever. Today Maria Callas is held in nearly unanimous adulation; in her lifetime, however, she was the object of the most brutal criticism.

The castrato voice is certainly not alone in owing a large part of its

[82]Published in English as *Observations on the Florid Song*, trans. J. E. Gaillard (1743; rpt. London: William Reeves, 1926); the 1874 French translation by Théophile Lemaire is titled *L'Art du chant*. The last quotation is Lemaire's footnote on the state of contemporary singing in France.

current fascination to the fact (apart from its strangeness, its monstrosity even) that it is a voice forever lost, a voice to which access has been barred, so that we have no point of reference that might give us some way of approximating it (the wretched recording made by the last castrato provides no basis on which to reconstruct it). But there is every reason to expect that attempts to yield something that may once more conjure up its echo will continue.

Naturally, the voice is not alone in being subject to nostalgic idealization, but by virtue of its evanescence, its intangible nature, it is so susceptible to this idealization that the implacable desire to capture this immateriality led humankind to invent the phonograph and the tape recorder—not very long ago, all things considered. But we mustn't forget that, however advanced this technology is now or may become, what the opera lover ultimately preserves in the precious recordings of his idolized diva is a degraded residue. Consider the curious history of the word "cassette," which in French once designated "a small casket designed to preserve papers and *precious* objects" or "a sovereign's private *treasure*,"[83] then passed out of common usage until modern technology revived it to function again as a case to preserve precious and royal objects: voices and sounds.

The Stolen Voice

The film *Diva,* by J.-J. Beneix, illustrates in a particularly pertinent—if entirely incidental—way the theme of the objectified voice (a term which, it must be emphasized, is not to be confused with the vocal object in the stricter sense that will be developed later). But what story does this film tell? Its point of departure is a singer's refusal to consent to having her voice recorded. Attempts to "steal" or "pirate" this voice start to multiply, their primary goal being to insert this object into the recording industry's familiar network of commodity values. A young fan accomplishes the theft, not for venal considerations but to appropriate the voice he loves. His recording then is coveted by those who seek to exploit the treasure for financial gain. The

[83]*Larousse de la langue française.*

convolutions of the plot soon collapse this first circuit, in which the recording of the diva's voice is the object of pursuit, into another, entirely different network, which involves the circulation of another cassette tape, this one of the voice of a prostitute indicting the political-bigwig-with-links-to-organized-crime, who in turn seeks to destroy the incriminating testimony along with anyone who has learned of its existence. The two pursuits eventually intersect, commingle, and interfere with each other in and around the same apparent object: "the" cassette, which for some is the voice of the diva, for others that of a whore. The ensuing events are dangerous, particularly for Jules, the young protagonist, who is caught in the deadly trap of having identified, of knowing this reified voice. In being detached and reified as a residue, prized by some, vilified by others, the voice is of course able to inspire quest or even conquest (the fantasy of possessing the elusive treasure is determined by this reification), but it becomes a trove of *illusions* to the extent that it engenders a misunderstanding,[84] for in fact it is always around some other thing that the protagonists' activities and lethal games revolve. The stakes of this pursuit may sometimes be high: indeed, as the following example will demonstrate, they may be death or madness.

The Broken Voice

"Her voice—her voice! They have destroyed her voice! A curse be upon them!" And he disappears through the door. . . . At once, a tremendous explosion shakes the whole plateau. Sheaves of flame leap to the clouds, and an avalanche of stones falls on the Vulkan road.

Of the bastions, the curtain-wall, the donjon, the chapel, of Carpathian Castle, there remain nothing but a mass of smoking ruins scattered over the Orgall plateau." . . .

The last words of La Stilla's song alone escaped from his lips,—

"Innamorata—mio cuore tremante. . . ."

Franz de Telek was mad!"[85]

---

[84]*Mal-entendu,* literally a mishearing. [Translator's note]

[85]Jules Verne, *The Carpathian Castle,* ed. I. O. Evans (London: Arco, 1963; rpt. London: Granada, 1979), 182–84.

Jules Verne's novel *The Carpathian Castle* is another illustration of what can come of the fantasy that dooms a subject to seek possession of the objectified voice: "But her voice—her voice shall stay with me! . . . Her voice is mine! . . . It is mine alone, and shall never belong to another."[86]

The Carpathian Castle is the story of a young Romanian count, Franz de Telek, smitten with love for a Neapolitan soprano, La Stilla, a figure of absolute beauty and vocal perfection. Each evening Franz attends the concert given by his beloved. But he is not the only one to demonstrate such devotion: also in the theater is Baron Rodolphe de Gortz, a disturbing, enigmatic presence: "the Baron de Gortz sat at the back of his box, absorbed in this exquisite song, impregnated with this divine voice, without which he seemed unable to live."[87]

La Stilla is eventually overcome by this presence: "Although she could not see him in the depths of his box, she knew he was there, she felt his look imperiously fixed upon her, and she was so greatly troubled by his presence that she no longer heard the applause with which the public welcomed her appearance on the scene." Finally she is so troubled by this silent intrusion that she decides to give up opera altogether and accept Franz de Telek's hand in marriage. A farewell performance is arranged at the Teatro San Carlo in Naples. Suddenly, toward the end of the concert, she stops singing: Baron de Gortz's face, "that ecstatic face, frightful in its pallor," appears in the light for the first time over the railing of his box; it terrifies her. "An inexplicable alarm paralyzes her. . . . She puts her hand to her mouth, which is stained with her blood. . . . She staggers. . . . She falls . . . ." She is dead.[88]

Franz de Telek, in an effort to put his tragedy behind him, leaves Naples. On his travels he meets up with Baron de Gortz, who has shut himself away in the Carpathian Castle to savor in solitude La Stilla's voice, which, along with her image, he had contrived, thanks to the technological genius of his faithful assistant Orfanik, to steal from her as she gave her last concert. Franz becomes the "delirious witness" to a session during which the baron treats himself to a performance by that voice and that image.

[86]Ibid., 181.
[87]Ibid., 112.
[88]Ibid., 111, 116.

Franz, too, stood intoxicated with the charm of this voice which he had not heard for five long years. . . . He was wrapped in the ardent contemplation of this woman whom he had thought he should never see again, and who was there, alive, as if some miracle had resuscitated her before his eyes!

. . . Yes! He could recognize the finale of the tragic scene in *Orlando*, the finale in which the singer's heart is broken in the climax—

"Innamorata . . . voglio morire.". . .

But the voice is beginning to fail. It seemed as though La Stilla were hesitating as she repeated those words of poignant grief,—

"Voglio mo . . ."

Would she fall on this stage as she had done on that other?

She does not fall, but her song is stopped on the very same note as it had done at San Carlo. . . . *She utters a cry, and it is that same cry* which Franz had heard on that very night. . . .[89]

In the course of the ensuing confrontation, the baron demonstrates to Franz the illusory nature of the scene by sacrificing its image: he breaks the set of mirrors used in the visual apparatus, as if to signify that loss of the image of the beloved is an easy grief to bear. But in the final struggle, "a bullet shatters the box he carries in his arms. He utters a terrible cry. 'Her voice—her voice! . . . They have destroyed her voice!' " The story ends with the cataclysm with which this section began.

However paroxysmal these events, they are sure to speak to those who love to record music; they will call to mind the genuine, over-powering anguish of recording a live broadcast, the anguish of knowing that it will be impossible to recover the original moment if the recording goes awry, that a transmission problem or a defect in the recording material may squander the opportunity. These events will also speak to all who, through their own fault or the fault of another (in which case it is best not to be that other), have felt that genuine sensation of death when one of these recordings, unique by definition, is lost or erased. Long-standing friendships have perished through such mistakes.[90]

---

[89]Ibid., 179–180. Notice that the cry does not figure in the initial description of Stilla's death; it is as though Jules Verne invented this cry when he came to describe hearing the recorded and thus objectified voice.

[90]If Jules Verne invents the tape recorder and even the video here, he is nonetheless not

The Vocal Object

When psychoanalysis speaks of the vocal object, however, it is not referring to these "reified" forms the voice can take, however useful they may be to illustrate certain properties of the voice as object. What psychoanalysis describes is something else, a process inherent in each individual, a process by which the voice is constituted as an object, an object of a drive, and thereby is constituted as lost from the very outset, independent of any reification into a tangible object of "reality," as that term is usually understood.

And if so many things are bound up together around this question, which in many individuals underlies investments every bit as strong as the quest for the sexual object, for example, it is because the process by which the voice is elaborated as an object dialecticizes an entire relationship with the Other, with the desire of the Other; in this respect, the vocal object occupies a fundamental place in the structuring of any subject, in precisely the same way and according to the same problematics as the other, more familiar objects of psychoanalysis: the oral, anal, and genital. Freud spoke only of these last three. It was Lacan who further identified the voice and the gaze as objects of a drive. But it is to the model presented by Freud in his *Project for a Scientific Psychology* that I will refer in an attempt to explain how the establishment of the vocal object in the subject is to be understood and how this object is from the outset established as lost. And if I qualify my explanation as an attempt, it is because nothing is more hypothetical than the formulation that follows, particularly by virtue of the way this phenomenon functions as deferred action.[91]

Speaking earlier of the blue note, I referred to proleptic action. Psychoanalysis is more often concerned with deferred action, that is, the rearrangement of psychic material situated logically and chronologically before other material under the *action* of this second material. This rearrangement may extend to the pure and simple invention of

the first to have fantasized the voice as a detached object: Rabelais had already imagined words that froze as they left the mouths of those who ventured into frigid lands and later could be heard in the air when a thawing ray of sunlight or a warm hand freed them from their icy solidity.

[91]I draw directly on the formulations of this process presented by the psychoanalyst Gérard Pommier in a France-Culture broadcast of 24 May 1984 (*La Voix*) and in a France-Musique broadcast of 2 March 1984 (*Psychanalyse et musique*).

the first situation, which then becomes mythical, a necessary postulate, independent of its actual locatable existence, enabling that situation to account for what occurs in an individual after the appearance and as a result of this second material, which alone is accessible to verifiable experience.

This is what occurs with the vocal object. But how?

Let us begin with the postulate, if only the hypothesis needed to hold together a construct based on what can actually be observed and analyzed, since in the presumed original situation, the hypothesis itself cannot be observed directly. The initial postulate is as follows: At the beginning of its existence, as a result of an inner tension, the baby, the *in-fans*,[92] marked by the characteristic human prematurity that makes it utterly dependent on the other for the satisfaction of its needs, emits a cry. It doesn't matter whether this "first" cry is "the" first or some other cry—as we shall see, this "first" cry is mythical or at all events hypothetical. What is important is that this cry is a pure manifestation of vocal resonance linked to a state of internal displeasure, and that this cry is answered by the Other (who may be and in fact usually is the mother, though it may be any other person), who *attributes* meaning to the cry, *interprets* it as a sign of hunger or thirst or whatever, and, in bringing the baby something to relieve the tension that provoked the cry, provides the child a first satisfaction.

A trace of this first satisfaction will remain in the child's psyche, associated with a trace of all the elements—whether feeding, physical contact, or the stimulation of sound, alone or in combination—that bring about the discharge of inner tension. Thereafter the child will have a representation of this object—or group of objects—of its first jouissance. In the same way, these mnemonic traces will be associated with another mnemonic trace, the resonance of the child's own cry— in other words, what surrounded the initial state of displeasure.

It must be understood that at this stage the "first" cry is not a priori a call, much less a demand; it is simply a vocal expression of discomfort. It is the Other, say the mother, who in attributing meaning to the cry raises it to the status of a demand and in so doing inscribes it with the mark of her own desire ("What does my baby want?" she says to her child, and behind that sentence several others can be made out, such as "What do I want you to want? To leave me in peace, or to have

---

[92]*Infant,* from the Latin *in-fans,* (one) who is unable to speak.

me pay attention to you?"[93] In extremely schematic terms, the nature and mode of the mother's "response"[94] can vary enormously and depends on the child's position in relation to her own desire, on whether or not she desired this child.

This first, pure cry is qualified as mythical or hypothetical because as soon as it is interpreted and elicits a reaction, its original "purity" is lost forever, as it is now caught up within the system of signification that is already in place with the intervention of the Other. From an experiential standpoint, there is only this state of the "demand cry"; as soon as the cry is uttered, its initial "resonant purity" has already disappeared forever.

But then comes a second phase, which begins when the baby, once more subject to some pressing need, cries out again. With this second cry, everything is different; this situation is not at all a repetition of the first, because the second cry is already inserted into a network of meanings emanating from the Other and into a dialectic marked by the desire of the Other. With this second phase, the cry, once "pure," now becomes a cry *for*—for someone, for something. It is no longer simple vocal expression but demand, a demand for the return of the object linked to the initial jouissance; the cry has once and for all attained the status of speech, for now it signifies. Now, when another object is brought to the child to appease its tension, this second object or second series of objects will never be completely identical to the first, if only because it is inserted into a situation that is no longer the same, if only because of the traces left by the first situation. The first object of jouissance can therefore never be recovered in an identical form: it is irremediably lost. As everyone knows, months of development are necessary before the child is able to recognize an object in different situations as the same object.

The voice set into play during this first experience of jouissance may be the child's own voice or that of the mother; the important thing is the voice, in its simple phonic materiality. When the second phase, the search for this phonic materiality, begins, it has already been lost behind the meaning the Other has given it and in its failure to be recognized as identical to the first object of jouissance, which now assumes

[93]The word "want" in this instance should not be interpreted as conscious volition.
[94]The term "response" is of course inappropriate, because no request has actually been made.

the value of a paradise lost. The child is literally "dispossessed"[95] of its cry as simple vocal resonant material because the cry really *exists*, at least from the standpoint of having an effect, only if and when the Other ceases to consider it as pure, gratuitous (or even ludic) vocal emission and inscribes it in the signifying order, gives it meaning, and comes to alleviate the child's displeasure by feeding it, changing its diapers, or singing it a song.

The voice in itself, its materiality, has for an instant functioned in much the same way as a bird call . . . attracting and exacting a response, an interpretation from the mother. This confusion of the cry through its signification has a divisive effect, for it is here that sound assumes the status of signifier. It leaves behind something useless (from the point of view of signification)—the skeletal remains of its phonic materiality. This residue is meaningless, it is a lost object, like the Freudian object that Lacan has designated as *objet petit a*, in view of its lack of meaning.[96]

Thus it is around this construct that the child's whole relationship with the Other is set up,[97] that its whole relation to language is established.

Another example, one drawn from the everyday experience of speaking, can help us better understand how vocal materiality is lost behind signification. Whenever someone speaks to us, the strictly phonic aspect of the utterance tends to disappear behind the meaning of what is being said. After a completely bilingual person has seen a film, he may find himself unable to tell you whether he saw the original or the dubbed version, especially if the question is asked some time after the screening, after the pure resonance of the language of the sound track is gone. On the other hand, he will have no trouble recalling which version he saw if a bad dubbing called attention to the specifically phonic dimension by failing to replicate the ambient sounds of the original sound track, or by some other inconsistency that became apparent as the film unfolded.

[95]Pommier, *La Voix* and *Psychanalyse et musique*.

[96]Gérard Pommier, *D'une logique de la psychose* (Paris, 1982), 40. Lacan would not let *object petit a* be translated. For an explanation, see the translator's note on page xi in Alan Sheridan's translation of Lacan's *Écrits: A Selection* (New York: W. W. Norton, 1977).

[97]Freud, in *Project for a Scientific Psychology*, calls this relationship one of "mutual comprehension."

A similar phenomenon occurs with accent in language and the dimension of jouissance that an accent can open up. Why is it that when a regional accent is heard outside its own region, and so takes on that slightly foreign ring, it tends to provoke laughter or value judgments (this charming lilt, that broad drawl, etc.)? Is it that accents evoke social or ethnic differences and the hierarchical values assigned to them? Probably. Yet it is also because the accent tends to bring to the surface vocal materiality, the vocal object as such; it becomes—as we have seen—an object of jouissance and this intrusion of jouissance into language subverts the signifying action of the spoken words.

An effect of this sort has undoubtedly led to the nearly universal exclusion of regional accents from the national broadcast media: national network radio and television announcers must have no accent—it is understood that the absence of accent is defined by the dominant accent—especially on news programs and in any other area where it is felt, rightly or wrongly, that the meaning of what is said is more important than the way it is said. From this standpoint, whatever might interfere with meaning is necessarily proscribed, beginning with the reintroduction of vocal materiality and the jouissance connected to it.

This example returns us to the question of jouissance in its relation to the vocal object. For the vocal object, in that first, hypothetical phase described earlier, is indeed an object of jouissance. Thereafter, any relation to phonic materiality will involve jouissance. The voice as object is thus constructed both as lost object and as first object of jouissance. It is thus not surprising that a *quest* for the object is set in motion, a search for lost phonic materiality, now dissolved behind signification.

It is important to note, however, that what is sought is not phonic materiality as such but only insofar as it frees itself from the domination of signification through a process of purification or expurgation that is never attained except at the asymptote of silence. Thus it now becomes possible to understand the basis for the antagonism between meaning and vocal object, an antagonism identified earlier not analytically but phenomenologically, in the emotion felt by the opera fan.

Nor is it surprising to see this quest advance into these regions of the cry and silence, regions farthest from the dominion of signification, for both cry and silence lie at the edge of this "lost" paradise. The futility of the search can be understood as well, and consequently the ever-increasing reinvestment it requires: there is no genuinely lost object to be retrieved. There is merely a "loss effect," a simple retroactive consequence of the symbolizing process brought about by linguistic signification: vocal materiality is never actually lost because speech is formed from this material; it is seen as lost only after the subject has unconsciously made it the representation of a totally purified transverbal state, experienced during the presumed primitive encounter with jouissance.

But if this quest is futile, if it is impossible, then the individual must be prevented from surrendering to it, from losing himself in it body and soul. It is here that the prohibition intervenes, the regulation whose insistent presence has been noted throughout this trajectory from speech to the cry along which I have arranged the history of opera. The prohibition is there to hide the impossible so as to limit the damage from the subject's commitment to the quest, damage that is not always avoidable because sometimes the only means the subject has to pursue the mythical lost object is to identify with it. The best way not to lose an object is to identify with it, to make oneself that object. To identify with the lost vocal object is to become loss oneself, to become supreme purification, to *be* silence; in other words, to die. Death becomes the only possible locus of return to that initial real that has not yet been elaborated by the symbolic. This is the tragic fate of the melancholic, as Robert Schumann, like many other composers, discovered.

Pathology reveals the extremes to which this search may lead; it points to the ineluctable fate of the desperate attempt to retrieve the impossible. But while the prohibition signals the impossible, it has another, secondary effect of revealing the jouissance that may be hoped for in it, a jouissance we must understand—as it should now be clear—in terms of an approximation of, an approach to a necessarily elusive object:[98] one never has jouissance of the object in the sense of "possessing" it, except in the embrace of death (whence, moreover, the constantly noted relationship between jouissance and death). Consequently the prohibition in a sense drives one toward jouissance, both fueling the wandering of the subject who is hooked on the fantasy of quest and marking out the path he must follow.

[98]When we speak of the "lack" of an object, we are speaking less of its absence than of its being missed or bungled.

The Eroticism of the Voice

With Lacan the voice takes its place alongside the other objects of drives identified by Freud: oral object (the breast), anal object (feces), genital object (the penis). This might help explain the frequent association of the vocal with the sexual—without reducing the former to the latter—and may clarify a matter usually addressed only with confusion: "The strange power of singing resides essentially in the emotion it sets off. And if we look more closely, we can see that this emotion itself has its origin in the 'strongest of feelings,' in those of sexual arousal."[99]

From the Lacanian perspective, it is as object of a drive (the "invocatory" drive) that the voice is inserted into an eroticizing system, which, like all systems built around the drives, consists of the object's source (structured as an orifice, as a rim: in this case, the ear); its goal—a satisfaction; and its "impetus"—the tension it engenders by being sought, its characteristic circular trajectory ("to make itself heard"). The eroticization of the voice follows from its elevation to object status according to modalities that I have attempted to describe and has little to do with its role as a mark of sexual difference, the feminine voice signaling the female sex, the masculine voice the male sex. In fact, the voices considered most erotic, those that hold the greatest fascination for the listener, whether male or female, are voices that may be called trans-sexual—the deep voice in a woman (think of Kathleen Ferrier, or Marlene Dietrich, the "blue angel"), the high voice in a man (the castrato, the tenor). The familiar relationships between eroticism and voice originate simply from the participation of the voice as such in a network of drives. There is no need to establish a "direct link between the voice and the genetic instinct" or to hear it as "an echo of the ancestral love cry" to account for this association.[100]

Strangely enough, Heinrich Schütz's fourth *Kleines geistliches Konzert*, or Little Oratorio, despite its religious subject, has something to say about the eroticization of the voice: in a rather unaccustomed way, a play on words in the Latin (*in ore*, in the mouth, *in aure*, in the ear) joins oral pleasure to aural pleasure, suggesting that beyond the voice of the

[99]Victor Andréossy, *L'Esprit du chant* (1949; rpt. Plan de la Tour: Éditions d'Aujourd'hui, 1979), 122.
[100]Ibid., 122, 125.

diva, the supreme vocal object is the Name of God or, in this case, the Name of Jesus, son of God, he who uttered a *loud cry* as he died on the cross:

> O nomen Jesu, verus animae cibus,
> in ore mel, in aure melos,
> in corde laetitia mea.
> Tuum itaque nomen, dulcissime Jesu,
> in aertenum in ore meo portabo.

> O name of Jesus, true nourishment of the soul,
> honey in the mouth, melody in the ear,
> joy in my heart.
> That is why, sweetest Jesus,
> I shall forever carry your name in my mouth.

Between Speech and Silence:
Moses und Aron

To conclude the second part of this work, centered on the tension between speech and singing and on the jouissance that is inextricably at stake in it, I would like to dwell for a moment on Schoenberg's *Moses und Aron*, which in a way brings to the surface the problematics developed in the preceding pages.

This too-often neglected work by the Viennese composer is nonetheless one of Schoenberg's—and opera's—masterworks. For while objectively unfinished (Schoenberg never wrote the third act he had planned), it is in fact a perfectly *accomplished* composition, in the sense that by the end of Act II, Schoenberg has been led to a conclusion by a logic that, though unconscious, is nevertheless sufficiently operative to block him from composing the third act, now redundant or superfluous. There are no "objective" reasons for the interruption of his labor: Schoenberg lived nearly twenty years more after he finished the second act, in March 1932, and time and again in his correspondence he refers to his desire to complete the work. On 26 May 1933 he even specifies "in six to eight weeks." Nor can his failure to finish the opera be ascribed to a lack of inspiration, since he went on to compose a number of important works after 1932. Schoenberg was anything but capricious, and unconsciously he must have known that his *Moses und Aron* was in fact a finished work.

The explicit themes of this opera are not what concerns us here. They have to do with a philosophical questioning of the relation to the divine and of divine representation. But a number of the solutions and situations that Schoenberg finds to translate his subject into music and drama happen to lend themselves to straightforward reinterpretation in terms of the problematics that has been described here. And this is not a mere coincidence, because at the heart of Schoenberg's work, fundamentally at issue in it, is knowledge of God, access to the divine— what the mystics call *"the ecstasy of God."* These intersections between the trajectory Schoenberg displays and the one I have tried to trace out here in the domain of opera is not at all surprising: it is not the first time that mystical jouissance encounters musical jouissance, nor will it be the last.

Schoenberg's opera is notable for the radical and systematic way the respective positions of the two central characters, Moses and Aaron, are differentiated by the musical material assigned to the two roles. The part of Moses is entirely spoken—in *Sprechgesang*—while Aaron's is entirely sung "to an extremely ornamented melody in the most extensive of tessituras."[101] Invested in the opening scene of the burning bush with the prophetic mission of transmitting to the Jewish people the knowledge of the one, the inconceivable and unrepresentable God, who will free them from Pharaoh's yoke, Moses calls upon his brother Aaron to be his spokesman, as he, Moses, lacks the gift of speech.

Note that elementary reasoning could have led the author to make the opposite choice: singing for Moses, speech for Aaron; singing for what is beyond speech, for the unsayable, and speech for "communication," as a mind-set quite common now probably would have suggested. The truth of the situation rests on a different logic, however, one we have seen at work in sacred singing: transmission of the divine word, but in a medium of jouissance, on condition that the latter be kept carefully in check by the former. This is exactly what Schoenberg sets up. Yahweh, who himself is both singing and speech (in the burning bush scene he is represented by a choral sextet and a spoken chorus simultaneously), reveals his law through Moses's speech, supported by Aaron's singing. Moses's exhortation, when he finally convinces the Jewish people of the omnipotence of the invisible God and of their liberation if they accept his law, comprises a sort of speech with melodic simultaneous translation by Aaron, and with miracles for good measure. Here is religion in all its guises: law and the Word on the one side, and on the other, in delicate submission to the Word, a certain jouissance. The latter dimension literally breaks its bounds when in Act II the Word is in default, absent (Moses has withdrawn to

---

101Bourgeois, *L'Opéra des origines à demain*, 357.

Sinai and is long in returning). What follows is the Dionysian debauch of the Golden Calf scene: orgiastic, erotic excess associated with the mystical excess of sacred violence, a human sacrifice on the altar of that rerendered figure of divinity, the Golden Calf. It comes as no surprise to find that in the strange musical construction, at once icy and complex, of this long scene to which Schoenberg attaches such importance, the chorus lets loose the most paroxysmal of vocal outbursts, the scream and the cry, ("a whole succession of naked people, screaming and yelling, run past the altar . . . and disappear into the background").[102]

On his return from Mount Sinai, Moses, carrying the tablets of the law, reasserts the order of language and has Aaron *bound up in chains*. But earlier Moses is profoundly shaken by his brother's suggestion that those tablets he holds in his arms are themselves no more than images of the "Idea": the word in stone is but another stone god. Moses then shatters the tablets of the law.

Finally, Moses is left alone with his despair, and this inspires Schoenberg to a note of sublime simplicity and shattering emotional power. His last monologue ("Inconceivable God! Inexpressible, many-sided idea, will you let it be so explained? Shall Aaron, my brother, my mouth, fashion this image?") is set against a completely bare melody on violins in unison, one of the great marvels of inspiration in all of music. And a long, solitary F-sharp pedal prolongs the resonance of his final exclamation: "O Word, thou Word, that I lack!"[103]

This long F-sharp pedal on the strings is perhaps the most perfect musicalization of the silence that imposes its absolute presence when all words fail. It is the pendant, in a way, of the E-flat that begins *Das Rheingold*. It speaks the truth that Moses unknowingly has just discovered: this lack, this gap—which gapes at the very heart of language and which humankind has tried to overcome through such figures as God-the-Word—this gap is silence: God is silence. From here on nothing more can be said: opera can go no further.

[102]Schoenberg's stage directions in the libretto.

[103]Harry Halbreich, brochure notes for Schoenberg, *Moses und Aron*, dir. Pierre Boulez, CBS.

PART THREE

ANGEL, WOMAN, AND GOD: THE SEXUAL, THE TRANS-SEXUAL, AND JOUISSANCE

The third part of this work will attempt to locate the ways in which the problematics I have just delineated takes flesh and form on the operatic stage in figures, themes, and situations whose presence, revealed or disguised, makes itself felt throughout the history of the genre.

I will thus be defining a second axis for this study, a second vector that will determine an approach to these figures, themes, and situations, with an eye to what the repetition or, conversely, the singularity of their characteristics can reveal of their relations to what I have described as being at stake vocally in opera. For although, as I have argued, the cause of the listener's emotional upheaval does not reside strictly in the signification of the situation, it is still possible to read opera's characters and themes for what they can tell us about the genre's deeper stakes. This is how it is when sometimes we awaken from a dream with a profound feeling, perhaps of anxiety, that bears no relation to the words spoken in the dream or even to its explicit incidents. All the same, it is by analyzing those words and those incidents that we can arrive at what Freud called the "navel," the kernel, which fundamentally organizes the dream and constitutes the cause of its affect.

This second path through the history of opera leads first to the Angel, then to the Woman, and finally to an encounter with the Divine, in the place assigned it by the "divine" voice itself, that of the diva—particularly in her cry.

Opera, or The
Angel's Passage

We left Schoenberg-Moses in the anguished paroxysm of silence. While we may be somewhat unaccustomed to the idea of silence as a divine attribute, silence is far more familiar in connection with the figure intermediary between the human and the divine, the angel: when silence descends during the course of a conversation, the French say that "an angel has passed." Opera was born beneath this angel's wing.

The Castrato's Voice, the Angel's Voice

In the Mozarabic church in Spain during the ninth and tenth centuries,[1] a strange encounter takes place between the angelic voice, whose chorus, according to the Catholic liturgy, sings the praises of God on high, and the castrato, the eunuch singer that Islamic culture introduced into Spain in the ninth century:

The appearance of castrati in Spain and Portugal by way of the Moslem world is more certain and more easily verified. The arrival at the Moslem court of Córdoba of the great singer, lutanist, and composer Ziryab (789–857), who had pursued his musical studies in Baghdad, sanctioned the use of castrato singers in the new musical forms developed in the Islamic cap-

---

[1] "Mozarabic," meaning "would-be Arab" or "among the Arabs," refers to the Catholic church in Spain during the Moorish period.

ital. . . . Moslem chronicles from the ninth century until the Reconquest of Spain by the Christians in the fifteenth century note the presence of castrato singers destined for this elegant music that could be heard within the walls of the Moorish courts.[2]

The Catholic liturgy had identified the function of the choir with the traditional function of the angel—the glorification of God—and had associated the high voice, the so-called treble voice, with the angelic position. In the Mozarabic church, "the angel's voice intervenes and this voice can only be high."[3] There is good reason to inquire as to the basis for this association, for its very familiarity tends to mask a radical absence of an obvious rationale.

Only at the end of this chapter will I consider some possible hypotheses, because on the path we shall travel in the company of the angel and its various operatic avatars, some light will no doubt be shed on the nature of this relationship. In any case, it was imperative that the singing angel of the Mozarabic church have a high voice. Now the prohibition against women as liturgical officiants also entailed their exclusion from singing in the choir of the secular church. (I say the secular church because in the convent, among themselves, women were allowed to sing: there was no prohibition against female singing per se). And so male voices modified through training in falsetto and countertenor techniques to increase their range or juvenile voices were invested with the angelic function. The presence of the Moslem castrato singer in Spain was to offer an exceptional solution to the problem of representing the angel's voice. That is how the Mozarabic church came to embrace the castrato singer: "A careful reading of the old texts points to the existence in the twelfth and thirteenth centuries of castrati in the Spanish and Portuguese Mozarabic liturgy. Chapel registers for the fifteenth and sixteenth centuries from various cathedrals in southern Spain and in Portugal confirm the presence of these singers in remarkable numbers."[4]

This angelic voice spread throughout Europe but principally in Italy, either directly to Naples, under Aragonese rule in the fifteenth century,

[2]Christian Gaumy, "Le Chant des castrats," *Opera International,* December 1984–January 1985.
[3]Christian Gaumy, France-Culture lecture, October 1978.
[4]Gaumy, "Le Chant des castrats."

or indirectly through the Papal Chapel. The latter (which in the nine-teenth century would become the "Sistine" Chapel) brought French, Spanish, and Italian singers together. By the end of the fifteenth century the "treble" voices were sung by the famous Spanish castrati. Yet "a century later, the first Italian castrati gradually replaced the Spaniards in the choirs of Rome, following disputes over seniority and musical and national rivalries. In the latter half of the sixteenth century, in southern Germany as throughout the Italian peninsula, the Italian castrati were the rule in most church choirs."[5]

By the beginning of the seventeenth century, baroque Italy had taken over this angelic voice incarnate and ushered it away from the sacred scene toward the secular stage, just at the time when the operatic genre was taking form. The latter was something of an immediate success, owing in large part to the fascination wielded by this voice:

Between 1600 and 1640, from the beginnings of opera until it began to reach a largely popular audience, all the great Italian noblemen responsible for the production of lyric spectacle insisted on using the castrato, so great was their fascination with a voice that seemed fabulous to them. And so—and this is a revelation as remarkable as it is recent—for the first performance of Monteverdi's *Orfeo,* at Mantua on 24 February 1607, while the title role was played by the tenor and composer Francesco Rasi, it was a castrato, and a monk no less, Padre Girolamo Bacchini, who played Euridice.[6]

By this time, conscious reference to the angel as a being who sings the glory of God had of course disappeared. But the presence of the angel can be glimpsed in the foregrounding of another attribute of the angelic nature: its "trans-sexual" character. In opera, the angel's voice is a trans-sexual voice in the sense that the castrato voice and hence the high voice is assigned to *male* roles and even to *virile* roles, without the least regard for the "real" sex of the character. "Have you never noticed this strange fact—that castrati always shine in the roles of kings, emperors, captains, warriors? . . . Why is what is least masculine in the voice chosen to express what is most masculine in the character?" asks a fictional Mozart in Dominique Fernandez's novel

[5]Ibid.
[6]Ibid.

Porporino.[7] Of course "the castrati played female roles since the origin of opera . . . but the practice was not as common as it is sometimes thought to have been."[8] It was essentially to compensate for the scarcity of female singers sufficiently trained in the new genre, who nonetheless were a presence, albeit a rare one, on the Italian opera stage. For, contrary to the received wisdom, in Italy at the time there was no general prohibition concerning the presence of women on the lyric stage. That prohibition did not extend beyond the Papal States during the period 1688–1798. Everywhere else and particularly in the Kingdom of Naples, one of the great training grounds for castrati of the day, women did have access to the stage. The castrato was not a substitute woman. Therefore the rise of the castrato must derive from motivations entirely specific to the voice and to what is played out through it.

This phenomenon is a clear indication of the autonomy of the voice, particularly the high voice, as an object of jouissance detached from its usual functions of signification, communication, and the marking of gender difference. For ultimately, the principal feature of the castrato voice is not that it is the voice of a woman in the body of a man, but rather its extraordinary, literally *unheard*-of quality. The strenuous ten-hour days of practice demanded of the young boys who were subjected to the operation after they were singled out for the beauty of their voices made exceptional singers of them, quite apart from their vocal uniqueness: "They had to be able to wield these vocal pyrotechnics across the full extent of a vocal range that often spanned three octaves."[9] We find mention as well of the displays of athletic virtuosity of which they were capable. Charles Burney reports the following anecdote about the famous Carlo Farinelli, who was

born at Naples in 1705. . . . He was seventeen when he left that city to go to Rome, where during the run of an opera, there was a struggle every night between him and a famous player on the trumpet, in a song accompanied by that instrument. . . . After severally swelling out a note, in which each manifested the power of his lungs, and tried to rival the other in brilliancy and force, they had both a swell and a shake together, by thirds,

---

[7]Dominique Fernandez, *Porporino, or The Secrets of Naples,* trans. Eileen Finletter (New York: Morrow, 1976), 150.

[8]Gaumy, "Le Chant des castrats."

[9]Gaumy, France-Culture lecture, October 1978.

which was continued so long, while the audience eagerly waited the event, that both seemed to be exhausted; and, in fact, the trumpeter, wholly spent, gave it up, thinking, however, his antagonist as much tired as himself, and that it would be a drawn battle; when Farinelli with a smile on his countenance, shewing he had only been sporting with him all this time, broke out all at once in the same breath, with fresh vigour, and not only swelled and shook the note, but ran the most rapid and difficult divisions, and was at last silenced only by the acclamations of the audience.[10]

The entire fantasy of the quest for the vocal object, which I have defined as a radically purified voice, is mobilized with unmatched intensity around this voice that seems to depart from all the usual references, becoming not only pure instrumental sound but *supreme* instrumental sound. It is the *divine* voice par excellence, and we needn't marvel at the infatuations it elicits. In his preface to *Porporino,* Dominique Fernandez writes:

The fame of Callas in our day doesn't approach the splendor of [the castrati's] renown in their time when audiences were overcome with joy, madly enraptured listening to them sing and aroused to unforgettable passions. Nevertheless, they left the world scene on tiptoe; memoirs of contemporaries mention them vaguely in passing; there remain no more than a few anecdotes and, unfortunately, no biographies. Such neglect, or rather such censorship, shows that for a slight gain in morals they were ready to sever an immense source of pleasure.[11]

We needn't marvel either at the extremely negative value judgments leveled against the castrato voice; it was condemned not only for the immorality of the practice that made this voice possible but also, on a strictly vocal level, for what was deemed the "gratuitousness" of the pure virtuosity I have been describing. It is interesting to note the attitude of the Catholic church in this regard: "The Church forbade castration, but church authorities had no reason to intervene in the operation itself. What to do, then, with those children who were

---

[10]Charles Burney, *The Present State of Music in France and Italy* (1773; facs. rpt. New York: Broude Bros., 1969).
[11]Fernandez, *Porporino,* 8.

operated on by necessity? Why not accept them into the choirs?"[12] The church discreetly looked the other way as these operations "for medical reasons" increased considerably, amply meeting the requirements of church choirs and opera stages. Christian Gaumy cites the following rather remarkable reasoning by a seventeenth-century casuist: "The voice is a faculty more precious than virility, because it is through the voice that man distinguishes himself from the animals. Therefore, if, to embellish the voice, it is necessary to eliminate virility, this can be done without impiety. So necessary are soprano voices to sing the Lord's praise that one must not set too high a price for their acquisition." The situation the castrati met with in France is just as revealing and entirely consistent with what I have said about the place of the spoken word in French lyric culture and the rejection of any autonomy of the purely vocal dimension. The castrato is accepted, but only in the choir of the Chapelle Royale (and here only until 1830) for the performance of religious music—that is, in a clearly circumscribed place in which the production of jouissance is made to serve the religious project from a consecratory perspective. Yet as might be expected, France was fiercely hostile to the presence of "capons" on the lyric stage. Gluck, for example, decided to rework his *Orfeo* for its Paris production, assigning a tenor to the title role initially written for a castrato alto voice in the original Vienna production twelve years earlier. And so with one more turn around this question, we meet up again with the author of *Émile,* in yet another of his contradictions:

"Do you know what Jean-Jacques Rousseau wrote in his *Dictionary of Music?*—'In Italy there are barbarous fathers who sacrifice nature to money and permit their children to undergo this operation, merely to give pleasure to cruel voluptuaries who cultivate these poor creatures' voices.' "

"We must not forget that Rousseau is not always consistent," Don Raimondo retorted. "When he edited the articles for his *Dictionary of Music,* he was thinking only of pleasing his Parisian readers. But when he was in Venice, all he had to guide him was his own pleasure. Did he not then write that he took back everything he had said against Italian opera after going to Venice's San Crisostomo to hear the castrato Giovanni Carestini sing Jomelli's

[12]Gaumy, "Le Chant des castrats."

Semiramide, where he experienced such ecstasy as he had never felt until that moment and realized that before this he had never heard real singing."[13]

Enlightenment philosophy, various European progressive movements of the day, and advances in female vocal technique, which eventually came to compete with and even supplant that of the castrati, dealt them a fatal blow. All the same, they lasted on the stage until 1844, at which time the world saw "the last documented appearance of a castrato on the stage . . . one Pergetti, in London."[14] After that date, the castrato could still be found, but only in the choirs of the Roman basilicas, reintegrated into his original angelic function, attesting once again to the truth that the religious apparatus is generally very tolerant toward the question of jouissance on condition that it participate in the religious project. It was not until 1903 that Pope Leo XIII definitively forbade the recruiting of new castrati for the Sistine Chapel. In writing the end of this extraordinary vocal adventure, he makes the castrato voice the Lost Voice par excellence, fueling the kind of nostalgia and fantasies that haunt the operatic imagination of the present era as no others do, nostalgia and fantasies always somewhat defeated by the pitiful recording left by one of the last castrati, Alessandro Moreschi—made in 1903/1904 on wax cylinders.

The *Travesti*

The passing of the angel in opera was to make way for the appearance of another figure, which continues into the twentieth century: the *travesti,* the character played by a member of the opposite sex. It is important here to avoid possible confusion: if I associate the *travesti* with the castrato, it is not because castrati, by virtue of the quality of their voices, played female roles. For as we have seen, the castrato voice was assigned to essentially virile roles. It is rather for another reason that I associate the two: they share in the "alchemy" that purges the voice of its sexual denotation, makes it angelic. In opera, moreover, the *travesti* appears almost exclusively as a woman assigned to a male role—

[13]Fernandez, *Porporino,* 146–47.
[14]Gaumy, "Le Chant des castrats."

so exclusively that in German such a part is called a *Hosenrolle*, or "trouser role." One may of course speculate as to the reasons for this unidirectionality in the dissociation of the voice from its appendant function of marking sexual difference. After all, the autonomization of the voice could just as well appear through the opposite substitution: the assignment of a male voice to a female part. Yet this is found only now and again in burlesque. This question ties in with one raised earlier as to the self-evident grounds on which it is held that the angel's voice can only be a high voice and will be addressed later. Here I will merely point out that the "trans-sexual" voice and the high voice—and therefore the woman's voice—seem to come together at this juncture.

Given the diversity of perspectives from which it can be construed, the theme of operatic cross-dressing would seem to warrant a study in its own right. Here I shall consider the *travesti*, however, only as a trace of the angelic *voice*, leaving aside the question of angelic *role*, or character. Certainly one of the attributes a character must have for the composer to assign it a female voice is youth (Cherubino, Romeo in Bellini's *I Capuletti ed i Montecci*, Octavian). But sexual nondifferentiation, a distinctive feature of the angel, is a trait they do not share. Two of opera's most famous *travestis*, Cherubino in Mozart's *Nozze di Figaro* and Octavian in Richard Strauss's *Rosenkavalier*, come with explicit reference to the angel, yet they are anything but angelic. Cherubino, whose name is that of an order of angels, is what Larousse defines as "a type of adolescent who awakens to love, though more as a libertine than as a romantic." It is not without reason that Kierkegaard relates the page's position in *Figaro* to Don Giovanni's, that he considers Cherubino a Don Giovanni in the bud.[15] As for Octavian, it is certainly not his character traits that make him angelic: his erotic function in the work could hardly be more explicit. And if in the amorous dialogue between the Marschallin Princess von Werdenberg and the young knight, the qualifier "angel" appears twice, it is Octavian who pronounces it in speaking of her, not the other way round. Octavian's association with the angel resides in the mission he is given to perform in this work, the typically angelic mission of annunciation: he is to bring the future bride a message—the traditional silver rose of a marriage proposal—from her suitor. It must not be forgotten that the

---

[15]Søren Kierkegaard, *Either/Or*, pt. 1, ed. and trans. Howard V. Hong and Edna H. Hong (Princeton: Princeton University Press, 1987), 100–101.

angel is etymologically the *messenger* of God (*angelos* in Greek means "messenger"). And in Richard Strauss's work, Marianne, Sophie's duenna, makes no mistake: upon seeing Octavian arrive with the silver rose intended for her charge, she exclaims: "Now they open the door! He alights! Dressed all in silver from head to foot, he looks like *an angel from heaven.*" (In a way, Octavian's position can be compared with that of the angel Gabriel, who announces the coming of the Messiah to Mary. The similarities end there: Baron Ochs is hardly a holy spirit!) Incidentally, it is in this marvelous duet of Sophie's encounter with her "angel" that her singing reaches stratospheric heights, with her one and only high C-sharp, as though in this tender confrontation with the angel's voice, Sophie's voice, the voice of a woman, transcends itself to hover for an instant on the verge of the musical cry whose emotional impact I have described so often.

Another confusion to be avoided is the one between the *travesti* and the character in disguise. The *travesti* does often assume a disguise: Cherubino, a young man played by a woman, disguises himself as a woman to meet the demands of the plot. Octavian, to avoid the scandal that his presence in the Marschallin's chamber would have caused, masquerades as her maid and in this guise leads Baron Ochs to his doom. This position is nonetheless different from such situations as that of a Fidelio or of a Zdenka in Richard Strauss's *Arabella,* in which a woman plays a female character who for whatever reason appears as a male. But here again, the substitution is still unidirectional: there are very few instances in which the vicissitudes of plot lead a male character to disguise himself as a woman. One exception that comes to mind is Achilles in Scyros, a theme that was widely used in Neapolitan baroque opera. Metastasio's drama recounts the episode in the life of the impetuous hero in which his mother, Thetis, hides him in woman's garb among the daughters of King Lycomedes of Scyros, to keep him from leaving for the Trojan War with the men Ulysses has assembled for the expedition. Ulysses reclaims the impulsive warrior by a trick: all the while pretending to take Achilles for one of Lycomedes's daughters, he slips in a sword among the gifts he has brought the king; unable to resist the attraction of this attribute so essential to his nature, Achilles immediately seizes the sword, casts off his feminine attire, and rejoins Ulysses' expedition. Such a situation is the exception rather than the rule and has to do with the assignment of the castrato voice to the character Achilles. The dissociation between the character's voice and its gender seems indeed to function only in one direction, for the character in disguise as well as for the *travesti*. Sexual indeterminacy thus appears to admit of only one possible voice: the high voice, which because it also happens to be the voice of the child, of the prepubescent male child, of the supposedly presexual or "trans-sexual" child, establishes a filiation between angelic voice, juvenile voice, and female voice (insofar as the latter may also be fantasized as "trans-sexual." I will return to this point later.)

No doubt a feminist argument could account for the asymmetry in the dissociation of the character's voice and gender where disguise is concerned. The simple fact of male supremacy may explain the difficulty of finding heroes or male singers willing to sink to putting on petticoats. By the same token, young female protagonists or singers could be expected to aspire to wearing trousers. This argument, however, fails to account for the much more radical asymmetry exhibited with the *travesti*. If the male is so highly valued, why not cast male voices in female roles? What better way to ensure male supremacy than by depriving the woman of her own voice? Yet the male character is sung by the female voice. The feminist argument might of course still obtain if one assumed that the determining factor was the character's gender: the female voice will rise in stature by singing a male role. Yet everything in operatic history attests to the fact that the supreme value in opera is the voice, the vocal aspect by far surpassing all anecdotal, ideological, and even moral considerations as they bear on the signification of the dramatic representation. As I noted earlier, the hierarchy of value among the characters is organized as a function of vocal values: the high voice at the top, assigned to the principal character, regardless of its gender. This strict hierarchy will last until the age of Mozart and Rossini. Then it will split down the line into a female hierarchy presided over by the coloratura soprano and a male hierarchy ruled by the tenor. With Mozart, opera ceases to be vocally asexual, angelic. And then with romanticism, the Angel becomes Woman, Woman driven to death.

The Angel's Traces

Before proceeding with this third phase or third avatar of the angelic figure, I would like to signal some traces its passage has left in aspects of particular characters or works. Every cultural construct, even long after its creation, continues to bear the marks of the circumstances of its origin. More or less disguised, more or less effaced references to the angel abound in one form or another in all of the major moments of operatic history. Such a reference can be found first of all in—Beethoven's Ninth Symphony: the climactic moment in the Ode to Joy before the final *allegro assai,* when the entire chorus joins in with the orchestra's *tutti* in a *long pedal multo tenuto,* is anchored in the following verse: "und der Cherub steht vor Gott" (and the angel[16] stands before God). Recall the function of pedal point. In this instance it is followed by a half measure of silence, which many conductors prolong (in the Jochum version on Philips it lasts five seconds). All the elements of the angelic problematics—voice, music, silence, and angel—come together here. This observation, incidentally, tends to bear out Richard Wagner's contention that the Ode to Joy is the paragon of music drama as he conceived of it.

One could go on like this, flushing out the presence of the angel at almost every turn in operatic history, beginning with the angel at whose feet Richard Wagner lays the first act of *Tristan:* "Thrice happy, out of reach of pain, free and purely ever thine—Tristan and Isolde, what they bewailed and forwent, their tears and kisses, in music's chaste gold I lay at thy feet, that they may praise the angel who has lifted me so high."[17] This angel, of course, was Mathilde Wesendonck. The angel's gaze crosses Wagner's oeuvre time and again: the prelude to *Lohengrin* depicts the flight of angels carrying to Montsalvat the vase of Joseph of Arimathea: the Grail. It is this silent flight evoked by the long legatos on the violins that seems to have first sent Ludwig II of Bavaria plunging into the ravishing ecstasy he then obsessively

---

[16]It is best not to translate *Cherub* literally: the grandeur of this passage is ill served by the connotations of this term.

[17]This is Wagner's dedication of Act I of *Tristan und Isolde* to Mathilde Wesendonck, in a letter sent on New Year's Eve 1857 along with a draft of Act I, in *Richard Wagner to Mathilde Wesendonck,* trans. William Ashton Ellis (1905; rpt. New York: Vienna House, 1972), 17.

pursued in the surging tides of Wagner's music, before being con-
clusively engulfed by the real waves of the Lake of Starnberg. A "madness" had found its echo in music, and this music was a music of
silence. The character of Lohengrin contains the angelic structure in its
entirety: "sent by God," "borne upon the breezes," he appears first as
silence (twice not answering the herald's call), then as a protector. It is
Elsa who points out this aspect of his nature: "My protector! My
angel!" she says. Finally he is "unnameable"—in other words, trans-
verbal and "trans-sexual," divorced from language and from gender.
Two things could cause him to lose this status: having to speak his
name and losing a piece of his body. "If you had torn off his finger in
battle, just a piece of finger, the knight would have fallen into your
power!" (Ortrud to Friedrich, II.i). Lohengrin must escape all naming, must avoid any "castration," lest he fall to the status of a desiring
man. From then on Elsa's desire, the desire of the woman who seeks to
name its object is unbearable to him: he prefers to return to the imaginary plenitude of the Grail, in which all desire is silenced.

Another music of silence, if ever there was one, is the prelude to
Parsifal. It, too, organizes an angelic substance (which Wagner will
carry to its extreme as he stretches phonic continuity to its limits). This
is how Wagner explains his prelude to Ludwig II: "First theme: Love
. . . repeated softly by angelic voices as though lost in the air. . . .
Faith descends from the gentlest heights as though carried on the wing
of a white dove."

There are many examples of this kind in which an angelic form
appears on the scene for the space of an instant in what sometimes can
seem improbable guise. In Verdi's *Don Carlos,* for example, in Act I (or
Act II, depending on the version), Don Carlos sees his friend Rodrigo,
marquis of Posa—who in the final act will sacrifice himself for him—as
a kind of angel: "Heaven has sent you to me in my suffering, consoling
angel." Another, stranger example is found in Benjamin Britten's *Billy
Budd*. Captain Vere, speaking of his cabin boy, Billy Budd (baritone),
whom he must sentence to hang for the murder of Claggart, his tor-
mentor, says: "The angel of God has struck and the angel must hang—
through me."

But here I will leave my readers to their own devices to discover for
themselves the angelic contour, explicit or implicit, in the situations,
qualifiers, and characterizations of numerous works.

The Angel Appears

Having been so ceaselessly invoked, the angel was bound finally to appear, as such, on the stage in flesh and blood, as it were. And in fact this is what happened at the Paris Opéra in 1983, in Act II of Olivier Messiaen's *Saint-François d'Assise*. Tableau 2, titled "L'Ange musicien," which follows "L'Ange voyageur," sets to music Francis's ecstasy at the appearance of a viola-playing angel. The musical style Messiaen uses for this effect is particularly illustrative of what I have been saying. While the work is fashioned on the whole of phonic material marked by discontinuity, by rhythmic irregularity, by the use of great percussive, flashing, "pointillist" masses of sound, what signals the appearance of the angel, apart from its soprano voice, is the steadiest and most continuous of possible sounds: the crystalline, long-drawn-out high tone produced by the *ondes musicales*. The contrast is striking. Francis of Assisi expresses his jouissance in specific terms: "I am not ill . . . only stunned, overwhelmed by this heavenly music. If the angel had played the viola a little longer . . . Ah! the *unbearable sweetness,* my soul would have left my body." Everything is said here, in the words as in the music of this deadly call, in the jouissance (and not pleasure: *unbearable* sweetness) of the angelic silence.

Mozart, the Angel, and the Divine

This review of opera's angelic battalions would be incomplete without a pause to examine the significance of the constant references to Mozart as angelic and divine. Such stereotypical imagery, incidentally, can irritate great fans of Mozart intensely, and for good reason, given the association of the angelic with the insipid. But as I have said before, traditions always speak the truth, a truth that is not always where common sense expects to find it. The fundamental truth of Mozart's relation to the problematics of the angel—once it is rid of the image of Mozart the child, which undoubtedly plays some part here—appears to lie in his singular relation to the question of silence, of the other silence.

"The silence that follows Mozart's music is still Mozart." Sacha Guitry's splendid remark is so well known and so often repeated that its profound meaning eludes us (and perhaps eluded Sacha Guitry himself; no matter: one always says more than one means). What does this statement disclose, if we take it literally? It makes us aware that the silence that follows Mozart's music is literally *overwhelmed* by the presence of Mozart, of his music, that his silence and his music are interchangeable, that Mozart and his music come in fact to fill the place of the angel, of the "consequent" silence—as Jankélevitch says—the divine or angelic silence that comes after the music. And by occupying that place of silence, Mozart's music makes it possible to avoid that agonizing and mortal stupefaction which religion avoids, as we have seen, by putting God or his angel there. Just as God and the angel are imaginary figures invented to fill the intolerable chasm of the unnameable silence where all words fail, Mozart's music—and this is what Sacha Guitry's remark points out—permits it to be forgotten, or even denied, in somewhat the same way a little tune is hummed or belted out for reassurance against the anguishing silence of night. Mozart's music functions at its best when it plays the role of the magic flute that allows Tamino and Pamina to face the ultimate ordeal: the fear of death. Let there be no mistake, this is not a simple role, for denial is another form of recognition. To say, "This is not silence, this is still music," is to admit to the presence of silence and then pretend it is not there. A fool's bargain? Probably, but also a challenge, like the one Don Giovanni defiantly accepts.

With this question the antinomy noted earlier between the "Mozart effect" and the "Wagner effect" reappears. In Wagner, the evocation of the unnameable and the ecstasy of silence—an ecstasy that always carries the risk of self-loss for those who pursue it—derive from his music itself. If Mozart's silence is music, in Wagner it is the music itself that reverberates to the silent continuum in which his devotees seek the bliss they fear to find. Where Mozart situates himself at the side of an often jubilant pleasure procured by the release of tension, Wagner is resolutely on the side of the quest for that unnameable residue which Lacan calls the Real. We have seen the musical means by which these paths are distinguished. If the "blue note" joins the desire of the listener to that of the composer, in Mozart that encounter takes place on the note, the expected cadence, prepared for by the rhythmic scansion it produces; in Wagner it is bound up with the long-held note or the cry.

The Angel Musician

The angel musician is a familiar figure in both the imaginary and medieval religious iconography. Its relation to silence and divine silence has often been posited as well, in ways that go far beyond the effect of its "passage" in language signaled by the common expression "an angel has passed." This relationship is the object of an extraordinary study by Pseudo-Dionysius the Areopagite, the fifth-century Christian Byzantine thinker and author of *The Celestial Hierarchy.* In this treatise he spells out both the role of the angel as messenger and the silence that accompanies it. At the summit of the celestial hierarchy, he explains, the seraphim dance around God while endlessly singing hymns in his praise. But these hymns are so marvelous, so utterly beyond human language, that they are imperceptible even in the ranks of the celestial hierarchy directly below, a fortiori to mere mortals.[18] It is the seraphim's task to transmit these divine and silent hymns down through the celestial ranks, one sphere at a time, until the musicians of the terrestrial church, discerning the faint echo of the heavenly songs, convey them, in the form of a now audible music, to human ears. It is in this sense that the Areopagite speaks of the angels as "colporteurs of the divine silence," and that one can speak of "the angel's silent song."[19] This theological construct connects the trans-verbal, singing, silence, and the divine in a way reminiscent of my schematization of the tension between words and music and the connection between music, singing, cry, and silence. All of this becomes even clearer in Jean-Claude Milner's formulation of the angel's figurative role: "The angel has long served as the image of what becomes of a subject when it is reduced to its purely enunciative dimension."[20] The subject then becomes sheer voice, incorporeal, sexless, and speechless. Here we are approaching the limit of its transformation into a "vocal object." The extraction of the "purely enunciative dimension," disengaged from all content and everything that gives it bodily substance, is something like

---

[18]See Henri Corbin, *L'Homme et son ange* (Paris: Fayard, 1983), 17: "[the angel Gabriel] is for humans the Hermeneut of this superior angelic world, which, being beyond their confines, is said to proffer only eternal silence."

[19]Françoise Ferrand, "Penser la musique au Moyen Age," in *Histoire de la musique occidentale,* ed. Jean Massin and Brigitte Massin (Paris: Messidor/Temps Actuel, 1983).

[20]Jean-Claude Milner, *L'Amour de la langue* (Paris: Seuil, 1978), 8.

the grin of the Cheshire Cat in *Alice in Wonderland,* a grin that persists for a few moments after the cat himself has gradually and finally disappeared.[21]

The Cheshire Cat's grin may perhaps help us understand how it may be possible to imagine the emergence of that other entity—a smiling one, too, as one can see in Reims Cathedral—called the angel. The angel is in a way the emblematic figure of the vocal object, inasmuch as the vocal object is produced by the disengagement of those aspects of the voice that give it body and sense. It should come as no surprise, then, to find that figure so present in the question that concerns us here.

The Angel-Voice

This analysis also allows me to formulate several hypotheses that might account for the supposedly self-evident idea, noted and rejected at the beginning of this chapter, that the angel's voice, in Christian Gaumy's words, "can only be high." Many factors converge to establish this correspondence. I will take them up one by one.

First a "topological" hypothesis: given that angels traditionally dwell "in heaven on high," it is perhaps conceivable to imagine a slippage by which the voice "on high" becomes the "high" voice. There is a problem with this hypothesis, though: it merely displaces the problem of the association of angelic voice and high voice; it does not, in other words, explain how the voice comes to be called "high" (or "low") in the first place. There is nothing self-evident about this metaphorical qualifier—or about other qualifiers that describe a voice as "sharp" or "piercing," for that matter (the universe of descriptions of sound is awash in metaphor). And yet it can be found in any number of languages totally unrelated to each other (the Romance languages, Arabic, Chinese . . .).

I therefore decided to undertake a somewhat unscientific investiga-

---

[21]Lewis Carroll, *Alice in Wonderland:* " 'All right,' said the Cat; and this time it vanished quite slowly, beginning with the end of the tail, and ending with the grin, which remained some time after the rest of it had gone.

" 'Well! I've often seen a cat without a grin,' thought Alice; 'but a grin without a cat! It's the most curious thing I ever saw in all my life!' "

tion, and asked those around me the following question: "Why do we use the word 'high' or 'low' to describe a voice in terms of its pitch?" The response most frequently offered was that it had to do with the place of the notes on the staff: the higher on the staff, the higher the note. The obvious problem with this explanation is that the qualifier was used in reference to the voice long before music was written on the staff (it occurs in Latin, for example). In all probability, the position of the notes on the staff lines followed from the qualifier "high."

Several people offered a rather colorful explanation: Animals of the sky have shriller songs and cries than those of the earth. The hypothesis is contradicted by the crow and the mouse, but it has a certain statistical validity and could be seen as consonant with the angelic anatomy. The association between the angel and the bird is well established by their wings if not their songs. Still, the idea of grounding a metaphor descriptive of the human voice in an animal cry seems somehow a little farfetched.

A final explanation, also frequently encountered, and one I am inclined to adopt, relates the adjective "high" to the proprioceptive sensations of movement in the larynx and in areas of the body that resonate when the voice moves from the lower to the upper registers, from the "chest voice" to the "head voice," these expressions clearly indicating a perceived sensation of an upward rise along the body's vertical axis.

The Angel and the Child

A far more interesting hypothesis, one I have already touched upon, establishes a relationship among the angelic voice, the high voice, and the child's voice. The supposed innocence of children, their supposed asexuality, makes them ideal incarnations of the angelic—at least before Freud. And the younger the child, the less corrupt and more like an angel. The religious folklore that sees the ranks of angels filled with stillborn and aborted infants expresses this notion. The idea seems to have historical merit, as evidenced in the church's turning to the singing of children to realize its idea of a music "in the image of the angelic choirs in heaven that sing high praise to the divine glory that halos them in light."[22] This notion, however, seems not entirely satisfactory on two counts:

First, the church was quick to turn to other ways of approximating the supposedly angelic voice, to the castrato in particular and to falsettists—that is, masculine adult voices trained in a particular technique that allows them to sing high. Did the inherent imperfections of the juvenile voice make it fall so far short of the desired ideal that this in itself was reason enough for the church to accept a moral contradiction as messy as the one into which it was led by the use of the castrato? It seems not, because with proper training the voice of the adolescent or the child can in fact achieve an acceptable level of excellence, the English boy choir being a case in point.

But there is a second reason that seems to confirm the merely contingent nature of a hypothesis that makes the supposedly innocent nature of the child the intermediate term between the angel's voice and the high voice. That hypothesis requires that childlike purity, associated with the child's (presumed) situation outside of sexuality, be itself the principal attribute of the angelic nature. Nothing is less certain: the primary function of the angel is, as its name indicates, to be the intermediary, the messenger—a role that is not specifically childlike. The problem of the sex of the angels is a relatively recent and secondary consideration and does not seem sufficient to support most of the connotations surrounding the figure of the angel and to regulate the modalities by which its human incarnation is fantasized.

Without necessarily excluding these hypotheses, I think it is the very peculiarities of the high voice that make it the medium for the angel's voice. And so I return once again to the observation that one of the characteristics of the high voice is that it destroys meaningful articulation. The high voice is a privileged site where all the tension between words and music produces its most striking effects. We have seen what is at stake in this opposition and how it works; there is no need to tell it again now. The purification of the voice, its separation from the "enunciative dimension," can be manifested most completely here because of the concomitant and gradual disappearance of the signifying dimension. One and the same voice, if it can reach the high notes, can stand at two poles, that of the intelligible signifying message and the other pole, the summit where, verging on the cry, the

[22]Ferrand, "Penser la musique au Moyen Age."

voice tends in the direction of becoming sheer voice, just as the Cheshire Cat became nothing but a smile.

Angel and Demon

At many points, then, this survey of the angelic intersects the course traced out around the vocal object in the second part of this book. Yet a fundamental intersection between these two paths is missing. That point is the cry. And except insofar as the cry can be associated with the sound of the trumpet, the angels' instrument of choice (an association not altogether baseless, as we shall see), the cry is indeed wholly alien to the angelic structure. Recall the diabolical markings of the cry. The devil, Lucifer, is a fallen angel, and one of the ways those possessed by the devil are identified is by "crying out like those possessed."

The question of the cry in opera is first addressed explicitly in Mozart; that is, at a stage in the development of opera at which the genre undergoes sexual differentiation, where the angel's voice definitively quits the castrato to be distributed, quite unequally, between the male tenor to some extent and the female soprano for the most part. Is this what gives Satan his foothold on the opera stage? Is the singing woman then the *diva,* a medium for the angel, or *demonia,* a medium for the devil, or is she both at once? This is what we must explore.

When the Angel Becomes Woman

Jacques Brunschwig observes that Mozart,

with his astonishing ability to enter into musical sympathy with the female experience and to break through the sexual barrier with his wit . . . , in *The Marriage of Figaro* singlehandedly brings about something entirely new that could be called an intrinsic sexualization of musical language. . . . *The Marriage of Figaro* goes so far with the sexual differentiation of musical discourse as to establish lasting and genuine musical stereotypes of virility and femininity, with their diverse variants reflecting social position (the Count, Figaro) or sentimental position (the Countess, Susanna); we have only begun to understand their melodic, rhythmic, instrumental, and vocal underpinnings.[23]

Mozart, furthermore, sets out the relationship of the masculine and the feminine in the thematic construction of his operas. That thematic construction first takes form in characters and story (*Le Nozze di Figaro, Don Giovanni, Così Fan Tutte*) before it is finally addressed as such in *Die Zauberflöte*, which through allegorical characters explicitly addresses the relationship of masculine and feminine at its very source.

Mozart thus sets the stage for romantic opera, which somehow divides the figure of the angel into a masculine side (the tenor) and a feminine side (the soprano), the latter receiving the lion's share of the initial angelic substance.[24] Operatic romanticism establishes Woman as the last avatar of the Angel, makes her the privileged ground of the quest for the vocal object. Situations in which the libretto explicitly

---

[23]Jacques Brunschwig, "L'Hymen de Suzanne," *L'Avant-scène Opéra* 21: *"Les Noces de Figaro"* (May–June 1979), 127.

[24]The two aspects always seek reunification in their duet.

assigns the angelic position to a female character are so numerous that I
need cite only a few examples. To call a woman (or a man, for that
matter) an angel is certainly common in everyday language, but this in
no way diminishes its deeper significance, especially when *five* times in
a single act, the last act of *Tannhäuser*, the female protagonist (Elisabeth) is referred to as an angel. This is obviously neither fortuitous
nor a sign of the exhaustion of Wagner's poetic inspiration. Further
examples: Elsa (*Lohengrin*); Leonor (*Fidelio*); the heroine of Donizetti's
La Favorita (also called the angel of Nisida). And Verdi's *Otello*, in
which Otello's characterization of Desdemona shifts explicitly between
the angelic and the demonic: "Were your demon to see you now, he
would think you an angel and not touch you" (III.ii). And Senta, in
The Flying Dutchman, where the same sort of double reference appears.
The Dutchman to Senta: "You are an angel, and an angel's love may
comfort even the outcast soul!" (II.iii). Later, Erik to Senta: "Come to
me! You are in Satan's clutches!" (III.ii). And Violetta in *La Traviata*, a
unique case in that when the tenor Alfredo invests her with angelic
imagery, she responds in kind: "No man or devil, my angel, shall ever
part you from me again," they sing in alternating duet, when in the
third act the exhilaration of their reunion peaks. Lulu, too, can now
take her place in this roster, which could go on and on. I will return to
it in greater detail later.

Lulu, Desdemona, Violetta—these are characters who insist on following the procession of female sacrifice, murder, madness, and death
which parades all along the history of opera, especially since the
romantic period. For when the angel's voice inhabits Woman, the
result is not merely woman as such, but Woman driven to death and
sacrifice. Of course this dominant theme of the sacrificed woman is not
confined to this period alone. It is one of the inaugurating themes of
the genre, Euridice being one of its first victims. Many others took
their places beside her in heaven or hell long before romanticism
(Clorinda, Armide, Alceste, Dido . . .).

To bring the weight of these numbers to bear more specifically on
the danger of the opera stage to the physical and mental well-being of
the female characters who nonetheless continue to venture forth upon
it, I decided to undertake a small statistical study.

The Opera Necropolis

I thus undertook a quick autopsy of the heaps of bodies strewn across the opera stage since the beginning of the genre, drawing my sample population from the 257 works composed between 1597 and 1973 and analyzed by François-René Tranchefort.[25]

I should first specify the extent of this study's validity. These 257 works in no way make up a representative sample of the operas that have been created since the genre began. Omissions are numerous, especially for the baroque period. The prolixity of the baroque composers, as well as their sheer numbers, make an exhaustive inventory impossible, especially in view of the many works that have been lost. The effects of these omissions are mitigated, however, by the fact that the same themes were used repeatedly. A handful of Metastasio's dramas serve as libretti for dozens upon dozens of compositions. Something like an overview may therefore be possible without undue distortion of the statistical fate of the operatic characters.

The first observation from this analysis reveals that the "objective" mortality rate for male characters equals that of the female characters (around 85 cases) and is even higher than theirs if a few giants, dwarfs, and dragons are included and if each of the suitors dispatched by Ulysses is counted individually. In a purely global sense, therefore, if opera is considered simply as a vast cemetery, male and female graves appear with equal frequency. This seems counterintuitive. But if to the class of strictly "biological" deaths we add the category of what could be called "characters in torment"—that is, characters who are subject to a particular kind of suffering such as madness, unjust condemnation, self-sacrifice in response to unrequited love (I love you; you do not love me; you love her/him?: go, follow your heart!), then female deaths begin to predominate (with 30 such cases for female characters, as against 15 for the males).

Another salient difference emerges if one considers the importance a particular death assumes by virtue of its timing as the plot unfolds.[26] Thus of some 85 female deaths counted, more than 60 conclude the

---

[25]François-René Tranchefort, *L'Opéra*, 2 vols. (Paris: Seuil, 1978).

[26]Deaths that occur before the action begins have not been included in this statistical tally, even if they constitute a fundamental motivation of the plot or figure "materially" in the work (as in Schoenberg's *Erwartung*, for example).

operas in which they occur as opposed to only 40 male deaths that do so. All the other male deaths (out of a similar universe of about 85) punctuate the peripeteias of the action: among these deaths are, notably, the deaths of traitors and deaths that cause other deaths, usually of women, as in *Pelléas et Mélisande,* when Pelléas's death in Act IV anticipates Mélisande's at the conclusion. Also to be noted are deaths that take place together (Aïda/Radames, Norma/Pollione) or in immediate succession (Isolde/Tristan, Tosca/Mario, Roméo/Juliette)—a dozen in all.

Turning now from this global analysis to a more detailed breakdown, we find an appreciable historical change in the distribution of male and female deaths. If actual deaths and characters in torment are grouped in a single category, then of some 120 female characters that fall into this category, 60, or half, occur in operas written between 1800 and 1900, that is, in what may be called the romantic period: the nineteenth century alone accounts for as many as the other three centuries together. In the same period only 37 male characters fall into this category, and 30 of them are heroes, while the rest are either nonspeaking roles or traitors. They therefore make up 30 percent of the total and correspond roughly to their proportion in the entire period under consideration. Modern times, on the other hand, are lethal to the male hero: of the 40 operas that *conclude* with the death of a male protagonist, 22 were written after 1900. These numbers thus confirm, even as they qualify, the commonly held idea that opera stages the suffering and death of women—what Catherine Clément has called their "undoing"[27]—especially in the romantic period.

The Voice of Sacrifice

But if we readjust the criteria and tally these fallen characters not by sex but by voice, we can observe a massive and almost unqualified phenomenon. That in itself is quite remarkable in a cultural expression stretching over four centuries and therefore subject to a multiplicity of decisions made year after year at various levels of this curiously com-

[27]Catherine Clément, *Opera, or The Undoing of Women* (Minneapolis: University of Minnesota Press, 1988).

plex construction that is opera. We find that male characters destined for death, at least those who perish with honor, all have high voices; this is not always the case for the traitors who die. One even sees an explicit pursuit of voices higher than tenor for male characters destined for sacrifice. Thus Bellini, in 1830, turns to a female voice (alto) for the role of Romeo, and his fate we know. Similarly, Rimski-Korsakoff in *Le Coq d'Or* makes the astrologer, killed by the king to whom he has given the magic bird, a countertenor, and this in 1909, well before infatuation with ancient and baroque music revived interest in this kind of voice.

There are few exceptions to this dominant feature. We find them in Russian opera (Boris Godunov, of course, and several others, including Ivan Susanin), in some of Verdi's protagonists (Simone Boccanegra, for example), and in the great Mozartian hero Don Giovanni. We find them too in more contemporary operas. Indeed, with the modern period the "heroic" operatic death tends to become more and more a masculine affair, not only in the characters' gender but also in their voices. Aside from the four or five exceptions I have noted, the twenty-two male characters killed off since 1900 make up the totality of non-tenor and noncountertenor deaths in operatic history, at least according to François-René Tranchefort's inventory.

These statistical findings—which need to be interpreted with caution, given the nature of the sample from which they were drawn—support the argument for the absolute preeminence of the high voice over all other factors that have shaped the evolution of opera, whether sociohistorical, ideological, or anything else. Perhaps there is a lesson to be drawn from these findings in respect to certain contemporary compositions that seem to have lost the intuition that it is the processes set in motion by this preeminence that allow the melomane's jouissance to emerge.

But then one must wonder why in these imaginary situations the extraordinary predominance of the voice and of the high voice is associated with death. An analysis of the emergence of the cry, but from a different angle, may shed some light on this question.

Woman's Cry/Man's Word

"Why does he not cry out, this man?"[28]

A somewhat more rigorous census once again confirms the expected: the cry (read "pure cry") in opera is, almost without exception, the cry of a woman. Male cries are rare, and the criteria must be broader yet if such cries as Don Giovanni's—noted musically on the staff but unsupported by the text—are to be included in the category of "pure" cry. Even in this broader sense, they seem to number fewer than ten. Even the death of the male protagonist at the conclusion of an opera is rarely the occasion for even a "melodic" cry. The opposite is true for the deaths of women: silent deaths (Mimi, Mélisande) are the exceptions. La Traviata's death is particularly significant in this regard. A certain elementary logic of "realism" (the breathlessness of the consumptive, for example) could have led Verdi to have Violetta expire *parlando,* which would have singularized "the wayward one's" final intervention: a woman who dies speaking—that would have been unprecedented in opera history. That was not the logic which prevailed; once more the logic of jouissance holds sway with the inevitable upheaval that besets the listener on hearing the extraordinary lyric flight to which the initial words give way, thereby marking the reaffirmed and terrible victory of the cry over language.

Now, it seems that this reaffirmation is forbidden when a man is the locus of these vocal stakes. If it is the cry that is prohibited, as we have seen, the injunction is particularly strong for the cry of a man. The following example from contemporary opera, coming therefore in the sizable wake of musical transgressions of that prohibition, offers a striking illustration.

In 1969 Krzysztof Penderecki composed *Die Teufel von Loudun,* bringing to the opera stage the famous case of "possession" of the Ursuline nuns in the convent of Loudun in 1634 and the torture of the curé of Loudun, Urbain Grandier, which marked the end of these events. In the context of contemporary musical composition, such a theme could be expected to lend itself exceptionally well to intensive treatment of any vocal or musical material that might involve the cry. And indeed, Penderecki uses the cry unsparingly for the chorus and for

[28]Richard Strauss, *Salome.*

certain female characters. But what is quite astonishing—at least in the recorded production[29]—is that while Urbain Grandier's torment is depicted down to its smallest detail, no faintest cry escapes his lips, even as the libretto again and again seems to demand a response of this kind: we hear the blows of the torturer's hammer breaking the victim's legs, but not a single cry. This is a tour de force that Puccini approaches but does not quite achieve in *Tosca,* where Mario Cavaradossi's cry under torture is heard, but offstage, from the wings. His cry keeps its distance, its impact is muffled. This kind of censorship of the male cry can be related to the divergent evolutionary paths of male and female singing through the history of opera.

In the second part of this work I characterized the evolution of opera singing in general as a trajectory from speech to cry, a trajectory that Violetta's death condenses into a single instant. This formulation should now be qualified. It really applies only to female singing. The further one proceeds in operatic history, the more the great lyric displays of female singing are located in the zone of inevitable unintelligibility, in the upper and extreme upper registers of the voice. Not only is there no such evolution in male singing—notwithstanding certain tenor arias where it undergoes similar treatment—but on the contrary, male singing tends, strikingly in the cases of Wagner and Berg, to reemerge as pure speech. Then finally, in Lulu, for example, we have those strange duets, such as Jack and Lulu's in Act III, which gives the impression of a man who speaks (so weakly is the musical line of his part stressed) and a woman who answers him with many extreme variations on a long musical cry. This striking contrast comes to a head in the final confrontation in which Lulu's sheer cry is followed by Jack's pure speech, in quasi-recitative.

Pure speech is of course not entirely absent from female opera singing, but its extreme rarity makes it particularly expressive whenever it does occur: the letters that Violetta receives and reads to herself, for example, and the lines from Racine that Adriana Lecouvreur declaims are in each case somone else's words. Lulu will finally counter this tradition. For her, speech punctuates the enunciation of the profound truth of her being; it is her genuine declaration of love in Act I: "meines Mannes . . ." It is the horrific finale of Act II, where she

[29]Krzysztof Penderecki, *Les Diables de Loudun,* conducted by Marek Janowski, Philips.

reminds Alwa that he is caressing her on the same sofa on which her father died. But in opera, where woman is concerned, singing and the cry inevitably prevail over speech and words, for if music is a woman, the woman is also music. That is what Alwa sings to Lulu: "Under your dress I feel your form as music.—These ankles—a grazioso. This gentle enchanting swell—a cantabile. And this knee—misterioso; and the powerful andante of love's desire" (III.i).

Conversely, the evolution of male singing in opera is marked by the victory of the word: *Sprechgesang* is a virtually omnipresent feature of contemporary opera. The 1985 Paris production of Konrad Boehmer's *Doktor Faustus* perfectly illustrates this tendency. *Parlando* or *Sprechgesang* or even pure and simple theatrical declamation is the rule for all the male characters in this opera. When singing reemerges (to some surprise), it comes by way of Maria, practically the only female character to sing in this work. Then we are reminded that we are at the opera!

From this perspective, then, what might the man's cry signify when from time to time it does manage to break forth?

The Dwarf's Cry, the Devil's Cry

> *Wotan forcibly tears the ring from Alberich's finger.*
> *Alberich:* (*with a horrible cry* [*Grasslich aufschreind*]) Ah! Vanquished, destroyed!

In the production he directed at Bayreuth (1976–1981), Patrice Chéreau draws out a fundamental truth in *Das Rheingold* by going beyond Wagner's explicit stage directions: in Chéreau's production Wotan does not merely pull the ring of absolute power from Alberich's finger; he severs that finger with a blow of his lance, the lance bearing the runic inscription of the law of the world. What better metaphor for the cutting function performed by the text, by the law (and the law of the Father) as it is brought to bear against absolute power, a law of unbounded madness symbolized by the ring—that is, by an object attached to the body, a part of the body (as Alberich explicitly proclaims: "hand, head, eye, and ear are no more mine than is this ruddy ring"). This is castration in precisely the sense that Lacan has given the word: the necessary severance that constitutes the human being as a "speaking being," a "*parlêtre*" (a being-through-language), the severance by which the human being renounces absolute, unregulated jouissance, and thus accedes to the desire inscribed in the law of language. The price of this renunciation is the loss of "the pound of flesh," as Lacan says, referring to the forfeiture that secures the Merchant of Venice's debt to Shylock. Behind these thoughts occasioned by Alberich's cry we can glimpse the outlines of our problematics that sees speech or words as a limit that checks a certain implicit jouissance. The dwarf's cry is somehow the final echo of this implicit unbounded jouissance when it confronts the obligatory loss that comes with the act of speaking.

Opera has a story about another dwarf, and this story too, oddly enough, is an occasion for a cry of absolute terror. Alexander von Zemlinsky, the Viennese composer who was the teacher of both Berg and Schoenberg before he became Schoenberg's brother-in-law, composed in 1921 a short lyric work titled *Der Geburtstag der Infantin*, or, alternatively, *Der Zwerg* (The Dwarf), after Oscar Wilde's short story "The Birthday of the Infanta." This opera tells the story of a dwarf presented as a gift to the Infanta of Spain. An object of scorn, subject to the Infanta's cruelty, he nonetheless falls and remains in love with the princess until one day, upon meeting his reflection in a mirror for the first time, he screams a terrible cry of horror at the sight of his monstrousness. The dwarf cries out again at the end of the scene, introducing a real *Liebestod*, a death by love, as the Infanta comments with bitter sarcasm. "His heart has broken," says the maidservant. "My present already broken!" the royal child complains. "Then I want a toy without a heart!" This powerful and very beautiful one-act work seems to have made a vivid impression on Alban Berg. Indeed, after one hears the dwarf's cry, it is difficult not to think of the cry Lulu later utters—a cry preceded by the same dramatic tension and followed immediately by the same orchestral overlay—just as it is difficult at the end of this opera not to think of the ending of *Wozzeck*.

This encounter between the dwarf and the cry is rather strange, especially given the rarity of this kind of character in opera, and calls for interpretation. But before I venture one, I had best go on with the census of the male cry: what we discover there may allow us to see our way to it more clearly.

In view of the preceding findings, it was inevitable that the search for the cry should lead to the devil, the angel's fallen counterpart. Meyerbeer, in *Robert le Diable*, provides the occasion for this encounter in the character Bertram. When this earthly incarnation of Satan sees his works undone, he is swallowed up in the chasm that opens beneath him, "uttering a terrible cry"—much like Don Giovanni, whose fate

Bertram's calls to mind. Yet Bertram is a singularly humanized devil, and his annihilation, unlike that of Don Giovanni, takes place entirely within the thematic structure of sacrifice so characteristic of the destinies of women in romantic opera. Indeed, after using spells to try to gain the soul of Robert, his son, Bertram gives him the freedom to choose between his father the Devil and the woman he loves: "Be free. Myself I sacrifice and henceforth I am in your hands. . . . Go! Flee! You can flee your wretched father. Your fate and mine are in your hands. My son! Robert! O my only fortune." The son of course opts for his beloved Isabelle. The Devil, his father, is defeated, and his cry punctuates his loss: "Ah! Vengeful God, you win!"

The cry of a wretched dwarf, the cry of a "poor devil," and in Richard Strauss's *Elektra* the cry of Aegisthus, under Orestes' dagger, an Aegisthus ridiculed and feminized by Elektra:

Chrysothemis [Elektra's sister]:   They [Aegisthus and Clytemnestra] are plotting hideous treason.
Elektra: Those two women?
Chrysothemis: Who?
Elektra: Why, our mother and that other woman, the coward, Aegisthus, that daring assassin, heroic only in bed. . . .

It is worth noting that Aegisthus is given a tenor part, which produces a somewhat strange effect: a tenor part for a character of paternal rank opposite a baritone stepson.

The Cry of the Deceiver

Those are among the more remarkable of the rare male cries in opera. In the mere description of their dramatic circumstances we can see that they have more than one trait in common with the female cry.

But what, then, of Don Giovanni's cry, that cry I called the "original"? Don Giovanni, an object of pitiful scorn? Certainly not! A dishrag, and womanish? Even less! A devil incarnate? That would perhaps be easier to argue but would nevertheless ignore the fact that one of Don Giovanni's dominant traits is that he believes neither in God nor in the Devil, but simply that "two and two are four, and four and four are eight" (Molière, *Don Juan*, III.i). In its uniqueness—this is the cry of a baritone, and Don Giovanni is the character archetype of a certain kind of masculinity, the "Don Juan" ("What a man!")—this unforgettable cry resists inclusion in the feminine category in which I have tried to group the few male cries that opera offers.

And yet a study undertaken from an altogether different perspective will perhaps allow Don Giovanni's D-minor cry to take its place within the logic of this analysis without too much coaxing. Though this perspective, which brings together linguistics and psychoanalysis, has nothing at all to do with the cry or with opera, it treats the nature of Donjuanian language and in analyzing this language makes it possible to give Don Giovanni's cry a consistent place within the structure of my analysis.

In her *Literary Speech Act* Shoshana Felman undertakes a study of Donjuanian speech in light of J. L. Austin's linguistic theories concerning the category of utterances Austin terms "performative." Very briefly, "performatives" are utterances such as "I insist," "I proclaim," "I promise," "I swear"—utterances that need only be spoken to accomplish the designated act. When a speaker says, "I insist it's a lovely day," for example, the act of insisting is entirely accomplished in the utterance of the words "I insist." Felman then demonstrates that Donjuanian discourse is fundamentally this kind of performative speech. "With the exception of the end, that is, of the supernatural conclusion, the action of Molière's *Don Juan* is made up entirely of performative events."[30] Most of these events are bound up with the idea of promising: one section of Felman's work, moreover, is titled "The Perversion of Promising." For "now it is Don Juan himself who does not believe in his own promises. Unbelieving, the mythical seducer refuses to be seduced by his own myth, refuses for his part to be seduced by language, *to believe in the promise of meaning.*" Then, imagining Don Juan's credo after his assertion "I believe that two and two are four," Felman has Don Juan speak the following words: "I believe in a truth that is obtained only from the reduction of the linguistic system of meaning; I believe in the arithmetic system insofar as it has, strictly speaking, no meaning, insofar as it is an entirely self-referential system, determined by its own axioms, and one that therefore depends neither on language nor on reality for its validity."[31] The entire Donjuanian

---

[30]And we know that this is the *Don Juan* that served as the basis for Mozart and Da Ponte's *Don Giovanni.*

[31]Shoshana Felman, *The Literary Speech Act: Don Juan with J. L. Austin, or Seduction in*

discourse of seduction is thus based, according to this analysis, on a perversion of meaning. Don Juan's seduction functions, then, through its relation to perverted and subverted meaning, which, in producing a purely self-referential utterance, creates in the other an illusion of meaning and of reference. What ultimately interrupts this operation is the statue of the Commander:

And no doubt the outcome of the myth, the very figure of the statue that *takes Don Juan at his word,* is a symbolic way of expressing the hold—the empire—of the referential over and within Donjuanian speech, the impress or the trace that the real leaves upon meaning. . . .

[Don Juan's death] seems to eliminate the scandal; in addition, its fantastic aspect dramatizes the symbolic elements of a kind of poetic justice: the commander, representing both the authority of the Law that commands and that Don Juan flouts, and the return of the repressed, the haunting return of the supposedly dead past, the statue, the immobile figure of death that stops Don Juan's transgressive movement: "Don Juan, that's enough" (IV, vii); "stop, Don Juan" (V, vi); the fire, representing the fire of desire through which Don Juan is consumed. . . . Heaven, symbolically made concrete as a hole in the earth, a hole in reality: "Earth is opening and swallowing him up; and great fires are coming out of the place where he fell" (V, vi). . . . "Thus Heaven is another stage," as Claude Reichler writes: "what is at stake, in *Don Juan,* is the irruption within a spatial continuum of a radical gap."[32]

Thus completely caught up in a certain form of linguistic transgression, Don Giovanni, in defying the Commendatore's injunction to recognize and obey his law, has recourse only to that supreme transgression of speech which is the cry, which occurs here as an upsurge of the voice at the edges of this gap in meaning.

After this detour by way of Don Giovanni's cry, I will now return to those other male cries and venture some interpretation that might allow them to find their place in this argument without endangering its coherence.

Two Languages (Ithaca: Cornell University Press, 1983), 25, 35, 36; Felman's emphasis.

[32]Ibid., 80, 54; Felman's emphasis.

Angel, Devil, Woman, Dwarf

The quest for the angel's voice, for the vocal object, began in romanticism, as I have said, on divided terrain, with a feminine side and a smaller masculine side. But the farthest reaches of this quest, the cry, or at least the "pure" cry, has been heard only in its feminine aspect. It would be tempting, then—and it is Elektra's mockery of Aegisthus that points to the following hypothesis—to assert that the few male cries in opera issue from "loci" or characters that have something in common with what may be called a female position, in the sense, however, that the position of The Woman in operatic fantasies is not a female position per se but a trans-sexual position.[33] Some explanation here will help avoid the misunderstandings that are so quick to arise with regard to such matters.

Perhaps the way to begin is to specify just what I mean when I describe the character as a "locus," as a terrain onto which the quest for The Voice ventures forth. What this means is that it is not the particular traits of a character that will determine the musical material, the little stretch of road in this quest that will be taken in his or her company; rather—and this may seem paradoxical—it is the desire for, the path toward the sought-after vocal jouissance that fundamentally will determine the nature of the character chosen to sing this music, who becomes in a way the mouthpiece, or more precisely the outer envelope of the underlying desire that is bound up with the voice. It might be said that characters do not sing but are sung. As in a dream, the characters who come forward, the words they utter, the relationships they maintain among themselves are determined not by their own characteristics but by the repressed desire that has fashioned them.

That is what I mean when I speak here of the absolute preeminence of the vocal dimension in opera, and it seems to be one of the fundamental axioms of the genre—an axiom that baroque opera, with its systematic noncorrespondence between voice and character, has allowed me to bring to the fore. To take an extreme position (before dialecticizing it), one might even say—contrary to what is typically proposed by musical commentary—that it is not the vocal expression of a particular

---

[33]Lacan's contraction of *hors-sexe* to *horsexe* here indicates a connotation of the horrific, since he coins this neologism with reference to Maupassant's "Horla." The Woman's position in operatic fantasies has nothing to do with the place of the "real" woman.

passage that reveals the underlying motives of the character at a given moment; rather it is what takes place in and what gets said by the character at that moment that can shed light on the underlying truth of what is vocally at stake there. In opera, the voice does not express the text—that is what theater is for; the text expresses the voice. To schematize with a simple example: it is not because the dramatic logic of the libretto has led the female character to her death that she cries out at that moment; it is because a logic of vocal jouissance is at work and is driving at the cry that the dramatic conditions necessary for its occurrence are created, demanding a death, for example. This holds so systematically that frequently the narrative structure of a work may fail (under the burden of an incoherent or implausible libretto, say) without in the least imperiling the vocal composition, which may still be a masterpiece (Verdi's *Il Trovatore,* for example, or in another vein, Kundry's cry, which has no narrative justification at all).

It is because so much of what claims to be opera analysis forgets this fundamental axiom that it ends up as textual commentary, which, while valid in itself, can be annoyingly lacking in a specifically operatic dimension.

That said, these remarks must immediately be qualified and above all resituated in a much more complicated dialectic. For dramatization has its logic, too, its own particular constraints and developments, which in turn determine the situations in which the voice will be displayed. The voice, then, bends to the "desires" of the characters, to the words they speak. In this way it can be said that the voice expresses these desires. I should like to insist once again that the relationship between voice and character is not unidirectional, with character determining voice, even if that is how this relationship is most often conceived. That is why I have formulated this relationship—somewhat goadingly and paradoxically—from the other direction, envisioning the properties of role, dramatic situation, and text as the deferred action of what is in play on the vocal level.

The operatic work, then, is the product of an interaction between these two movements, from the dramatic to the vocal and vice versa. The great achievements of the genre always result, it seems, from a particularly tight overlapping of these two trajectories, when both music and voice "speak" deeply to us of the beings moving about on the stage and at the same time the words, the actions, the profound truth of these beings illustrate and somehow stand as metaphors of what is at stake in terms of the jouissance that opera wagers on the voice.

With that in mind, I will return to my point of departure, to the question of what it is that can summon the angel, the devil, woman and the dwarf and bring them together around the cry. In the case of Don Giovanni, the answer is now clear. As for the others, there are several possible and not mutually exclusive approaches that may help answer that question.

The Locus of Lack

In several articles dealing with infantile sexuality, Freud identifies and analyzes the unconscious fantasy that forms the basis of the genital organization of the child,[34] or more properly, that of the boy, Freud having confessed to his puzzlement with regard to the girl. From his clinical experiences Freud learned that the little boy at first imagines that, like himself, everyone has a penis. Then[35] he discovers that there is an entire category of beings, "little girls," whom he imagines not as having a sex organ *different from* his but as *lacking* one. And if little girls do not have a sex organ, it is either because they do not have one yet or because they no longer have one. The discovery that adult women, too, lack a penis is taken as confirmation of the second hypothesis. And if they no longer have a penis, it is because it has been removed, cut off; it is because they have been castrated, and if they have been castrated, the only explanation is either punishment or some act of aggression against them. The Woman, as a castrated being, is therefore either bad, guilty of some misdeed and punished for it by a Great Judge, or the victim of a supremely wicked being. By the same logic, this phantasmic construct yields the notion of the Woman as unsexed and therefore trans-sexual, as a guilty victim and therefore singled out for punishment and suffering.

We are coming very close to something I pointed out in the destiny of women on the opera stage. The filiation between the figure of the

[34]Sigmund Freud, *Three Essays on the Theory of Sexuality*, trans. James Strachey (New York: Basic Books, 1962).

[35]This "then" is not chronological but *logical*. The process of sexuation is in fact an unconscious logical process.

angel and that of the doomed woman has its logic in the male fantasy
that posits The Woman as a site of lack and suffering. Her relation to
the figure of the dwarf suddenly becomes clear: the dwarf is fantasized
as monstrous—therein lies his drama—but his monstrousness resides
not in excess but, like that of The Woman, in deficiency, in lack: the
dwarf, in a way, is a metaphor of castration, and thus he, too, is seen as
guilty and therefore destined for punishment and suffering. Alberich's
situation in *Das Rheingold* is quite explicit in this regard: guilty of an
original crime, the theft of the Rhine gold, he is reduced by Wotan's
lance to the status of wretched refuse, a status he thought he could
overcome through the power of the ring. His cry marks his return to a
position of lack. With Wotan's victory, he is cast back into what in this
context may be described as a feminine position (as it is construed by
the fantasy described above).

As for the relationship of the angel, the woman, and the devil, it,
too, originates in that fantasy: if The Woman is envisioned as lacking a
sex organ, then she, like the angel, is also trans-sexual. As for the devil,
he is none other than the angel's fallen counterpart.

If Freud's interpretation provides an apt model for my own findings, the question still remains as to the role of the voice in this
structure.

The answer seems to lie in the fact that once the vocal object is, as
we have seen, constituted as a lost object, it functions precisely as a
lack, whence the desire to bridge it or recover it. If this quest is
doomed to failure, it is precisely because its object is a missing object,
an object that is always missed: it is thus entirely consistent that this
search for an object registered as something missed should find its
incarnation in a figure that is itself marked by the sign of lack. The
imaginary figure of The Woman takes her place as queen of the opera
stage. As queen? Isn't there some contradiction between this notion
and what I have just said? The phantasmic Woman has a second avatar,
one that, like the first, is perfectly consonant with the quest for the
first object of jouissance.

The "Lack of Lack"

The same fantasy that constitutes The Woman as a locus of lack also
casts her as something desired (no doubt a more familiar role), but

impossibly so—something to fill the lack, the cause of the man's desire. This second aspect was the basis for a particularly elaborate cultural artifact in medieval Europe—courtly literature. This cultural product deserves to be explored in some detail here because it is at work on the opera stage and in fact determines—and not by accident—the shape of what might serve as the keystone in the edifice of opera, Richard Wagner's *Tristan und Isolde*.

Henri Rey-Flaud's study *La Névrose courtoise* (Courtly neurosis) will serve as guide in this excursion through the realm of courtly love.[36] Rey-Flaud is concerned with literary texts, so his examples are not drawn from the operatic repertoire. Yet some of his analyses and even specific formulations apply directly, word for word in some cases, to opera. This is why I will engage in a little game that consists in substituting operatic examples for the instances Rey-Flaud cites in support of his thesis.

Deepening Lacan's own analysis of courtly love, the *fin'amor* of the troubadours, Rey-Flaud organizes his characterization of it around two poles: "the mastery of the lady and the asymptote of masculine desire."

"The aim of courtly love is to purify jouissance of pleasure through a univocal relationship in which the man pursues the woman with a desire maintained in essence as fundamentally *impossible*. . . . Desire is caught up in a hunt-the-slipper game and surfaces only in *death*, for which the Lady, because she does not respond, is a stand-in." In this formulation of courtly love[37] we find concepts we have seen before: jouissance ("purified" of and distinct from pleasure), impossibility, death.

One of the consequences of her being installed in this position is that the Lady occupies the place of the law, but in this case a law antithetical to the law of "rational" desire, of "the logos," the law that elsewhere I have referred to as the law of language. The Lady in courtly love embodies a deranged law, a law of "nonresponse," of enigma; hers is an unruly, dangerously whimsical law, a law of the love-passion

---

[36]Henri Rey-Flaud, *La Névrose courtoise* (Paris: Navarin, 1983).

[37]It is important to note Rey-Flaud's comment that "courtly love is never more seriously misconstrued than when it is supposed to illustrate the *historical* relation of man to woman in the twelfth century. For the literary work and courtly love draw their support solely from, and take form only in, the field of the imaginary, in their translation of the structure of the subject" (ibid., 30).

proclaimed by Carmen: "Love is a gypsy child, heedless of the law. If you do not love me, I love you; and if I love you, *beware*."

In this respect, the words in which Rey-Flaud describes Lancelot's muteness upon seeing Queen Guinevere for the first time can be applied verbatim to Calaf as he first sets eyes on Turandot: "Perceiving the Queen among her retinue, he is *drawn in* by her the moment she disappears from his sight. . . . The Queen is henceforth his only point of reference, all symbolic reference having been abolished: he is literally thought, spoken, and acted through where courtly love is manifested as mad love." Prince Calaf and his entire entourage experience something that could not be more similar: as the Princess arrives with her retinue, Calaf catches sight of her: "O Divine beauty! O marvel! O dream!"

Then later, once he has resolved to submit to the lethal test demanded by Turandot: "I am all fever, delirium. Each of my senses is fierce torment! Each fiber of my soul a voice that cries out . . ."

Whereupon the ministers, Ping, Pang, and Pong, answer: "Death! Death! Death!"

The Prince replies: "Turandot, Turandot, Turandot."

The ministers continue: "Death! Death! Death!"

As for madness or folly, eight times in the first act alone Prince Calaf's state of mind and his resolve are described in those terms. But nothing will sway him, he will give himself over to the law of the Princess, lady of absolute beauty, death's human face, "white as jade, cold as the sword," and holder of the key to the deadly riddle.

Before this absolute Woman, *The* Woman, compared constantly in courtly literature with the cold evanescence of snow, or in *Turandot* with moonglow, whose intensity fades in the light of day— "It's the dawn! It's the dawn! Turandot is fading away"—or even with pure and simple nonexistence— "Turandot does not exist" (Ping and Pang, in Act I)—before Woman, thus "installed in an elsewhere that puts her beyond reach," the man's desire in courtly love

is manifested as fundamentally *impossible,* not unsatisfied, but *impossible.* . . . The troubadour, too, finds his jouissance in the asymptote of an impossible desire maintained through a delicious and painful holding back at the threshold of transgression. But it would be a mistake to speak here of a "mastery of desire." For this holding back of desire knows no master, other than death itself, always present as third party to the courtly relationship. The troubadours must be taken at their word when they insist that "they die of love." . . . For the man what is called into question at that moment is precisely his jouissance, insofar as it depends entirely on the prohibition imposed by the Lady, who sustains it to a point of paroxysm in an asymptote whose infinitude the prohibition supports. . . . The queen, like the Mother, is forbidden as woman.

Which, moreover, explains the strong presence of more or less oedipal situations in opera (*Tristan, Don Carlos, Semiramis, Hippolyte et Aricie,* and so on).

In this brief detour through courtly love in twelfth-century literature, illustrated here with quotations from *Turandot* and to be encountered again and in greater detail in connection with *Tristan* and *Parsifal,* all the key concepts that have made it possible to describe the voice as an object of jouissance can be found: loss; inaccessibility; evanescence; impossibility and therefore prohibition; the source of a quest, of an asymptotic desire; the deified object (with its two faces of good and evil), dangerous if not deadly in its seduction.

The neurotic avatar of masculine desire described by courtly literature is especially apt to underpin the quest for the Voice as opera structures it. The Woman may be a stand-in for "Nothingness," for that which, like Euridice, immediately disappears when exposed to the human gaze or to the light of day; or her Absolute Beauty, which is supposed to satisfy man's every desire, at the cost of the death of his desire or quite simply his death, may make her a stand-in for the divine. In either case, The Woman, thus fantasized, incarnates the "lack of lack," the emblematic figure that is supposed to bridge the gap that causes desire. For Woman, imagined as Voice, is ever elusive, whence the intensification of desire ad infinitum. Whether divine, angelic or satanic, the Voice, like Woman, imposes its law and its ordeals on those who give themselves to its quest: "Tonight no one must sleep in Peking!" orders Turandot (III.i). Is this not the capricious command obeyed by those who give up a night of sleep to get a seat at the opera? And as for the call of this voice, like the call of Woman, it can be a deadly call, like that of the sirens who charmed unwary sailors and lured them to their death.[38] Woman, Voice, and Death once again converge in the profound consistency of a fantasy.

[38]Charm: from the Latin *carmen,* magic spell, incantation, song.

Impossible Jouissance

"Immer zu, immer zu": Again! Again! says Marie as she dances with the Drum Major in Act II of *Wozzeck*.[39] Wozzeck knows exactly what this "again" means:

" 'Again, again,' " he repeats. "Twist and spin! Why doesn't God put out the sun? Everything spins about in lechery: man and woman, man and beast . . . Woman, Woman, the woman is hot! She is hot, hot! How he paws her with his hands on her body! And she just laughs!"

Once again, Marie calls out: "Again, again!"

Wozzeck, as we know, will put an end to this intolerable "again" by stabbing Marie to death. And when Don José stabs Carmen, is it not this same supposed infinite amplification of feminine jouissance that he seeks to kill? Lawless desire, limitless jouissance; all of that is dangerous, it is best destroyed. Exactly like that embodied presence of lack to which I referred above: it is best done away with.

That is another way of approaching the lethal fate that opera accords Woman. Indeed, opera can be envisioned not as a ritualized "undoing of *women*," to use Catherine Clément's expression,[40] but as a ritualized elimination of that which is supposed to embody the lack that, according to Freud, plunges the man into dread and anxiety. Another possibility—and this need not exclude the former interpretation—is that the ritual is the sacrificial destruction of that which bears witness to something of an impossible jouissance, that so-called feminine jouissance with which the man maintains such complicated relationships, a feminine jouissance emblematized by that very adverb "again," which happens also to be the title of the seminar (Encore) that Jacques Lacan devoted to this question.

---

[39]The translation of this *Immer zu* may vary: Michel Vallois's translation (*Avant-scène Opéra*) renders it as *"Encore, encore"* (Again, again); *"Encore, va toujours"* (On and on we go), which expresses much the same idea, is Marthe Robert's version in her translation of Büchner's text (*Théatre complet* [L'Arche]); P. J. Jouve's translation, "Pour toujours, pour toujours" (Forever and ever), bends the idea in a direction that seems consonant neither with the lines that immediately follow nor with the character of Marie and the general context of the play.

[40]The term "undoing" or "defeat" (*défaite*) suggests a power relationship in a determinate sociohistorical context; in other words, a confrontation that can be settled with the failure of one of the two parties and that could quite conceivably go either way.

In a manner at once terrible and compelling, the crushing of Salome beneath the shields of Herod's guards illustrates this dual interpretation of the fate of women in opera. I will dwell for a moment on *Salome,* a particularly powerful and important work, composed in 1905 by Richard Strauss, after the play by Oscar Wilde.

Voice/Mouth

First of all, it may be of some interest to note that quotations from *Salome* would have served to illustrate Henri Rey-Flaud's analyses just as well as those from *Turandot. Salome* makes the same reference as *Turandot* to the lunar pallor of death, a reference made subtly through a parallelism in the initial dialogue between Narraboth, officer of the guard, and the Page.

Narraboth:　How beautiful is the Princess Salome tonight!

The Page:　Look at the moon, how strange the moon seems. She is like a woman rising from a tomb.

Narraboth:　She has a strange look. She is like a little princess who has little white doves for feet. One might fancy she was dancing.

The Page:　She is like a woman who is dead. She moves very slowly.

Like *Turandot, Salome* refers to the danger posed by The Woman, thus fantasized:

Narraboth:　How pale the princess is! Never have I seen her so pale. She is like the shadow of a white rose in a mirror of silver.

The Page:　You must not look at her. You look at her too much. Something terrible may happen!

Narraboth ignores the warning and for this he will die, stabbing himself in despair over Salome's passion for Jokanaan.

In both cases desire is dissolute: Salome, like Turandot, demands a head: "I ask the head of Jokanaan," she repeats seven times, giving the words every possible vocal inflection, from the most charming and melodic to the most savage.

To these dimensions that Salome shares with Turandot she adds another: a jouissance as dissolute as her desire. Let us listen to the voice of Jokanaan (John the Baptist), a baritone voice, the voice that is a call to order, that reaffirms the incest prohibition: "Go, order her to rise from the bed of her immodesty, from her incestuous bed, so that she may hear the words of him who prepares the ways of the Lord and may repent her evil deeds."

It is not enough merely to silence this man's voice—and that is not even where Salome's problem lies. She must seek her jouissance not only in this voice but—the height of transgression—in the real physical source of that voice, that material medium of the murdered word: the mouth of Jokanaan's head. We can now understand Salome, whose own voice transgresses limit after limit (Richard Strauss withholds from her only the pure cry) as she wonders: "Why does he not cry out, this man? Ah! if any man sought to kill me, I would cry out, I would struggle, I wouldn't suffer. . . . Strike, strike, Naaman, strike, I tell you."

Beyond this limit lies the horror: jouissance in the pure real, the piece of dead flesh: "I have kissed thy mouth, Jokanaan, I have kissed thy mouth." Faced with the absolute anxiety unleashed by this living vision of an equally absolute jouissance, there is but one recourse: "Kill that woman!" Herod says. "Crush her, suffocate her, destroy her," he might have added. The strange manner of her execution ("The soldiers rush forward and crush her beneath their shields," reads the libretto) signifies the necessity of covering and stifling, of bringing into play, apart from real death, another death, symbolic death, just as the orchestral *tutti fortissimi* covering the cry permit the reintroduction of words and singing.

But Salome's trenchant and deadly desire casts the man back upon another of his fundamental anxieties. For if The Woman, as a "locus of lack," is imagined as castrated and therefore, according to the logic of the fantasy discussed above, as guilty or as victim, why should the man always be spared this fate? Especially a Herod, guilty himself of transgressing the fundamental prohibition against incest. By the same token, why should The Woman not be—particularly by reason of the transgressive display of her own desire[41]—the agent of this castration? That is undoubtedly what motivates Herod's long refusal to satisfy Salome's desire: he is afraid of God because he has sinned, but he is also afraid of seeing Woman in her labors of castration. Salome, the visible embodiment of that danger, is therefore ordered destroyed.

[41]See the film *Empire of the Senses.*

Much more could be said about the psychoanalytic structure of the Salome myth as Oscar Wilde and Richard Strauss elaborate it. My concern here is not to pursue this analysis as such. It is simply, as I said before, to consider how the emergence of certain themes, certain figures, squares with a particular perspective on the problematics of the voice in opera. In this regard *Salome* is particularly illustrative because the axis of the present analysis, positing the voice as the stakes of jouissance, explicitly predicts the trajectory of Salome's desire even as she transgresses the limit of the impossible and of the prohibition beyond which lies the horrible and deadly attainment of a "real" object of jouissance—not merely the "aimed-for" object of jouissance that I have been describing.

At issue here is not the vocal object, the object as voice, but rather, quite literally, the object as the mouth itself. Salome is peculiarly fixated on Jokanaan's mouth; that mouth, however, is a metonym for the voice.[42] For Salome's burning desire does focus on Jokanaan's voice, a voice that rises up from the depths of the "cistern" in which John the Baptist is locked away; a voice, therefore, that functions as a detached object. In fact, during the greater part of the opera Jokanaan sings offstage, the score indicating *"the voice* of Jokanaan."

"What a strange voice," says Salome as she hears the prophet's imprecations for the first time. "I would speak with it."

Then, shortly afterward: "Speak again, Jokanaan. Thy voice is as music to mine ear."[43] And finally, presented with the severed head: "In the whole world, there was nothing so red as thy mouth. Thy voice was a censer, and when I looked on thee, I heard a strange music."

Jokanaan's baritone voice speaks the law, manly, honorable words in prophetic and sententious phrasings (at times musically reminiscent of Wotan, whom Siegfried in Act II of *Siegfried* charges with being a "sententious old man"), and Salome's perversion is that she seeks jouissance in the reified medium of this voice, the incarnate mouth of a severed head. Jouissance also means enjoyment, in the sense of possessing.

"Thy head belongs to me," says Salome.

---

[42]For other interpretations see *L'Avant-scène Opéra* 47/48 (January–February 1983), devoted to Strauss's *Salome*.

[43]The French text of Oscar Wilde's play gives it an even more voluptuous turn: "Ta voix m'enivre" (Your voice intoxicates me); Georges Pucher, *L'Avant-scène Opéra* 29: *"Salomé"* (January–February 1983), 110 (textual and musical commentary).

Consequently, the most direct way of enjoying an object, in that sense, is to incorporate it and to identify with it. Salome's words signify this incorporation explicitly:

"Ah! thou wouldst not suffer me to kiss thy mouth, Jokanaan. Well, I will kiss it now. I will bite it with my teeth as one bites a ripe fruit."

As to the process of identification, it seems to be heralded by the strange anticipatory *Sprechgesang* in which Salome registers her astonishment at John the Baptist's silence in death as she declaims: "Why does he not cry out, this man?"

As if, in the presence of the man's noncry, she herself became speech. And finally, it is through something again on the order of speech that at the end of the work she brings about her ultimate amorous fulfillment—or more exactly, her nonfulfillment, unless killing and dying are her satisfaction—what commentators of this opera consider a genuine *Liebestod,* a love-death. The whole trajectory of the voice is traversed in an instant: from speech to the very highest vocal limit. Only the pure cry is shunned. On the verge of transgressing the rules of tonality (Strauss often uses polytonal composition), on the verge of transgressing the limits of the voice, Strauss refused to take the final step.

The Woman-Voice

And so we have a series of analytical elements that converge in the coronation of the phantasmic figure of The Woman as queen of those lands where opera devotees are led in their search for the lost Voice. I will briefly reiterate those elements.

The first is the necessity for tension in the lyric material between sense and non-sense, a tension verging on the dissolution of sense, on the isolation of the vocal material from the meaning it normally conveys. We have seen how the upper register of the voice was a privileged instrument in this process. The female voice appears as the most "natural" candidate for this function. But that alone cannot account for the preeminence of a particular kind of feminine position in opera ever since the romantic period. Indeed, other periods pursued the high notes in voices other than those of women (castrati, falsettists). Moreover, the female voice can be easily separated from the female role and assigned to a male character; we have seen many examples. Finally, it is not at all clear why the woman cannot establish her dominion over opera simply as herself, why she can do so only if she is put to death or sends others to theirs, suffers herself or causes others to suffer.

At this point there emerges another element: the similarity between the structure of the object, resulting from the way it is constituted, and the structure of certain fantasies, particularly but not exclusively male fantasies concerning the Feminine.[44] This parallelism permits a particularly precise overlapping of these unconscious constructs, with the Woman, thus embellished, taking on the same contours as the object—in this case, the vocal object. Elusive and inaccessible, evanescent or nonexistent, the cause of desire, the locus of lack, and the nullification of lack, locus of jouissance both infinite and impossible, alluring and forbidden, death-ridden and deadly, trans-sensical and trans-sexual, heavenly voice or hellish cry, angel or demon, The Voice and The Woman come together in these tightly woven fantasies; they fuse, completely justifying Wagner's aphorism that music is a woman. For only the alchemy of music allows the voice to be purged of the meaning it usually conveys.

This lofty encounter of The Woman and The Voice in what is principally a male fantasy can also be related to the almost total masculinization of opera on two levels: reception (specifically, the extraordinary investment of the opera lover) and composition.

There are few observable differences between the male and female contingents of the operagoing public: statistically, the audience for opera seems to be made up of roughly equal numbers of men and women. That, of course, is an impressionistic assessment, but at all events, any difference between the respective numbers of men and women is not overwhelming (as it is, for example, at a soccer game). And yet as far as personal investment in opera is concerned, very few women, it seems, are so deeply invested in this quest as some men are. If indeed one were to establish an audience hierarchy according to level of individual investment (whether financial or emotional) and undertook to differentiate men and women within the pyramid, one would find that the pyramid becomes proportionately more male as it pro-

---

[44]Not to be confused with the idea of "woman as object" as it is commonly understood, though "female object" and "objectified female" are not totally unrelated.

gressively approaches its apex. I have no way to conduct a proper tally, but the makeup of the more demanding box-office queues (those requiring a wait of ten hours or more, say) seems to bear out this assumption. And if there are fewer women than men in these queues, it is certainly not because "the missus has had to stay home minding the children while Monsieur has gone to spend an al fresco evening on the steps of the Palais Garnier." Nor is it because the gentleman has gallantly consented to sacrifice himself while Madame enjoys the sweet repose of hearth and home. Most fans who are this hooked are in fact unmarried (which isn't surprising!), or in any case—whether men or women—manage to arrange things so that material contingencies will not hinder the pursuit of their passion (remember the colleague Anne spoke of, who was always on her way to the four corners of Europe, wherever there was a performance she felt she had to see). In any case, the phenomenon is equally apparent on the other level, that of composition.

Here again, it is not enough to interpret this finding in purely sociological and ideological terms, positing the place to which our culture assigns women as its sole cause, for a number of reasons. The first is that between the seventeenth and twentieth centuries, that place has changed appreciably, while throughout the entire period opera composition has remained a strictly male endeavor, uninflected by developments in social attitudes and in the respective status of the sexes. The second reason is that under the same conditions, some women have managed nevertheless to become poets, writers, painters; a few even ventured into musical composition (Clara Schumann, for one); and one or two found the energy to become sculptors (even at the sometimes heavy cost of madness: consider the case of Camille Claudel). But no woman ventured into opera (should Pauline Viardot's *Cendrillon* be counted as an opera?). Of course, an opera is not like a poem, something that can be composed at the corner of a writing desk. And furthermore, for an opera to exist, it is not enough for it to be composed; it still needs to be produced, which is an entirely different matter from persuading an editor to publish a novel. But ultimately, the fact that there are virtually no exceptions to be found, the fact that music should so long have remained an exclusively male affair (hardly a woman is to be found among the rolls of composition students at the Conservatory before the first decades of the twentieth century), suggests a deeper reason for this state of affairs. Moreover, generally speaking, no social practice, however dubious or even repugnant it may be, can endure if it has not found some profound moorings within the subject. To condemn these practices on their ideological dimension alone is to miss the mark and may even contribute to their perpetuation by continuing to obscure what sustains them. This underlying reason, as we have seen, seems to lie in the close structural correspondence between the voice as object and the male fantasy that, revolving around a certain imaginary construction of the Woman, makes her a particularly likely candidate to embody that object. Wagner's *Tristan und Isolde* seems an exemplary illustration of this consonance.

Tristan, or Bitter Desire

"But to this day I am still looking for a work that equals the dangerous fascination and the gruesome and sweet infinity of *Tristan*—and look in all the arts in vain," wrote Friedrich Nietzsche in *Ecce homo*.[45] Henri Barraud writes:

Surely no other work holds so complete a fascination for so vast a public. That a performance of *Tristan* leaves spectators literally spellbound is an empirical certainty. But ultimately, what have they seen? What have they heard? The Germans admit that they can make out less than a third of the text of a Wagnerian lyric drama. All the more reason to say that the French do not make out a single word [*un traître mot*].[46]

Traître mot: nowhere is the word's reputation for cunning and deceit—a reputation so familiar that it tends to disappear behind the figure of speech—more warranted than in connection with *Tristan*. In opera the word is a traitor because, like Melot the *losengier*,[47] it is what permits the law, the king's law, to be rewritten as a restriction on the outlaw jouissance to which the lovers are led by their incestuous transgression in the queen's gardens. King Marke, figure of Day, and Queen Isolde, sorceress, figure of Night: not unlike *Die Zauberflöte,* except that here the values are reversed, since *Tristan* is in fact a long "Hymn

---

[45]In *The Basic Writings of Nietzsche,* trans. and ed. Walter Kaufman (New York: Modern Library, 1968), 706.

[46]Henri Barraud, *Les Cinq Grands Opéras* (Paris: Seuil, 1972). *Traître mot:* literally, a traitorous word. [Translator's note]

[47]Melot, Tristan's "friend," who betrays Tristan's and Isolde's liaison to King Mark (in Wagner's version). In the Middle Ages, the *losengier* was the character with the false tongue, the maligner.

to the Night," a protracted refusal of the law of Day. Still, in *Tristan* the truth of this forbidden jouissance is spoken aloud: impossibility and death.

The music and singing in *Tristan* embody that truth in sound and make Wagner's masterpiece, in the words of Ernest Bloch, "a transcendent opera."

The dramaturgical particularities of the work, as, for instance, the relegation of the action to the periphery of the three acts, the almost complete omission of all 'local colour' and the transference of the incidents of the action to the psychic 'interior' of the characters—*all these qualities tend to bring about the absolute domination of the score, making the personal constellations almost into an emanation, as it were, of the musical flow.*[48]

From this perspective, *Tristan* is a perfect demonstration of that first and more fundamental of the two movements in which opera is caught up: the preeminence of the trans-sensical, of lyricism, in the jouissance that it brings about.

"The truth that the visionary composer desires and respects defies narration. . . . Into what had taken on meaning, the myth of Tristan and Yseut, [Wagner] introduced an excess of meaning, in other words, music."[49] The author of this article uses the word "excess" in the sense of that which exceeds, of that which is beyond, if I understand him correctly. Yet the word *excéder* has another sense: that which inflames meaning, drives it to distraction, within the logic of the antagonism described at length in the second part of this work. "This is why the verses of *Tristan* resolve into music. The words ultimately no longer have much importance in themselves, they are at most a sort of incantation grounded in the symphonic orchestration of Isolde's death song."[50] "The music combines not with the libretto but with the music of the libretto. For Wagner never sets a text to music, he plays the music of the verses he writes."[51] Indeed:

    [48]Jürgen Maehder, "A Mantle of Sound for the Night—On the Score of *Tristan and Isolde,*" *Bayreuth Festival Program* (1982).

    [49]J.-P. Krop, "Le Sillon de Gottfried," *L'Avant-scène Opéra* 34/35: *"Tristan et Isolde"* (July–August 1981), 14.

    [50]Edward Sans, "L'Amour dans Tristan, ou Le Romantisme surdimensionné," *L'Avant-scène Opéra* 34/35: *"Tristan et Isolde"* (July–August 1981), 20.

    [51]Krop, "Le Sillon de Gottfried," 16.

To the indignation of many, Richard Wagner's texts display in their formation, word-formation and syntax, peculiarities which reach the point where language ceases to be language, and make his language into a special language. This special language occurs, however, essentially in association with the musical articulation. . . . Richard Wagner thus created an artificial language for his works which functions like a natural language, but the polysensuousness, which naturally prevails between a word and meaning, becomes more complex in this triangular relationship of sound-word-sense than in natural language.[52]

Thus despite the conscious project Wagner sets forth in *Opera and Drama*, *Tristan* brings explicitly to the fore the undermining of language itself which I have attributed to the vocalise. In *Tristan*, the music, the desire at work in it, goes beyond the subversion, the dissolution of the meaning of an idiom that would otherwise conform to the laws that govern it and makes its mark on language itself by bending it to its own demands. This very special relationship, that of text to music and not music to text, is undoubtedly one of the first fully "emerged" manifestations of this fundamental telluric tension at work in the operatic genre. Subsequent developments in contemporary lyric forms following the decisive shocks that Berg brought to the genre have of course made pure vocal emission, the isolated phoneme, all modalities of expression of breath, and literally unheard-of vocalic inflections the very mainstay of the lyric musical project, to the exclusion of all reference not only to meaning but to the word itself. (Listen especially to the works of Berio, Kagel, or Aperghis.)

Tristan's compelling power over its audience thus rests essentially on the way Wagner shapes his musical and vocal material. Without entering into a detailed analysis of this most distinctive of musical compositions, I will merely point out among the elements emphasized by commentators those that seem particularly relevant to my perspective here. Some of these features, moreover, while not specific to *Tristan*, are nonetheless characteristic of the "Wagner effect" in the way they seem to approach the "phonic object" as such. I will turn once again to Jürgen Maehder's article about one of the most intense moments in the work, Brangäne's warning song in Act II. Maehder analyzes this most

---

[52]Karl Bertau, "Tristan and Narcissus," *Bayreuth Festival Program* (1982), 89.

radical way of tendentially obliterating the meaning effect: through the suspension of time. All language is in fact inscribed in diachrony and in the periodic breaks that occur within it: the points of silence at the phrase or the word that lock in their meaning. With the suspension of the temporal flow, with the absence of the rupture of scansion, the meaning effect is no longer possible, and it is then that we come upon the phonic continuum of the Other Silence:

Wreathed about by an unusual number of orchestral parts which conflict with the metric pattern, Brangäne's part runs through the passage as, so to speak, a mainstay; the stretching of the regularly measured melody dictated by the tempo marking—and the superimposition of a highly concentrated orchestral passage full of inner movement—obscure the contours and give the impression of time at a standstill. The 'knowing orchestra' does not comment on the warning function of the singer but suspends the course of time in order to lend duration to the 'fulfilled moment' of love. The suspending of musical time in Wagner's later works has a precisely definable range of application; passages in which the attention of the listener is directed to the development of a static sound by the arresting of the progress of the cadence together with much inner movement in the instrumentation, are first encountered in *Rheingold.* . . . In contrast to this, Wagner created in *Tristan,* with a similar technique, the musical symbolization of enchantment; while at the peak of complexity fifteen independent strings produce a band of sound which completely envelopes the voice of Brangäne coming from the back of the stage, Tristan and Isolde are silent. The orchestra lends them its eloquence. . . . Nietzsche recorded—as the first one to do so—the realization that the suspension of musical time is capable of casting a spell on the listener: '*The significance of* metre *as the limitation of music in conflict with its greatest effect. In Wagner one can experience at times what music is like without it: herein he is also* idyllic.'[53]

Wagner in this sense is indeed the composer of the immeasurable, a term that should be understood here with reference not to colossal scale but to the limiting function of measure, or meter.

Along with detemporalization, another Wagnerian discovery participates powerfully in the process of purifying the phonic object,

[53]Maehder, "Mantle of Sound," 100.

which may be understood as a variant of the vocal object, and that is the discovery of spatial "delocalization" of sound, brought about by the principle of the covered orchestra pit, as practiced at Bayreuth.

The general reduction of the intensity of sound of the covered orchestra allows a 'close-up' of the unfiltered voices; the differentiated manner of dampening the louder instruments furthermore effects a revision of the orchestral sound and produces a 'synthetic' over-all sound in which the 'de-individualized' instruments are merged. . . . In this the 'Bayreuth sound' reinforces an inherent tendency of Wagner's instrumentation; the technological perfection of the project, i.e., the orchestral sound aims at the virtual disappearance of the producing agent in order to achieve—as Novalis (1772–1801) already envisaged—an apparent immediacy of the product.[54]

Therein doubtless lies the source of Bayreuth's acoustical "magic" that is always so imposing: the Festspielhaus hall constitutes a veritable athanor for the refinement, the purification of sound into a pure object of jouissance.

The major feature of the Wagnerian musical material, however, particularly in *Tristan,* is of course chromaticism, repeatedly characterized by commentators as "exacerbated."[55] This adjective refers directly to the idea of pain, or to be precise, of irritation, of painful tension. It almost has the connotation of asymptotic intensification, of being pushed to the edge, as well. In Wagner, chromaticism, like desire, is exacerbated. On a melodic level its role of destroying points and frames of reference as well as harmonic limits is analogous to the role played by the suspension of time on a rhythmic level, as discussed above. There is no mode of composition better than chromaticism for allowing the melody to unfold unhampered as it shifts from one note to the next, from one tonality to the next, smuggled in like contraband in defiance of the laws and limits of the tonal system.

Arnold Schoenberg spoke of 'vagrant chords' here which were 'forms which drifted, homeless, between the territories of the keys.' And he asked: 'why should the return to a key be established at all costs by these particular vagrant harmonies?' The 'comparison with eternity could hardly be brought

---

[54]Ibid., 97.
[55]From the Latin *acerbus* (harsh, painful) and *exacerbatus* (irritated).

closer than by an unresolved, so to speak, endless harmony which does not
constantly carry with it a certificate of domicile and Passport, carefully
showing the country of origin and the journey's destination.'[56]

This style of composition has its supreme expression in Isolde's Transfiguration. I have already referred to this music repeatedly as one of the
most productive of that lyric jouissance which leaves the listener at the
verge of emotional collapse. I will now return to it one last time.

It is striking, first of all, to see how commentators on this opera
begin systematically by apologizing for taking on its final page: "Here
more than anywhere else, if possible, the analyst feels the solecism, not
to say the bad taste, of commenting on one of the most sublime pages
in our musical heritage . . . ."[57] "On this celebrated page of such lofty
inspiration I will offer only a few words of commentary. It would be as
inappropriate to turn this music into analysis as it would be to turn it
into literature."[58]

As though their words, even at critical remove, could somehow
impinge upon the sublimity of this music, or rather, as though—
conversely—they feared that their words might dissolve in the musical
flood at the mere mention of Isolde's voice, let alone its actual sound.
And incidentally, there is no better example of that peculiar phenomenon of "the libretto that falls from your hands" that I described at
the beginning of this book. How many Wagnerians, those who are
Germanists, can say exactly what it is that Isolde sings in that supreme
moment? Perhaps the first words, because they are sung in the lower
register: "Mild und leise, wie er lächelt . . ."; but then the process
already described at length gradually begins to take over:

. . . the manner in which this immense expansion is husbanded, in which
the breath that sustains it is prolonged, is ultimately glaringly obvious; and
that is why it is so effective. Everything is organized around two themes,
the *exacerbated* chromaticism of the death song to which we are introduced
at the end of the duet in Act II, and the diatonic and descending theme of

---

[56] Arnold Schoenberg, *Harmonielehre* (Vienna, 1922), cited in Bertau, "Tristan and
Narcissus."

[57] Dominique Jameux, in *L'Avant-scène Opéra* 34/35: *"Tristan et Isolde"* (July–August
1981), 144 (textual and musical commentary).

[58] Barraud, *Les Cinq Grands Opéras.*

the *Liebestod,* clearly reminiscent of Berlioz's *Roméo et Juliette.* The former lends itself to an ascending movement and drives it perpetually upward. The latter is naturally oriented in the other direction, but its three notes of anacrusis that prepare its tonic and expressive accent contain an ascendant principle that Wagner seizes upon for the final climactic surge. And here we reencounter his cherished method, and the infinite repetition of a thematic cell that he carries *progressively higher* finally creates in us a nervous tension from which we are delivered, at the very moment we can no longer bear it, through the expansive slackening of the melodic tide that this repetition held out as its promise."[59]

The perfect fulfillment of the blue note's "proleptic" action, of the "promise it bears." The perfect expression of an asymptotic progression of melody through "canonic structure,"

in which the orchestral and vocal parts rise together but at a certain interval apart. . . . The image that immediately comes to mind is that of a chase, in which the orchestra closes in on the voice until they finally meet on the G of "in Düften." The voice will go no higher . . . while the orchestra continues to climb until finally and for the first time it reaches the note and chord of B, the point at which the motif is fulfilled, the point where all the accumulated tensions in the work are resolved.[60]

Chromaticism, as we have seen, was considered too tainted for religious music in the Middle Ages. This is understandable: as that which carries the disintegration of the boundaries and breaks necessary for the preservation of meaning, it adroitly helped break the spine of the law of the word and thereby opened the door to excesses that could not be controlled. Chromaticism is too strong a metaphor of the tension of desire and the onset of jouissance.

The pure cry is absent from Isolde's Transfiguration, which peaks melodically in G; the orchestra, continuing its progression, takes over from the voice where it can go no further, takes its place at the point where the cry seems to be imminent. The presence of the cry is figured, however, by the movement of the musical line with as much precision as the infinitely distant vanishing point in a painting is fig-

[59]Ibid.
[60]Jameux, in *L'Avant-scène Opéra* 34/35: 145.

ured by converging lines of perspective. Indeed, in the analogous musical structure of the end of the love duet in Act II, the cry actually does occur. It is uttered by Brangäne and not by Isolde, although a distracted ear could easily attribute it to Isolde, since its place is so clearly carved out in the climbing musical spiral of Tristan and Isolde's duet, which prepares its appearance: "Perched above an abyss, in the sense that it becomes clear that these two beings are sinking into each other, a violently dissonant chord covers the entire orchestra above which rises Brangäne's cry."[61]

The substitution of the orchestra for the voice to complete the trajectory of Isolde's Transfiguration is the very image of the function of music in opera, which is to implant the horror of what is in fact sought after within a system that remains beyond its reach, to avoid that final step where perfect beauty turns into horror. This horror is there, however, in Brangäne's cry. The dissonance of the orchestra announces it. This is Wagner at his most effective: toying constantly with points of intolerability and always avoiding them, for even when he seems to transgress the prohibition, it is always sidestepped at the last moment. For while Dominique Jameux speaks of the orchestra as being *surmounted* by Brangäne's cry, what occurs most often in actual performances is that the orchestra's fortissimo *drowns out* that cry. As for dissonance, Jameux indeed notes that this "chord sounds more dissonant than it is." Be that as it may, if the cry in *Tristan* does not have the same insistence that characterizes its appearance in *Parsifal*, in Kundry's part, still its formal purity as well as its melodic form makes it a genuine vocal keystone, the locus of fulfillment, for the two most powerful moments of the work, prepared for long in advance and foreshadowed by the musical and dramatic material.

This is the right moment to turn to the mythical and dramatic material, the mainstays of the construction of sound and voice, to see what it is that allows it to be shaped with singular precision to the contours of the process in play in the quest for the vocal object.

The quest in *Tristan* is explicitly announced, though much less explicitly than in *Parsifal* (Wagner had, moreover, once imagined an encounter between Parsifal and Tristan in Act III of *Tristan*). For Tristan, the quest becomes a quest for Night; a search for the obliteration of his coming into the world, his seeing the light of day, the abolition

of the rupture and the primordial lack that results from it, since his
mother died in *giving him light*:

> The land that Tristan means,
> Where sunlight casts no beams;
>   It is the sacred
>   Realm of night
> From which my mother
> Sent me forth.
> I was conceived
> In death and darkness;
>   In death to languish,
>   In light she left me.
> And the refuge on earth
> Of her who gave me birth,
> The wondrous realm of night
> From which I came to light:
> I offer now to thee
>   Yet I must go there first.[62]
>   [Tristan, II.iii]

The Night, site of the Mother, of Woman; the Day, site of the
King:

> What you perceived
>   In the waning night [Isolde, love]
> You were forced to surrender
>   To kingly might
>   Haloed in diurnal light [*des Taggestirnes*
>   *Königsmacht:* King Marke].[63]
>   [Isolde, II.ii]

On one level, the Tristan myth is a variant of the Oedipus myth,
particularly in Wagner's reshaping of it: King Marke, the uncle who

---

[62]Libretto translation by Andrew Porter, in *Tristan and Isolde,* English National Opera
Guide 6 (London: John Calder, 1981).

[63]These lines are translated to accord with the French translation that Poizat uses and
the interpretation he bases on it. [Translator's note]

adopts the orphan Tristan, is clearly a father figure, and Tristan, in search of his "first object of jouissance," the maternal object, offers the woman he himself desires to the King as his wife, thus casting her as his own mother and making her inaccessible and forbidden. The difference is that Oedipus acts unknowingly and blinds himself after his transgression is revealed, whereas Tristan knows from the outset but shuts his eyes to it. He blinds himself from the start, and the philter allows him to maintain his ignorance. In Act I, after drinking the potion, the "bewildered" Tristan hears the faithful Kurwenal hailing the arrival of King Marke: "Which king?" he asks, in all "bad faith." The potion allows the lovers to disregard the law. Wagner understood the potion's role perfectly well: not to create desire but to reveal it, a perverse permission to violate the law of incest, to seek freely narcissistic jouissance in the love-passion.

In his discussion of Chrétien de Troyes's *Érec et Énide* in *La Névrose courtoise,* Henri Rey-Flaud distinguishes three kinds of love: narcissistic passion, chivalrous love, and courtly love proper. Here again opera furnishes material that could serve as direct illustration of his remarks:

Chrétien's text demonstrates at this point that in narcissistic passion (*Verliebtheit*), it is through the woman that the lover finds his ideal image (ego ideal) realized in the other; that, all things considered, it is always with his own reflection that this passionate lover falls in love. We should further specify that this radiant image of himself is not one that he perceived (how could he have?) one (mythic) day but rather one that all along he has read reflected back to him in the gaze of the mother, a function held here by the queen.

The woman of the love-passion is the "woman-mirror: the mirror in which the man suddenly finds his own image magnified." This analysis is applicable word for word to Richard Wagner's *Tristan;* the function of the gaze is the same:

> *Isolde* (I.iii):
>   Over him I stood
>   With shining sword,
> to slay the rash intruder.
> For Morold's death take vengeance.
>   But as he lay there

> he looked up
> Not at the sword,
> Not at my hand,
> He gazed in my eyes.
> And his anguish
> Wounded me so;
> The sword then fell before me.

The love potion is in the end merely the element that allows the mirror play of their gazes: "She drinks, then throws away the cup. Both, seized with shuddering, gaze with deepest emotion, but fixed expressions, into one another's eyes, in which the look of defiance to death fades and melts into the glow of passion" (stage directions, I.v). J.-P. Ponnelle's staging at Bayreuth in 1981, 1982, and 1983 brought this out with particular clarity: the potion has become just a large silver chalice in whose polished surface Tristan and Isolde gaze upon each other, side by side. Just as in Act II they gaze upon each other in the reflecting surface of the spring that flows at the base of the tree that marks their meeting.

This mirror effect is signified in the work on many other levels: in Tristan becoming Tantris at his first encounter with Isolde under conditions already described:

> I'm [that] "Tantris"
> He hoped that the name disguised him;
> As Tristan
> Isolde knew him plainly.
>
> [I.iii]

And in the end, of course, it is the exalting climax of their love duet:

Tristan	*Isolde*
Tristan, thou	thou, Isolde
I, Isolde	Tristan, I
no more Tristan	no more Isolde

Henri Rey-Flaud titles the chapter of his work devoted to this analysis "La Passion narcissique ou l'in-différence" (The Narcissistic passion, or in-difference). Once again, there is no better illustration of this fantasy of nondifference than Wagner's *Tristan:* the duet turns about the "and" in "Tristan and Isolde":

> *Isolde:*   But this conjunction
> "And" if it's destroyed
>
> . . .
>
> *Tristan:*   So let us die
> And never part
>
> . . .
>
> *Both:*   Nameless,
> Endless rapture sharing
> Each to each devoted
> In love alone abiding!

A rejection of separation along with a rejection of conjunction, in the imaginary of the other envisioned as the representative of absolute wholeness. An idea figured in Wagner's work by the nick in the edge of Tristan's sword; the missing piece, held by Isolde, allows her to reconstitute the original and fundamental wholeness.

In passion, the lover chooses a woman-queen who allows him to retrieve the image of himself (ego ideal) that his mother loved and to which she gave the status of imaginary phallus. The man's desire is merely a rediscovery of maternal desire. This relationship with the woman is also fundamentally always underlain by an imaginary homosexuality, and when Érec kisses Énide, it is to his own pure mirror image and to this alone that he desperately clings, it is in this image that he loses himself and drowns. In this sense passion is already in-difference.

Love can exist only through difference, particularly the difference maintained by the name. "Nameless" in the indifferentiation of their names, conjoined without the copula, Tristan/Isolde make of love a narcissistic passion, "love's shadow."

Echo and Reflection

The extreme richness and ambiguity of the myth of Tristan and Isolde, particularly in Wagner's revision, warrants long and detailed discussion.[64] But what is important here is to see how the emergence of the thematic network of this myth may relate to our focal question of the voice as object.

Their first point of encounter comes from the myth of Narcissus with its two aspects—the image, of course, but also sound, which figures explicitly in the relationship between Narcissus and the nymph Echo. Here, briefly, is the story as Ovid tells it in the *Metamorphoses.*

Narcissus was an adolescent whose great beauty incited the passionate longings of girls and boys alike. But his excessive pride made him indifferent to all. One day, one of those whom he had shunned cursed him thus: "May Narcissus, too, love this way one day, and never possess the object of his love." Now, the nymph Echo also loved him with the deepest love. Echo had once incurred the wrath of Hera, who condemned her, for speaking too much, to repeat forever the last sounds of everything she heard. One day Narcissus, having wandered away from his companions, began to call out: "Is anybody here?" "Here," answered Echo, rushing out of the woods ready to embrace Narcissus, who in disdain rejected her cruelly: "Not that! I would die before I give you power over me" . . . "I give you power over me," repeated Echo, who let herself pine away until *only her voice remained.* As for Narcissus, we know his fate: bending over a pool to slake his thirst, he sees his face in the water, and at the sight of such beauty he instantly falls in love. Lost in contemplation of this elusive image, he pines away (or in another version kills himself). But Echo, reduced to her voice alone, remains beside him, sharing in his sorrow. "Alas, farewell," says Narcissus to the beloved image. "Alas, farewell," answers the echo. "The fate of the nymph Echo represents the idea of the lover as the reflection of the beloved as an acoustical allegory."[65] Or, as B. This has put it, "A reflected glance, a resounded cry; that, in short, is the drama of Narcissus and Echo." The entire problematics of the voice as object is there in place on the stage of myth: the voice purified of its material source in a being who becomes pure voice, who dissolves into a final cry of pain. A voice whose existence is inexorably bound up with the word of the Other, issues from the word of the Other, and is inflected to his desire.

[64]See the bibliography in *L'Avant-Scène Opéra* 34/35, devoted to Wagner's masterpiece.

[65]Bertau, "Tristan and Narcissus," 80.

For Lacan, "as an object [the voice] is the voice of the Other, or rather, the voice in the Other." The entire dialectic articulated by Freud in his *Project for a Scientific Psychology,* on which I have based the description of the constitution of the vocal object, is represented in this myth, including the quality of elusive evanescence, which, like the narcissistic reflection, symbolizes what is forever lost, or forever lacking.

The echoed voice, or the voice as the pivot of Tristan and Isolde's relationship, appears quite explicitly in Wagner's opera: the dialogue-duet of Act II is punctuated throughout by alliterations, which are like slightly distorted echoes of the lovers' words, apart from any real coherence in the continuity of the dialogue, whose rapturous exaltation, it is true, lends itself well to the relatively deconstructed tenor of the discourse:

Dies dein Mund?	This thy mouth?
Hier deine Hand?	Here thy Hand?
. . .	. . .
Überreiche	Joy unequaled
Ohne Gleiche	All surpassing
. . .	. . .
All' Gedenken	All remembrance
All' Gemahnen	All reminding
. . .	. . .
Ohne Schmachten	No more pining
hold Umnachten	Night-enfolded!
. . .	. . .
Neid'sche Wache	Envious watcher
Nie erwachen.	I'll not waken

The duet ends in echolalia pure and simple as both sing:

Ohne Nennen	Ever nameless
Ohne Trennen	Never parting
neu Erkennen	Newly learning
neu Entbrennen	Newly burning
ewig endlos	Endless ever
ein-bewusst	Joined in joy
heiss erglühter Brust	Ever-glowing love
höchste Liebeslust.	Highest holy love.

Suddenly Brangäne's cry bursts forth, proclaiming the lethal truth of the passionate abyss in which Tristan-Isolde founders.

Yet the voice as such figures in still another instance, as the relational knot between Tristan and Isolde, expressed in the third act's pervasive theme of "the old sad melody" (*die alte traurige Weise*).

Act III of *Tristan* is punctuated by the interruptions of the shepherd who keeps a lookout for the arrival of the ship carrying Isolde, who has come at Kurwenal's summons. This melody, played on the English horn, serves as a signal and is what awakens Tristan from his comatose slumber. It should not be forgotten, even if Wagner, oddly, seems to have omitted this particular detail, that according to the legend, Tristan is a knight-musician, who, like Orpheus, has a harp as his attribute, and furthermore that it is with his singing that he charms King Marke's court:

Tristan took up the harp and sang so sweetly that the barons' hearts softened at the sound. And Marke marveled at the harpist from the country of Loonis, where once Rivalen had stolen Blanchefleur. When the lay was finished, the King was silent for a long time. "Son," he finally said, "Blessed be your tutor in the eyes of God and you together with him! God loves those who sing well, those whose song touches the hearts of men, awakening their cherished memories and making them forget their griefs and losses. You bring us joy. Stay long beside me, friend."[66]

Perhaps this detail gave Wagner the inspiration for the theme of the "old melody." When Tristan hears the tune, these are his words:

> Is that your song to me,
> O ancient, mournful piping,
> Is that your song of woe?
> Through evening silence
> Once it rang,
> When as a child
> I learned how my father perished;
> Through morning greyness,
> Still more fearful,

[66]Joseph Bédier, *Le Roman de Tristan et Iseut* (Paris: Union Générale d'Éditions, 1981).

When the son
Of his mother's fate was told.
When he who sired me died,
She died as I was born;
   The mournful piping
   Through their pain
   Once sang to them
   Its doleful strain;
   It asked me then,
   It asks me now:
What is the fate before me,
To which my parents bore me?
   What is my fate?
   That mournful piping
   Plainly tells me;
   'Tis yearning and dying!
   No! Ah, no!
   It is not so!
   Yearning! Yearning!
In dying ever yearning,
Though yearning brings no dying!
   What never dies,
   Yearning now calls
   For death's repose
   to the healer far away . . .
              [III.i]

    Throughout this despairing soliloquy, Tristan indicates with extraordinary specificity how literally fundamental this melody and this voice are to his relationship with his father, his mother, and the entire structure of his desire that it has produced. The shepherd's dirge makes direct reference to lack, is apprehended by Tristan as *loss* of the primordial maternal object, and functions at the same time as a call to overcome that lack: the dirge is sung at the approach of Isolde, the "healer far away" who comes to bridge the gap, to replace the missing sliver from Tristan's sword. From the voice that commands Desire, that means Desire (in the sense that "to mean" can also mean to order), and the voice as cause of Desire the distance is not great. Ultimately, it is again the voice, the object of plenitude ("what never dies"), that designates the "healer far away" in Isolde, that literally activates the fantasy of the Woman as "desire overcome," as mode of the imaginary reconstitution of narcissistic wholeness.

Tristan's neurosis represents an original departure from the "passionate" dimension of the "courtly neurosis" by virtue of the role played by the love potion. Tristan is perfectly aware that the philter functions as yet another cause of desire, as yet another cursed and sought-after object of jouissance; in short, as a drug—as the term is understood today—whose substance derives from the same source as his desire (the modern-day Tristan might be a heroin[e] addict!):

> That dark fatal drink,
> With anguish imbued,
> By me, by me
> That potion was brewed,
> From father's grief
> And mother's woe,
> From lovers' tears
> Of long ago
>
> . . .
>
> My hand distilled
> The poison of madness.
> Poison I brewed,
> Poison I tasted,
> That moved my mind
> To limitless rapture,
> I curse you,
> Dark fatal drink!
> And curse
> Him by whom 'twas brewed.
>   [III.i]

The thematic structure here is rigorously parallel to that of the "old melody": both instances refer to the pain and the distress of the mother and father as the origin of the suffering. It may seem surprising that Tristan's meditation on the causes of his torment and jouissance fails to include Isolde; it was she, after all, who served him the magic brew. But this omission is consistent with Tristan's understanding of his situation. Once he realizes that he alone is responsible for his fate, the other, Isolde, Brangäne, can be envisioned in no other way than as the instrument of fate. Isolde is no longer his poisoner, and her role is now exclusively that of his healer.

Explicitly posited here—and this is quite remarkable—is a certain desire, a desire linked to the voice, to the Woman, to the drug, which seeks its fulfillment only in death, since the goal of this desiring structure is not the satisfaction of desire, even less the fulfillment of love, but rather the death of desire.

If Tristan is thus engulfed by a bitter desire that the old melody has revived, Isolde too, in her Transfiguration, is engulfed by the fascination of a melody, of what may be called the "Tristan melody," a melody-plenitude, thereby realizing Tristan's fantasy:

> See you not
> How his heart
> So proudly swells,
> Full and bold
> It throbs in his breast?
> Gentle breathing
> Stirs his lips,
> Ah, how calmly
> Soft his breath
>
> . . .
>
> Can it be that I alone
> hear this wondrous, glorious tone,
>   Softly stealing,
>   *All revealing,*
>   Mildly glowing
>   From him flowing
>   Thro' me pouring
>   Rising, soaring,
>   boldly singing,
>   Round me ringing?
>   Brighter growing,
>   O'er me flowing,
>   Are they waves
>   Of tender radiance?
>   Are they clouds
>   Of wonderful fragrance?

They are rising
High around me,
Shall I breathe them,
Shall I hear them?
Shall I taste them,
Dive beneath them?
Drown in tide
Of melting sweetness?
In the rapturous swell,
In the turbulent spell,
In the welcoming wave,
Holding all,
I'm sinking
I'm drowning,
Unaware,
Highest love!

Isolde's Transfiguration is thus the dissolution in death of Tristan's fantasy, the fantasy of imaginary plenitude sought in The Woman, herself absolute, the maternal object, the initial object of jouissance, the lost object, impossible and forbidden even as she is sought in one's own image: the woman-mirror of narcissistic love. And it is a voice, the swelling strains of the old melody calling forth and anchoring Tristan's delirium, that becomes a plenitude at the very moment when the dying Tristan believes that Isolde has come back to join him. *Believes* she has come back, because the object always escapes, is always missed.

This is the truth that J.-P. Ponnelle brings out stunningly in his staging at Bayreuth to which I referred earlier. Without in any way compromising the logic of Wagner's music drama, Ponnelle imagines a denouement that clearly inflects what Wagner on the face of it had allowed for. In Ponnelle's mise-en-scène, Isolde does not actually disembark at Kareol and rejoin Tristan: her arrival, as well as that of Brangäne and of King Marke, and even her death are Tristan's hallucinations, hallucinations encouraged by Kurwenal, who literally enters into his delirium. This idea has its justification in an earlier delirium, this one explicit in Wagner's text, in which Tristan actually does hallucinate a first arrival of Isolde's boat. Ponnelle merely extends this dramatic idea and applies it to the arrival of Isolde that Wagner intended as an actual arrival. Isolde thus becomes an apparition, spanning with her singing and her radiance the figurative rent in the thunder-struck tree at whose foot Tristan lies. The death of Isolde is now no more than Tristan's death, the dimming of his desire, finally appeased in the fantasy of an impossible and forbidden love fulfilled. And when Isolde, *mater dolorosa,* takes Tristan into her arms for the last embrace, it is now Mary who holds her son in the pose of desperate consolation of Michelangelo's *Pietà.* Darkness falls on the stage, and as the final extended orchestral pedal fades, the glaucous light of abhorred Day reappears. And here the truth dawns, too: it is only Tristan's corpse, held thus by Kurwenal in his arms. Isolde has not come.

The Diva

If this quasi-Marialogical vision of *Tristan* gives a somewhat unex-
pected ending to this key work in which Wagner crystallizes most
purely the *mise-en-abîme* of the voice and The Woman whose imaginary
quest is structured by opera, it also serves as an introduction to that
ultimate transmutation where Voice and Woman commingle in a common deification: the *divine* voice of the female singer makes her a *diva*, a
goddess.

Note that in opera commentary and criticism the adjective "divine"
is reserved for the female voice. Laudatory superlatives addressed to the
male voice tend to describe it in terms of its distinguished *materials*—
the male voice may be golden, silver, or bronze—even when the voice
sings the role of a god. Even though Hans Hotter sings a brilliant and
inspired Wotan, it would somehow sound odd if his voice were
described as "divine." The only divine voices, it seems, are those of
women.

The diva herself appears at the moment the Angel becomes Woman;
her appearance reintroduces via the vocalist the attribute of divine substitution or identification that I noted earlier with regard to the objectified voice: the *Trésor de la langue française* indicates that the first
appearance in French of the word "diva" in its acceptation as "celebrated [female] singer" occurs in 1832, in a text by Théophile Gauthier
(*Albertus*), as a borrowing from the Italian, first attested in that language with this meaning at the beginning of the nineteenth century.
No mention is made of a masculine form—*divo*.

There is a twofold observation to make in this regard. First, explicit
reference to the divine occurs when operatic romanticism presents The
Woman not as such but as she is fantasized according to a logic that
condemns her to death. This reference then shifts to the singer herself.

From the beginning, the opera stage had been peopled with gods and goddesses, and the Wagnerian oeuvre resumes relations, as it were, with this early clientele (alongside his Germanic pantheon of the *Ring*, Wagner intended to create an opera about Jesus and another about Buddha). But what is new in the appellation "diva" is that now it is the female singer and she alone who is accorded divine status, as though it were her power to transform herself into pure voice, inasmuch as she is *one* incarnation of *many* successive roles, that allowed her to be characterized as divine.

The term "diva" admits of another, incidental connotation in its application to the great female vocal artists, a connotation of what I have referred to as "the mad law," the caprice. Behind the title "diva" there is often the somewhat pejorative idea of capricious behavior, bizarre demands, in short, the abuse of a position of absolute mastery. This idea can also be found in the concept of the "star" which comes from the movies (and wasn't Greta Garbo, moreover, called The Divine?).

Finally, it should be noted that it is just when romantic bel canto takes the singing of its heroines to higher and ever higher extremes, closer and closer to the cry, that the title "diva" comes into its own. This latter convergence may seem strange: God is more commonly associated with the Word than with the cry. And yet did not Jesus, too, son of God, God himself, die with a cry, like any opera heroine doomed to sacrifice in the last act?

Opera has always avoided the patently Christic theme. Nevertheless, a lyric musical genre that is linked to opera in many respects is the Passion, especially in the form given it by Johann Sebastian Bach (but in other forms as well). It is a fact that recent productions of such works as Bach's *Saint John Passion* (produced by P.-L. Pizzi and the Venice Fenice) evince no hesitation to stage them in the purest "operatic" style. It is certainly no accident that, along with the requiem liturgy, it is the Passion of Christ that has provided the material for the closest equivalent to opera in the realm of religious music. True, few other passages from the Gospels are so densely peopled with characters and events that lend themselves to dialogues of such dramatic intensity. The Christmas theme, one would think, could be adapted to opera every bit as easily. Yet notwithstanding several masterpieces of oratorio (Handel's *Messiah*, Bach's *Christmas Oratorio*), the richness that has characterized productions of the Passions has yet to be discovered in that theme.

"And Jesus cried again with a loud voice and yielded up his spirit" (Matthew 27:50). Three of the four evangelists note this detail of Christ's death on the cross. Only Saint John, the evangelist of God-the-Word— "In the beginning was the Word, and the Word was with God, and the Word was God"—makes no mention of it. Saint John says only that "When Jesus had received the vinegar, he said, 'It is finished'; and he bowed his head and gave up his spirit" (John 19:30); as if the initial insistence on the Word of God, God as Word, were incompatible with his final cry of death. The musical liturgy is very circumspect about this cry. Compositions on "the seven last words of Christ" abound, but his final cry is everywhere stifled, even in Bach's enormously expressive *Saint Matthew Passion:* Peter's sobs rend the skies, the Temple curtain comes crashing down, but the death cry on the cross resolves in a modulation closer to a plaint than to a real cry.

Be that as it may, as far as the cry is concerned, God in his second person and as a figure of sacrifice finds himself cheek by jowl with Satan the fallen angel, The Woman, the Dwarf, and the Goddess. Here again psychoanalysis offers a particularly coherent perspective on this reunion of God and the Voice in sacrifice. That perspective, developed by Jacques Lacan in his seminar on anxiety, has its point of departure in an essay by the psychoanalyst Theodor Reik on the shofar, an instrument of the Judaic liturgy.

The God-Voice

Theodor Reik, a contemporary of Freud and one of his most loyal disciples, was particularly impressed by the emotion that overcame him—as it does any listener, Jew or non-Jew—at the sound of the blowing of the shofar at the end of the ceremony that closes the observance of Yom Kippur. "The shofar," Reik writes, "is not only the sole primitive instrument which still plays a part in the ritual of Judaism, it is also one of the oldest wind instruments known." It is fashioned most often from a ram's horn or the horn of a wild goat. Reik ponders the following question: "Can the unusually strong emotion be due to the three sounds which are produced from the shofar? The three sets of sounds, which are only distinguished by the change of rhythm, have different names in the ritual: *Teki'ah* (long sustained), *Shebarim* (interrupted), *Teru'ah* (blare or tremolo). A fourth set, *Teki'ah Gedolah,* is only a longer *Teki'ah,* distinguished from the primary form by a long sustained fifth. . . . On the Day of Atonement [Yom Kippur], at the conclusion of the ceremony a single long-sustained note (*Teki'ah*) is sounded once in the sense of '*ite missa est.*' "[67] Reik does not stop with this purely acoustical characterization of the sounds of the shofar. In the present context, what is important to note is that aside from the *Shebarim* form, the fundamental feature of these emissions of sound is their continuity, their lack of scansion, their termination in a long *pedal point.*

In this regard, I should reiterate my observation that musical rituals often tend to explore, at times very insistently, the dimension of the continuous in sound. For a convincing illustration one has only to listen to the horns or "oboes" of the Tibetan Bon-Po ritual, involving the repetition of a single extremely long-drawn-out note, which requires the player to master a very specialized technique of blowing and breathing: certain notes can be held for almost a minute. Closer to home, one need only listen to the preeminent instrument of the Western Christian liturgy, the organ. The distinguishing feature of this instrument is that it is a "wind" instrument whose mechanization permits it to produce the continuum, an effect amplified by the reverberant qualities of church architecture which create a veritable spatial delocalization of the sound source, achieving the detachment of the sound as such that is so characteristic of its object function. But let us return to the shofar.

A particularly close reading of biblical texts leads Reik to conclude that the sound of the shofar is the voice of God, of Yahweh himself— the voice of God, that is, when in his ancient form as a totem animal *he was put to death* in a sacrificial rite.

The peculiarly fearsome, groaning, blaring and long-sustained tone of the shofar becomes intelligible in that it revives the memory of the bellowing of a bull; it derives its serious significance from the fact that, in the unconscious mental life of the listeners, it represents the anxiety and the last death-struggle of the father-god—if the metaphor be not too forced, one may say, his swan-song. . . . When the form of the father was recognized in

[67]Theodor Reik, "The Shofar," in *Ritual Psycho-analytic Studies,* trans. Douglas Bryan (London: Hogarth, 1931), 226, 237, 277.

the totem animal and was worshipped as a god, the believers imitated his voice by means of onomatopoetic sounds. The imitated roar of an animal signified both the presence of the god in the midst of his worshippers and their equality with him. In the course of centuries an instrument was evolved from the horn—the most striking emblem of that totemistic god— and was now used as a means to imitate his voice.[68]

Reik's analysis is Lacan's point of departure in his seminar on anxiety, in which he addresses the question of the voice as object, relating it, however, to a different aspect from the one we have been considering. I have dwelt at length on the fascinating call of the voice, its appeal, its "sirenic" dimension, feminine and maternal, and marked by desire and incestuous jouissance, its rejection of the law of the Word, the voice-cry of the Queen of the Night. Lacan, for his part, locates another presence in the objectified voice, the presence of a commandment: "The voice in question," he says, "is the voice as an imperative, as something that demands to be obeyed or believed." Or as Alain Juranville puts it: "The sound of the shofar is the bellowing of the bull at slaughter. A voice that is the very voice of the Father, the voice of that absent God who must be recalled and whose murder is repeated in the sacrifice. It is the voice of the prohibiting Father condemned to death."[69] Now as Lacan emphasizes, "It is from this [the original act inscribed in the murder of the Father], as a prohibition impossible to transgress, that the original desire is constituted in its most fundamental form." It is therefore through the sacrifice of God-the-Commander-and-Prohibitor that a sacrificial residue, the Voice, is detached from him. In this sense, the vocal object, especially at the extreme of the cry, is not only the decanted product of a speech purged or purified of meaning, it is the product that results from the murder of the Word (now as commandment), and thus is bound up with the entire problematics of desire, prohibition, and transgression.

It is this facet of the imperative voice in opera that is at work in the powerful and petrifying *recto-tono* of the voice of the Commendatore. What is Don Giovanni's response to the appearance of that imperative face of the objectified voice? He speaks its other face, its murderous

[68]Ibid., 256–60.
[69]Alain Juranville, *Lacan et la philosophie* (Paris: Presses Universitaires de France, 1984).

face, the cry. "Do not forget," Don Giovanni's cry might seem to say, "do not forget, Father Prohibitor, that we have put you to death."

Jean and Brigitte Massin, in their biography of Don Giovanni's composer, reveal the following curious detail from his childhood: "Certain sounds Mozart literally could not tolerate. That of the trumpet, for example." The authors cite a letter from Andréas Schachtner, a family friend and trumpeter at the Salzburg court: "Almost until he was ten, he had an irrational fear of the trumpet, especially when it was played solo, unaccompanied. . . . Your father [Leopold] sought one day to deliver him from this childish terror and he told me to play near him, no matter how he might protest. Mon Dieu! I should never have obeyed him! Scarcely had he perceived the instrument's piercing timbre than he went pale, began to faint away, and had I continued, he would no doubt have had convulsions."[70] Now the trumpet is in fact an avatar of the shofar: translators of the Bible chose not to retain "shofar" and translated it rather as "trumpet" or "horn." Reik further notes that the horn can be found again as a consecrated instrument among the Greeks and the Romans (as the buccina): "[We have many indications] that these instruments have all evolved from the simple horn of an animal, and have been perfected by technical improvements and the use of bronze, silver and gold."[71] At all events, the fact remains that in the Judeo-Christian mythology the sound of the trumpet becomes the voice of the Angel, when it ceases to be the Guardian Angel and becomes the Exterminating Angel—in this capacity, the Divine Voice in its paternal, prohibitive dimension, pronouncing the ultimate interdiction and Last Judgment. It may not be too farfetched to imagine that it is this unconscious resonance—it is a matter of record that relations between father and son were charged—that so impressed the young Wolfgang, a resonance against which he never ceased to struggle, in every aspect of his life, without ever freeing himself from it completely.

This object presence of the Voice, heard in its superego component, Divine and Paternal, is already to be found—and this is certainly no accident, given the theme of the work (a father driven to sacrifice his son)—in the voice of the Oracle in Idomeneo, composed by Mozart at

---

[70]Quoted in Jean Massin and Brigitte Massin, Wolfgang Amadeus Mozart (Paris: Fayard, 1970).
[71]Reik, "Shofar," 229.

the age of twenty-four, an "underground" voice, offstage and detached. In a letter of 29 November 1780, in the thick of composition, Mozart writes: ". . . the voice must be terrifying—must penetrate the soul— *the audience must shout out that it is truth itself.*"

Incidentally, Mozart goes on to make a remarkable association: he refers to the ghost in *Hamlet.* Now it is well known that Freud long saw the Hamlet myth, which on one level can be read as a version of the Oedipus myth, as the myth of the structuring of the subject's desire. The Ghost, Hamlet's father, assassinated (poisoned *through his ear*), is a failed and fallible father. Lacan says that it is in fact Hamlet who is poisoned through the ear, by his father's words.

Many other works turn to this type of "flat" vocal treatment to signify the commandment to which there can be no rejoinder. To the examples I have already given can now be added the voice of the Friar, the spirit of Charles V, at the end of Verdi's *Don Carlos.* And the sentence of papal damnation with which Tannhäuser returns from his pilgrimage to Rome:

> If you have partaken of such evil pleasures,
> warmed yourself by Hell's fires,
> and dwelt inside the Venusberg,
> you are eternally damned!
> Just as this staff on my hand
> can never be graced with fresh green leaves
> so, never out of Hell's fire
> will your redemption blossom forth![72]

The Cry of the Bull, the Bull-roarer

Theodor Reik associates the sound of the shofar with that of the bull-roarer or rhombos, an even more primitive instrument, examples of which have been discovered at Paleolithic sites and which is still used sacramentally by aboriginal peoples in Australia and New Guinea. "The instrument consists of a flat, narrow piece of wood in which there is a hole. It is whirled very quickly in the air by a long string threaded through the hole in the instrument, and a loud humming

---

[72]Richard Wagner, *Tannhäuser,* Trans. William R. Gann, Angel Records SDL3620.

noise is produced."[73] Reik compares the bull-like roaring this instrument produces (whence its name) with the bellowing sound of the shofar, and inscribes it within the same interpretive structure. One can also see this buzzing roar as yet another instance of the emergence of something like fixity in the realm of sound: a lethal fixity, the auditory face of the fixing gaze, which like the great big eyes of the bogeyman —a corpse's eyes—terrorizes the misbehaving child by evoking the supreme prohibition, the primal murder that cannot be repeated. If one day a composer finds himself with the task of illustrating the eye of Cain in the grave, he will find no better musical material than what he might draw on directly in these deep and primitive strata of sound.

This analysis of the God-voice, as a relic of divine sacrifice, has led to the paternal and therefore masculine prohibition, seemingly at odds with the feminization of the divine signaled by the term "diva." In fact, what occurs is a collapsing of one into the other, of the dimension of the voice as a resonant substrate of the commandment prohibiting the paternal sacrifice into that other dimension of the voice in which it functions as the substrate of speech, which from the moment of the infant's first cry bears the inscription of the desire of the Mother. As though in the field of opera, Woman-Voice and God-Voice amalgamate into Goddess-Voice, the voice of the diva. As Henri Rey-Flaud writes in *La Névrose courtoise*, describing Lancelot's emotional reaction to the queen's hair: "There is no doubt that at this moment the woman has taken the place of God and that the strands of her hair that remain caught in the ivory comb are indeed relics of absolute being. . . ."

Thus both in her voice and in her cry the diva would have the power to make audible the echo of the murder of a paternal God and the fascinating call for retrieval of a first object of maternal jouissance. In this sense, lyric jouissance is indeed divine jouissance, mystical jouissance. Whenever the diva on the stage begins to make herself pure voice for the jouissance of the spectator, the re-presentation of her sacrifice, in whatever anecdotal garb, has the effect of making this sacred resonance echo in such a way that the listener may enjoy it in the most radical way possible: by incorporating it. And indeed, the function of sacrifice is to prepare the divinity for incorporation by the faithful, and in the event to prepare the faithful for what Mozart called "the voice that penetrates the soul."

[73]Reik, "Shofar," 284.

It is to this conception of performance that Richard Wagner explicitly connects in composing his *Parsifal,* his *Bühnenweihfestspiel,* or "sacred festival play," which was initially to be performed exclusively in the only temple deemed worthy to receive this celebration: Bayreuth.

Opera, Holy Drama

From the beginning, opera has been closely related to Greek tragedy. The broad outlines of the aesthetics of opera, defined by the Bardi Camerati in Florence at the end of the sixteenth century, came in the wake of their research into the musical aspects of ancient tragedy. The first themes to be staged were drawn directly from Greek mythology; some derive from the tragedies themselves (Euripides' *Alcestis* and *Iphigenia,* for example). This flirtation with tragedy is protracted, continuing up though Stravinsky's 1927 *Oedipus Rex.* Now the ancient tragedy is precisely the final form taken by the celebration of the cult of Dionysus, commemorating the *Passion*—that is, the killing—of God.

The Dionysian Passion

Dionysus is a "suffering god," characterized in the various versions of his mythic story by a number of fundamental features, notably by a particular relation to the feminine, to madness, and to a certain mode of sacrifice. I will briefly summarize this myth as Grimal recounts it in his *Dictionnaire de la mythologie.*

From the union of Zeus and his daughter Persephone is born the god Zagreus, identified in the theology of the Orphic mysteries as the original embodiment of Dionysus. Hera, Zeus's wife, orders the Titans to destroy the child. They tear Zagreus to pieces, dismember and then devour him. His heart, however, is not consumed, and Zeus brings him back to life by impregnating Semele with the still-beating heart. Semele asks Zeus, by way of recompense, to let her see him in all his power and glory, and she is struck down by the burning light that no mortal can behold and perishes, with the child, in its sixth month of gestation, still in her womb. Zeus tears the child from his mother's belly and sews him into his thigh until the infant comes to term. That is how, from the thigh of Zeus, Dionysus, the "twice-born," comes into the world. Still pursued by Hera, he is given by Persephone to King Orchomenos to be reared as a girl. Then, transformed into a young goat, he is entrusted to the care of the nymphs at Nysa, and there he invents wine. Now grown to manhood, he is recognized as Zeus's son by Hera, who afflicts him with madness: he wanders the world with his female followers, the Maenads ("possessed women"). When he reaches Phrygia, the goddess Cybele (the "Great Mother") receives him and initiates him into her cult. Freed from his madness, he gradually conquers the world, inflicting madness on his enemies and drawing women into his orgiastic cult. He goes so far as to disguise himself as a woman, the better to make them follow. "On his return to Greece, he introduced the Bacchanalia, those feasts in which all the people, but especially the women, were overcome with mystic delirium and wandered about the countryside, calling out in *ritual cries.*" The rhombos is the requisite musical instrument for these ceremonies. Finally, having established his cult throughout the world, Dionysus ascends into heaven, now fully a god, almost as powerful as Zeus himself, at whose right hand he sits.

The followers of the Dionysian cult in ancient Greece, especially the women among them, reproduced the Maenads' rituals. During the ceremonies in honor of Dionysus, god of "mania," of the trance, female devotees would undergo a genuine crisis of mystic possession during which they would wander the countryside, chase down a small animal, dismember it alive and consume it on the spot;[74] this is how Zagreus had been torn apart and devoured by the Titans, so that his very identity was abolished, since once resuscitated and made whole, he appears with a new name—Dionysus. But beyond the incorporation of God or the sacrificial victim that represents him, the important thing to note is that through this rite of collective devouring, the Maenads as a group reconstitute the sundered divine unity, doing away with the suffering of dismemberment, of the multiple, through the ecstatic unity of the collective body. It is the whole collectivity of the Maenads, a veritable mystical body, that becomes the image of God. Underlying this cult, then, is a whole mystique of suffering in differentiation and jouissance in indifferentiation.

The excesses of this mystic cult were bound to trouble the social

[74]See Euripides, *The Bacchae.*

authorities, and a poeticized form of the Dionysian rites gradually came to take its place. Verbal expression replaced what had once been action: the dithyramb was originally a round dance performed by the initiates, interspersed with hymns and recitations. As Theodor Reik points out, the entire structure of opera is already there: "Opera and operetta have developed from the dithyrambic hymn which was sung and danced."[75] Celebration then became spectacle, the retelling and singing of the exploits not only of Dionysus but also of other mythological heroes, and finally gave birth to the ancient tragedy as we know it in the works of Aeschylus, Sophocles and Euripides.

With tragedy a new basic element appears: the actor now comes forward and separates himself from the chorus, the symbolic figure of the collective body of the Maenads, thereby reintroducing new dismemberment, new differentiation, new suffering. By virtue of this fact, the actor, as an object detached from a mythical and mystical Whole, becomes the living reemergent presence of a primordial rupture: he introduces lack into the Chorus. Condemned in this respect to desire and to suffer, he becomes the scapegoat who must be sacrificed so that the initial wholeness can be recovered. This is why the tragic hero whom the actor incarnates is a marginal being, rejected by the polis, set up in opposition to the Chorus-god and in defiance of both. Like a detached bodily organ, he becomes refuse, subject as it were to the whims of fate, until his supreme fall and ultimate elimination. But insofar as he incarnates the pain of differentiation, at the same time he comes paradoxically to represent the earlier, initial god, not in his reunified avatar but in the suffering of his dismemberment. And if the Chorus is a mystical unity, it is also the indeterminacy of anonymity. In distinguishing himself, however, the tragic hero wins a name and sometimes renown. That is the actor's twofold destiny, to be both object of refuse and divine object ("idol"). These observations point to new ways of understanding the actor's centuries-long ostracism by the organisms of social cohesion, especially religious ones, as well as the adulation often bestowed on him by the crowd.

This specific problematics will no doubt call to mind the analogous problematics of the object as Freud elaborated it and as I have reformulated it to bear specifically on the vocal object. From this perspective,

[75]Reik, "Shofar," 304.

the actor is ineluctably bound to become not only the *porte-parole,* the spokesman, or bearer of the word, but the *porte-voix,* the bearer of the voice of human suffering.

This entire structure is quite visible in outline if we know how to look for it, in the first operatic work that deliberately reconnects with holy celebration. That work is Richard Wagner's *Parsifal.* The last work by the composer of *Tristan* gives us a fundamental truth, which is that the primordial rupture, the suffering, the price the subject must pay for speech and name, is castration. But this work also leaves us with the illusion that this totality, primitive, beatific, and lost, can somehow be retrieved.

Parsifal, or The
Quest for Illusion

The theme of the Quest that has been encountered at every level of this study could not help but finally appear as an explicit operatic theme. It does happen that a dream will eventually bring forth and decode the desire that plagues the sleeping subject, whereupon he may awaken to a sometimes frightening revelation.

The Quest for The Thing

Wagner's *Parsifal,* as we know, was inspired essentially by the *Parzival* of Wolfram von Eschenbach, written in 1203–1204 and based principally on *Perceval* by Chrétien de Troyes. In a fascinating study of the relationship of Chrétien and Wolfram, Jean Fourquet shows, on the basis of what are clearly errors of translation in Wolfram's rendering of Chrétien's text, that Wolfram had not really mastered all the nuances and even the meanings of certain words in the French vocabulary; Jean Fourquet points in particular to those instances where Wolfram was unaware that the word "grail" was a common noun designating a kind of receptacle or vessel.[76] Wolfram thought the Grail was a proper noun, but what did it designate? For want of other words to describe the Grail, Wolfram rendered it as *"ein Ding,"* a thing. When the Grail is first unveiled to Parsifal, the reader, if he adheres to a literal reading of the text and forgets for the moment the images he already

[76]Jean Fourquet, *Wolfram d'Eschenbach et le Conte del Graal* (Paris: Belles Lettres, 1938).

has of the Grail, has no way of picturing what this "thing" might be like, because the attributes Wolfram gives it are abstract qualities: the Grail is "a thing . . . that surpasses all earthly perfection." Elsewhere "it is the flower of every happiness," or "that which bestows such abundance of the world's sweetness that its delights were very like what we have heard about the kingdom of heaven." "The august brethren received their entire sustenance from the Grail." What then is the Grail, if one takes Wolfram literally? It is *the* Thing, the lost Thing that sustains an endless Quest, because this Thing is inaccessible completeness; it is, in short, The Thing in the sense that Freud, Heidegger, and Lacan give to the concept, each in his own way. For it is precisely this Thing that in a fundamental way arouses desire—the causal "objects" of desire are stand-ins for it, taking its place after the original experience of lack, which is the locus of The Thing. Now that primal ordeal with which every quest, every desire, and the life of every speaking being begins happens to be precisely what we call "castration," the fundamental wound whence all desire originates, from the moment the first "Other," perhaps the Mother— in other words, he or she who will constitute the child's first object of jouissance—inscribes it in the order of language, of the signifier. "The Thing is therefore both a myth and anything but a myth. It is inferred, on the one hand, from the signifier giving rise to the idea of absolute plenitude (without which it would be impossible to speak of desire) and, on the other hand, from the fact that the very emergence of the signifier inflicts the ordeal of the lack of that plenitude."[77]

Parsifal's quest is thus the quest for that thing, his errantry is simply the ordeal of living and speaking, of being named and desiring. But Parsifal in a fundamental way misses his rendezvous with desire, with Kundry, the woman. Like Tristan, he opts for the death of desire. In his avoidance of the unavoidable wound, the price of desire, he remains trapped within the "courtly neurosis." "The courtly neurosis marks the moment when the man refuses this loss and recoils from this risk. The woman is then no longer the object of desire through which life opens up: she appears as harboring a secret, withholding an absent sign, as the site of prohibition. The man stops at the sanctuary door."[78] Conquest of The Thing, or more exactly the fantasy of its

[77]Juranville, *Lacan et la philosophie*, 215.
[78]Rey-Flaud, *La Névrose courtoise*, 76.

conquest, figured in Wagner's opera by the bloody spear, signified by the "renunciation of desire," can lead only to the death of the subject, in both real and symbolic terms. The theme of redemption, of regeneration, whereby the Wagnerian ideology attempts to glorify this illusory and deadly achievement, fails to conceal its more fundamental truth: the silence and death of Kundry, The Woman, and the return of Parsifal to angelic anonymity in the mystical indifferentiation of the collective body represented by the brotherhood of the Knights of the Grail.

The Tragedy of Amfortas

Some tasks of life can be carried out only at the cost of suffering and death. So it is with Amfortas, whose wound reopens at each feast of the Grail. Strictly speaking, Amfortas is in some way a tragic hero. For what, in fact, is the fundamental structure of *Parsifal*? A homogeneous brotherhood, the *circle* of the Knights of the Grail, who gather in ecstatic celebration around the Grail, which gives them substance and sustenance and, notably, divine nourishment. A point has become detached from the circle. That point is Amfortas, condemned to endless suffering because one day he met a woman and let her come too close. A wound in his side, one that will not heal, opens every time the ritual of wholeness, the ritual of the Grail, is performed. Amfortas thus represents, trait for trait, what I earlier touched on in connection with the situation of the tragic hero: inscribed by the group from which he is differentiated under the sign of wrongdoing, of guilt, he also embodies the sacrificed God (Amfortas suffers from a wound in the side like the one Christ received on the cross). Wagner's opera will then consist in fantasizing, as it were, the elimination of this suffering through the reconstitution of primitive wholeness in indifferentiation. That is the mission which falls to Parsifal, who in this respect is the opposite of the tragic hero, inasmuch as Parsifal aspires to restore the primordial circle. Claude Lévi-Strauss observes that "the 'Percevalian' myths reverse another equally universal model, that of the oedipal myths whose problematics is its mirror image."[79] The oedipal myth is

---

[79]Claude Lévi-Strauss, "De Chrétien de Troyes à Richard Wagner," *Programme Festival Bayreuth,* 1975, reprinted in *L'Avant-scène Opéra* 38/39 *"Parsifal"* (January–February 1982), 14.

the epitome of the tragic myth. Wagner's innovation is to make the forces that bring down the hero not "forces of destiny" or "fate" but clearly designated desire and castration. Woman, the Feminine Universe, is explicitly placed at the heart of the problem.

This universe is presented in two interrelated forms: the world of Klingsor and the character of Kundry.

Klingsor is a knight who once sought admission to the Grail sodality. But in his expiatory zeal, he castrated himself—a real castration that puts him on the side of the feminine, but in its phantasmic, malignant dimension, characterized by unrestrained and magical power—a universe like that of the Queen of the Night, peopled by Flower Maidens, vegetal women who, like the half-woman, half-beast sirens of Greek myth, derive their power from their alluring song. The chorus of the Flower Maidens is composed entirely of sopranos, and their heavily embellished and always high-pitched vocal line makes it impossible to understand the words they sing, yielding a vocal symphony whose effect on the listener is particularly powerful. This is the universe against which Amfortas, then the gallant knight of the Grail, whole and intact, took up the spear, the sacred spear that he believed to be the spear of the law that defended the brotherhood from Klingsor's threatening excesses. It was then that Amfortas met Kundry, the woman, and everything changed.

The extraordinary character Kundry constitutes the second mode of *Parsifal*'s feminine universe. Wagner's letters to Mathilde Wesendonck indicate that this character, a synthesis of several female characters who appear in Wolfram's epic, represented an important breakthrough for him in the composition of the opera. But is Kundry truly *one* woman? She is first of all the Grail *messenger:* Kundry is an angel. But she is also the temptress, the sorceress, Klingsor's slave and accomplice: Kundry is a demon. She thus represents in its purest form that image of The Woman ever present in opera, the privileged medium of The Voice in its purest embodiment as object. It therefore comes as no surprise that her vocal score calls for cry, plaint, moan, and then the silence to which the entire third act confines her despite her continued presence onstage. In no other opera role—apart from that of Kundry's future sister, Lulu—does there appear such a systematic inscription of the trans-verbal. To that vocal palette Kundry adds the laugh, with all its demonic shadings—an effect rarely used in opera with such violence as here.

The meeting of Amfortas and Kundry provokes the original catastrophe that introduces the original break in the circle of knights,
Amfortas's surrender to Kundry's desire.
"At the moment of jouissance, The Thing comes to be lost."[80] That
is the lesson of psychoanalysis, the lesson Amfortas learns through
Kundry: castration is nothing but the experience of that loss, a symbolic castration, to be sure, having little in common with the usual
meaning of the term, but Amfortas's wound is its perfect image. No
matter that Wolfram's description of Amfortas's wound as a castration
derives from an error in translation (which Wagner does not correct):
every wound, every severance is an image, a metaphor of the symbolic castration. It is significant, however, that Wolfram should have
"chosen" to err in this particular way. As a matter of fact, what Amfortas ultimately discovers is that the Grail is an enticing deception, a
lure; that the status of the human, of the speaking, living, and desiring
being, comes at the cost of resigning oneself to the loss of the deception and its symbol—the holy spear—and at the cost of an inescapable
suffering that is at the origin of the quest for that lost paradise where
man was not a man but an angel and where speech was divine silence.
   It falls to Parsifal, then, to cancel out Amfortas's trajectory and
retrieve the absolute jouissance of the Grail, a strictly neurotic undertaking that assumes that absolute jouissance is possibile precisely
because it is prohibited, precisely because those who seek it must
renounce their desire. Instead of acceding to the equation encountered
earlier—impossible and therefore forbidden—the neurotic concludes:
forbidden and therefore possible (read: if I do what must be done).
Parsifal's mission will be to repress or deny Amfortas's discovery, to
avoid both the castration inherent in this discovery and its cost, the
renunciation of jouissance, and to reconstruct at last the primordial
angelic brotherhood in the ecstasy of nirvana, forgetting that in the
death of desire it is the death instinct that ultimately is played out.
Hans-Jürgen Syberberg understood this perfectly when he ended his
film of *Parsifal* with a long close-up of a human skull, the death's-head.
Amfortas, too, understood this: " 'The innocent fool.' I think I know
him now: I would call him by his name: Death!" (Act I).
   Parsifal is at first a hero without a name and without an origin, like
so many of Wagner's tenor protagonists (Tristan, Sigmund, Siegfried,

[80]Juranville, *Lacan et la philosophie,* 227.

Lohengrin). In a sense, then, he is not really a man, or even genuinely a speaking being, inasmuch as he is governed by silence: the silence of Act I as he is first shown the mystery of the Grail, the silence of Act III upon his return to Montsalvat, the domain of the Grail. Parsifal, all things considered, is perhaps himself an angel, or at least terribly imbued with the "angelic" atmosphere in which the whole work is steeped. He is nevertheless something of an innocent,[81] and at the first presentation of the Grail he probably smiled. But of course it is in Act II, in the confrontation between Parsifal and Kundry, that everything is played out, when she, "the nameless one," exposes him to the ordeal of desire. At the outset Kundry appears as the Mother and for the first time in the work calls Parsifal by his name. With the lover's kiss she then gives him comes the knowledge Amfortas acquired under similar circumstances. But whereas Amfortas bore the consequence of that knowledge, notably the incurable wound, Parsifal fearfully refuses to acknowledge it. Freud speaks of such fear when he discusses the reaction of the little boy to his discovery of the mother's castration (and it is certainly not by chance that in this scene Hans-Jürgen Syberberg's film gives Parsifal a shield representing the shield of Perseus, in which, as in Caravaggio's famous painting, the head of Medusa is reflected: Freud, as we know, saw the severed head of the Medusa as an image of castration anxiety). The spear can now be recovered. Parsifal therefore knows, and so is subject to the curse and to suffering: his curse is to wander. But at the same time, he would rather know nothing about it and the original circle can be restored: at the threshold of manhood, Parsifal remains an angel in beatific indifferentiation. This trait, too, Syberberg has understood: that is one of the underlying reasons why, after Kundry's kiss, the filmmaker gives the character a double nature, one masculine and the other feminine:

After the kiss, while Parsifal I *invokes the wound,* Parsifal II advances like a shadow as Parsifal I disappears like a shadow. . . . Now it is this feminine Parsifal who will assume the difficult task of resisting Kundry. . . . This is no longer merely a case of male rejection of the feminine, it is as though the better part of Kundry warned her against herself, as in interior monologue. . . . The Kundry-Parsifal constellation—Parsifal in his first, mas-

---

[81]*Benêt,* from *benoît, béni,* blessed.

culine avatar—can grow more intense and therefore can be pushed as far as it
is in the direction of the mother-son recognition, initiatory catastrophe of
Wound and Desire (Sehnen), and the love torment after her maternal kiss
upon his breast, only because another Parsifal comes along to resolve all that
and to pursue it at another level.[82]

Syberberg, as it were, covers Parsifal's bets.

Kundry has revealed Parsifal's name to him, but it is of no concern
to him. It is as "The Pure" that he will be anointed king of the Grail;
he will assume Amfortas's functions without even once being named,
thus restoring wholeness to the Grail company, whose circle closes
round for the Last Supper, the final sacrificial meal beneath the unitary
sign of the now-recovered spear. Here Kundry is engulfed in the final
silence of death. Syberberg at this moment radically changes Wagner's
stage directions. Instead of placing the healed Amfortas at Parsifal's
knees in homage to the "redeemer," Syberberg associates Amfortas
with death by placing Kundry beside him on his deathbed, "at the
place of the Wound," in Syberberg's words. (Throughout the opera,
Syberberg in fact separates the wound from Amfortas's body, objectifies
the wound, making it a "pound of flesh," a palpitating and bloody
illustration of the knight's torment.) Kundry's taking his place now
assumes its full significance: she is indeed the locus of Amfortas's suffering. By making death the wounded knight's cure, Syberberg under-
scores a truth that Wagner chose not to see, though he may have
anticipated it. The logic of ancient tragedy entails the annihilation of
the guilty, of the marginal, of the point of suffering that has come
apart from the circle: the subject and site of this pain must be sup-
pressed; Amfortas and Kundry must both be destroyed.

Parsifal's journey, his return to the knights' domain, is completed
under the sign of black armor and in emblematic silence. The author of
Tristan ("that old Klingsor!" as Nietzsche called him) may well have
understood that completion of the Quest spells a kind of death. The
denial of the truth inherent in the severance necessary to exist and to
speak is echoed in silence, in the angelic and ecstatic anonymous jouissance of the Other Silence.

"Wagner's true genius in this work," writes Jean-Vincent Richard

---

[82]Hans-Jürgen Syberberg, Parsifal: Notes sur un film (Paris: Cahiers du Cinéma/Gal-
limard, 1982).

in a most (im)pertinent article, "is to have made us believe that we have encountered a 'human' by the name of Parsifal. Like the protagonists in Pier Paolo Pasolini's *Teorema* who never really met the Angel, not once have we chanced upon Parsifal. How could we have, since that man does not exist."[83]

If I have sought to clarify a certain problematics in *Parsifal*—one among many, as the extreme ambiguity of this work will tolerate diverse and even mutually exclusive interpretations—it is because this problematics seems to constitute the very metaphor of opera, the staging of what underpins the entire operatic "system"—the quest for a lost object and the illusion of its recovery in absolute jouissance. And if Wagner deceives himself or his audience by making us believe that that recovery is possible, his music tells us where all this will lead. No other orchestral material is so uninflected in time and meter, so little determined by them. Nowhere is the indeterminacy, the indifferentiation of sound taken to such extremes. Not content to create a spatiotemporal continuum of sound through the dissolution of rhythm (Gurnemanz explicitly states: "Time here becomes space"), Wagner goes so far as to create a continuum of *timbres:* "More than in the other works, Wagner plays here on the contrast between pure and doubled timbres. Here we *recognise* the instrument clearly in a soloist capacity—the orchestra becomes *transparent;* there, the doubling is intended to camouflage the identity of the different instruments, and by this fusion of different timbres to obtain a block sonority with a kind of imaginary continuum of timbres."[84] Nietzsche, for his part, had this to say about Wagner's music: "One walks into the sea, gradually loses one's secure footing, and finally surrenders oneself to the elements without reservation: one must *swim*. . . . [Wagner] overthrew the physiological presupposition of previous music. Swimming, floating—no longer walking and dancing."[85] Swimming, floating—or, like Ludwig II of Bavaria, dissolving—in the Other Silence.

From a strictly vocal perspective, what I have said many times about Kundry's vocal part still holds: Kundry *is* The Voice, the epitome of

[83]Jean-Vincent Richard, "L'Homme qui n'existait pas," *L'Avant-scène Opéra* 38/39: *"Parsifal"* (January–February 1982), 119.
[84]Pierre Boulez, "Approaches to Wagner," trans. John Bell, brochure notes to *Parsifal,* conducted by Pierre Boulez (Bayreuth, 1970), Deutsche Grammophon 2530 162–6.
[85]Friedrich Nietzsche, *Nietzsche contra Wagner,* in *The Portable Nietzsche,* trans. Walter Kaufmann (New York: Penguin, 1982), 666.

the vocal object; she is The Woman, locus of the Quest, whose impossible truth Amfortas discovers and Parsifal, who comes to conclude the Quest, denies.

Fifty years before Artaud's dream of a theater of cruelty, there could be heard on the stage of Bayreuth a range of procedures that would come into systematic use only with the twentieth century (in Berio, Cathy Berberian): modifications of the timbre of the singing voice; . . . transition from the sung laugh to the genuine laugh, . . . from the cried-out text to the true cry . . . and from the cry to the plaint. . . . It is perhaps no surprise to find in the musical composition of Kundry's role a direct precursor of *Sprechgesang*.[86]

This entire vocal palette unfolds with unparalleled vehemence, especially in the extraordinary final part of the Kundry-Parsifal encounter, which ends on Kundry's terrible cry as Klingsor's spellbound world collapses. The irrepressible emotion that cannot fail to grip the listener—if the singers are equal to their task—and echoes of which are heard in Claude's remarks at the Palais Garnier, has its basis here: never before in opera has the voice come so close to its object status as here in Act II, in the voice of the "nameless one." Only silence can follow the paroxysmal cries of this finale; in Act III Kundry can still produce a muffled moan, a final cry of alarm, two words—"Dienen, Dienen" (Let me serve, serve)—but that is all, despite her constant presence on the stage. Exit the word: enter silence, and, in silence, death. No other work comes as close as *Parsifal* does to being an opera of the cry and of silence.

His wandering now over, Parsifal himself enters the third act in silence, a silence signified by an extraordinary orchestral effect: the entire string section (with the exception of the double basses) swells up twice in unison and then tapers off in a very long-held note, diminuendo, for more than seven measures; a particularly illustrative example of this music of the "Other Silence" that has figured so often in these pages. And the male cry, too, is present in Wagner's last work: the entire chorus of knights cries out as the body of Titurel, the old king, is revealed. But the horror of this sight is circumvented forthwith: the pure hero, the Innocent, is there; with a touch of the now-recovered spear he abolishes chasm, fissure, suffering, all, in the ecstasy of the absolute jouissance of the Grail, without realizing that in doing so he abolishes life.

"An object—an object that man has never possessed—he comes to lack. Or perhaps he has once possessed this object in a mythic past and now has lost it. It is the same thing. The lack of the object becomes the object of lack, for lack is 'the bare necessity of life.' This lack is life-giving as long as it is not lacking."[87]

[87]P. Martin, "Pour un Perceval et son envers: La Perspective de la castration," *Lettre de l'École de la Cause Freudienne,* September–October 1982.

Lulu, or
The Angel's Cry

Klingsor to Kundry, *Parsifal,* Act II:
  Come up! Come up! To me!
  Your master calls you, nameless one,
  primaeval witch, rose of Hell!
  You were Herodias—and what else?
  Gundryggia there, Kundry here!
  Come here! Come hither! Kundry!
  Your master calls: Obey![88]

An esquire to Kundry, *Parsifal,* Act I:
  Hey, you there!
  Why do you lie there like a wild beast?

The animal tamer to Lulu, *Lulu,* Prologue:
  She as the root of all evil was created,
  To snare us, to mislead us she was fated,
  And to murder, with no clue left on the spot.
  My sweetest beast, please don't be what you're not!
  You have no right to seem a gentler creature,
  Distorting what is true in woman's nature.[89]

---

[88]Libretto translated by Lionel Salter in *Parsifal,* Pierre Boulez, dir., Deutsche Grammophon.
[89]Alban Berg, *Lulu,* trans. Arthur Jacobs (Vienna, 1977).

Lulu, I.i:
Painter: Nelly . . .
Lulu: My name is not Nelly. My name is Lulu.

Lulu, I.ii:
Schilgoch: My own little Lulu.
Lulu: You call me Lulu still!
Schilgoch: Lulu, yes. What did I ever call you but that?
Lulu: It was ages ago since my name was Lulu.
Schilgoch: What are you?
Lulu: . . . A beast . . .
Painter: Who is this you mean?
Schoen: I mean your wife!
Painter: My Eve?
Schoen: I used to call her Mignon.
Painter: I gathered her name was Nelly.
Schoen: That name came from Dr. Goll.
Painter: I called her Eve! . . .
Schoen: What her name really is I don't know.
Painter: She knows it, perhaps . . . .

Lulu, II:i:
Schoen (to Lulu):   You wretched thing, were you sent to drag me through
    the gutter to the grave? You black angel! My unavoidable tormentor! My
    joy and consolation! You hangman's noose!
Lulu: How do you like my latest dress?

A close kinship unites Kundry and Lulu in de-nomination and animality. Both of them figures of the "Eternal Feminine," of the phantasmic Woman, they go by names that men—history in Kundry's case,
successive lovers in Lulu's—have seen fit to give them. Lulu, who calls
herself a *Wunderkind,* creation's child (II.i), has neither origin nor
name. As for Kundry, the *Urteufelin,* her origin, too, is lost, in the
night of primordial mythic times. Cast from the beginning as beast or
angel—the demonic, dangerous, exterminating angel—neither Kundry nor Lulu is at this point a human woman. And despite their
reputations, they are not even seductresses. They never go out looking
for men, it is always the men who meet up with them along their way.
Kundry and Lulu merely embody the *locus* to which the men are led in
their quest and to which they come to lose their desire. Kundry and

Lulu are in this respect an ideal representation of the objective in the search for the Woman-Voice that is played out in opera. It comes as no surprise, then, to find in Lulu every facet of pure vocal expression.

But there is an essential difference between Kundry and Lulu, these two avatars of the Femme Fatale: Lulu, unlike Kundry, claims her name and speaks, first, her poignant declaration of love for Dr. Schoen (Act I):

Schoen has just sung: "I shall not permit our meeting, except in the presence of your husband." Lulu suddenly answers in *Sprechgesang:* "Of my husband . . ." Then in what may or may not be rhythmic *declamation:* "If I belong to one man in this world, then I belong to you." And now for the first time, above her voice, beyond her voice, through her voice, the most profound, most lyrical (and certainly the most Mahlerian) theme in all of opera swells up from the strings. . . . What is most striking here is the superimposition of a voice that *speaks* and an orchestra that has never been so bent on singing, so intoxicated with its own melisima.[90]

And finally her quadruple "Nein" in *Sprechgesang,* her final denial before Jack's knife, her final word before her death cry.

And with that word another line is crossed: after the Angel becomes Woman, Woman in turn becomes *a* woman, a being of flesh and blood, who speaks and desires.

Wagner had anticipated this step with Brünnhilde, the Valkyrie, virgin warrior, Wotan's daughter, who is willing to sacrifice her divinity to become a woman. He anticipates it with Kundry, too, though the ideology of the opera tends to mask it; Kundry's encounter with Parsifal in Act II is in fact anything but a seduction scene if "seduction" implies insincerity and calculation. It is indeed quite the contrary, a true love scene; the pure melodiousness of the orchestration bears this out: no antiphony, no afterthought, no friction; this might just as well be Act II of *Tristan.* But Parsifal rejects the emergence of the woman who, having revealed his name to him, now reveals herself in her desire: "Perish, miserable woman!" Kundry is lost in the cry that engulfs the fantasy. But Wagner cannot or will not hear this cry and he will consecrate the silence that follows it with the halo of redemption: murder is done, but the divine ecstasy of sacrifice abides.

[90]Étienne Barilier, *Alban Berg* (Lausanne: L'Age d'Homme, 1978).

In Lulu the line is crossed, and the truth of what is at stake appears as Horror, the horrible emptiness of the Thing: the Grail is empty, *Woman* does not exist, the Voice is a cry.

Indeed, it is as though once opera becomes woman, the Angel and all it represents can be recovered as the lost paradisiacal object only at the price of the murder of The Woman, as though the musical cry, the apogee of her singing, abolishes the woman at the moment of sacrifice and at that moment reintroduces the Angel, the Voice, in the jouissance that takes hold of the listener. But the more *Woman* becomes *a* woman, the more this lyric climax becomes the cry and the more this jouissance approaches horror.

Let there be no mistake: nothing is less liberating than that cry, because it does not make The Woman *a* woman; rather, it announces her return to the beatific circle of the angels, it marks the ultimate uprooting of what was properly human, feminine, and desiring before the ecstatic recovery of angelic transparency: a true experience of dread because what is revealed beyond this transparency is emptiness, the Unnameable—a void that human beings have always sought to bridge by bringing to it their whole array of divine beings.

In *Lulu* Berg exposes the violence of this truth, after having broached it in *Wozzeck*. But like Wagner (though without his ideological baggage), Berg fails to see his insight through. And how could he, without calling into question the entire system of opera, without making opera impossible? Nicolas Poussin said of Caravaggio that he had been born to destroy painting. Can it also be said that Alban Berg was born to destroy opera? He seems, at all events, to have taken every precaution to avoid that outcome: Lulu's terrible death cry under Jack the Ripper's knife is screamed out from the wings and is covered forthwith by the orchestra's fortissimo. With the Countess of Geschwitz's death song—Lulu's adoring companion, too, has fallen under Jack's blade—the opera retreats in returning to the purest of melodies, one that might have been sung by Isolde herself:

"Lulu! *My angel!* Appear once more to me! For I am near, I'm always near. For evermore!"

Frank Wedekind, author of the two plays that Berg combines for his libretto, ended his text with the word "Malediction!" This "malediction" was eliminated by Berg. Friedrich Cehra, who completed the orchestration of the work after the composer's death, reinstated the word for the complete three-act 1979 Paris production, perhaps overstepping Berg's desire but remaining faithful nonetheless to his trajectory.

Still, beyond his final resistance, Alban Berg makes it arrestingly clear that the beauty of the lyric flights of bel canto was—and here we rejoin Rilke—merely "the beginning of the terror" into which Lulu falls as she utters her cry. And this is the outcome that "somewhere" we were waiting for:

However monstrous the tearing apart it signifies, however terrifying the surprise it occasions at the end of Act III [Lulu's cry], psychologically and musically, could not be more expected, more anticipated. The surprise that this cataclysm provokes is all the more fearsome for its being expected, for its satisfying the unconscious desire that Berg engenders in us: all through the opera, these *tenuti,* these pauses, these waverings on two or three notes, these arrested tempos have heralded a violent event, a catastrophe. Now it is a certainty. There is "recognition" in our start of terror. (Even for those who know this work well, moreover, the "surprise" effect does not diminish. Quite the contrary. So it is in Greek tragedy, where the fact of knowing the outcome in no way hinders the spectators' anguished participation in the characters' fate.).[91]

This cry, were it not blood-red, could be blue, the color of the blue note.

Uttered from the wings, this cry is of course muffled; but at the same time it becomes pure vocal object in which Lulu immaterializes: "Lulu! My angel!" the Countess can now sing, and so indeed she is. But the profound horror of this transmutation by which, in the crucible of the cry, the woman again becomes angel has been revealed. In this sense, one can say that Lulu's cry literally overturns the entire operatic system: the jouissance felt as tearful and trembling joy at the sound of beauty is overturned as well, and topples into the shudders and tears of pure horror.

The only exit from this fantasy now ripped apart by Jack's knife is through the reintroduction of words. This is the function of the quasi-recitative, of Jack's almost pure unmusicalized speech that immediately

[91]Ibid.

follows the catastrophe: "Das war ein Stück Arbeit!" (That was quite a job!), he exclaims.

"That was a piece work!" the translation might also go, and working our way back through the etymology of the word, we might conclude: "That was opera!"[92]

[92]"Opera," from the Latin *opus*, work.

The Eternal Return

Lulu, the end of opera? Some will say so, despite the numerous and no less important works that have come after it. Paradoxically, there may be some connection between the idea that opera is a dead genre, finished, passé, and what has been called a renewed infatuation with the lyric arts. If it is indeed true that the opera fan's jouissance plays itself out in the quest for a lost object, and if the locus of this quest is construed as lost, then the quest for this jouissance must always be embarked upon anew. Opera's "new fans" devote themselves to what they consider a genre of the past, which may explain their curious interest in the resurrection of little-known works, particularly those that date from the beginnings of the genre. It may also explain the infatuation, in an era of high-fidelity sound reproduction, with old wax masters and first pressings, behind whose pops and scratches and hiss the passionate opera fan tries to recapture the essence of music and voice. A perfect illustration, incidentally, of the idea that the phonic object, the vocal object, is above and beyond pure sonority. This may also help account for audiences' relative indifference to contemporary composition, at least to some extent. In this regard it is interesting to observe how today's composers, too, sometimes play on references to a past genre in their own creations. Luciano Berio's *La vera storia* is a magnificent illustration of this tendency. This kind of reference seems to underlie the lyricism of this most contemporary of works, and perhaps may explain why *La vera storia* is one of the very few contemporary operas to achieve popular success.

But going beyond the limit, or at least approaching it so closely, had to have some effect. A certain disinvestment from the purely vocal dimension has clearly come about. The new appeal of opera often draws on purely visual values, such as those exploited by opera films;

or on the function of opera as a repository of meaning, of psychological or socio-ideological meanings that directors try hard to bring out. Significantly, many serious opera fans take strong exception to the opera film and are quite wary of or at least actively indifferent to the question of opera stagings, precisely because they feel that film and even the stage tend to obscure opera's specifically vocal dimension and can even destroy it altogether; witness that supreme contradiction, the silent-film opera.

But these fans and contemporary composers can rest assured. As long as there are human beings and therefore language, the quest for the vocal object will continue. The fantasy and its cultural expression that both organize and regulate this object may be modified, displaced, and diversified, may leave the lyric stage for the sports arenas and stadiums of the world, but through it all they will endure, in accordance with the deep structures whose outlines I have tried to trace in these pages.

Thus, if one were to examine the phenomenon of the Beatles, for example, from the perspective of this book, one could find there all the key elements that have been described in these pages, perhaps with a few modifications. The same appearance of a jouissance that looks for all the world like torment (turn off the sound on the film of the Shea Stadium concert in New York: the crowd shots—filled with raving fans, sobbing adolescents, screaming, grasping at the air, wringing their hands, collapsing in the *"petite mort"* of a swoon—will convince you that what you are observing is paroxysmal grief, like the grief that gripped the mourners at the funeral of Oum Keltoum in Cairo, rather than a concert audience's enthusiasm. Turn the sound back on: you will be struck by those voices of the Beatles, very high voices, almost head voices, a genuine call for the cry, a call that is heard and resoundingly answered by the thousands of cries and piercing screams of teenage girls. Therein lies the great difference between this situation and that of opera: in rock concerts of this sort, a type of quasi-identification with the vocal object occurs at the level of the spectator, or, to be precise, at the level of the young female spectator, as she herself becomes cry. A kind of jouissance is let loose, requiring chain-link fences and police to contain it. These are things that have yet to be seen at the opera.

Even reference to the divine can be found in phenomena of this kind, and not only in the emergence of the term "idol" to designate these "divas" of rock and roll. Remember John Lennon's claim, scandalous at the time, that "we're more popular than Jesus now." Why not the queen of England, or Napoleon, or any other world figure from this century or from the pages of history? As it happened, what came to his mind was divinity, God in his second person, Jesus Christ, doomed to sacrifice, to the cry. Bear in mind here, moreover, the tragic fate of John Lennon, murdered by a delusional fan.

But even though many other forms have come into being offering jouissance in the Voice, that in itself poses no threat to opera, in part because only opera, as a dramatic form, reproduces and reinvests the structure of the vocal fantasy.

Let us now return to the steps of the Palais Garnier on that January night, with Anne, Étienne, Renaud, Claude, and Guy speaking of their passion for opera and, now at the end of the interview, of their passion for Richard Wagner—an idol to some, an abomination to others.

Claude: To go to the opera is . . . to listen to life?
Anne: I'm absolutely certain of that.
Guy: Oh, yes! I feel that opera is a little like Plato, who turns to myth to explain things and stumbles upon the truth, who was able to explain the truth only through myth. I feel a little bit that opera is the same: a sort of higher truth that can't be expressed any other way, a sort of metaphor that is truly . . . It's because it's the most artificial of all arts that it is the truest.
Claude: The simplest, too. The voice . . . In the beginning, the first musical instrument was the voice.
Anne: Italian opera made me understand that.
Guy: For example, that's what I think Wagner understood to the *n*th degree at Bayreuth with the music coming from out of the ground: you feel as though it's a music coming from the body. It's unique, and you feel it there, you only understand once you're over there. And something . . . a kind of truth appears, a physical truth . . . an intellectual truth, even.
Claude: What do you mean by an intellectual truth?
Guy: When I see the *Ring* . . . something happens intellectually and at the same time emotionally. I'm not saying with every opera . . . *Tristan* for me is completely different. But *Parsifal* and the *Ring*, these are

extremely precise intellectual constructions. Something about them fascinates me.

Renaud: I'm beginning to notice something. We were speaking about opera and then gradually we got on to Wagner and soon we'll have been talking about nothing but Wagner for an hour. I find that a little . . . amusing. Take almost any debate, any book on opera: it's going to be talking about opera and then you'll see that halfway through the book they'll start talking about Wagner and when they're finished, they'll still be talking about Wagner! Really . . . Wagner always manages to dominate the discussion!

Guy: Something very surprising is taking place in Italy with opera now and soon it's going to happen in France, and that, I think, if it ever happens, is going to be fascinating: the second monster is coming!

M.P.: Which is?

Guy: The *Saint John Passion* as an opera. It was performed at Venice.

Anne: It's Wagnerian, too, in a way.

Guy: Precisely.

Renaud: Absolutely! Is Wagner the god of opera or what?

Guy: But to get back to Wagner, you have to admit he had great P.R.

Anne: And that's kind of troubling!

Guy: Bayreuth is a monster advertising agency! And then we're also susuptible to Wagner's mystical side, we fall into the trap. Sometimes I wonder . . . if it weren't for Cosima, would he be such a cult figure? Isn't it because of everything that was cooked up at the end of the nineteenth century? And now it's become self-perpetuating. . . . It's really a fantastic advertising coup!

Claude: I think about Wagner the same way I think about Puccini or Verdi. He's a composer first of all, and that's it. I distinguish completely between what I listen to . . . I listen to Wagner, but I also listen to Verdi. I just can't fall in with that Wagnerian indoctrination. And you, it completely fascinates you. I have to say that whenever I've gone to Bayreuth, it's been with Guy, and when we get to Bayreuth, we have to go on a festival tour so that . . .

Guy: I can't help it. I need to experience the building physically. And don't go saying it doesn't get to you, I know it does!

Claude: Listen. I get the shivers, it's true, but it's because of something I'm remembering, because the first time when the lights go down and you're there completely in the dark and the music begins . . . It's not like Renaud in his bedroom but it's the same sort of thing. You feel an incredible emotion. Then you remember . . . It may be emotional recall, but I don't have this fascination, this urgency for Wagner as a place or a figure. You've never once gone to the festival without stopping by Wahnfried.[93] Now, Wahnfried is very nice. I saw it once. It's interesting for me because I want to know about Wagner's life, but in an objective way, just as I'd go to see Verdi's house.

Guy: I find it extraordinary to be in his living room listening to music.

Claude: That has its pleasant side, intellectually, but beyond that, it doesn't interest me. When I go to the festival, I don't go to commune with Wagner!

Guy: But I don't commune with Wagner!

Claude: Listen, sometimes I wonder!

Guy: I don't commune with Wagner. It's a need . . . to retrace a kind of trajectory . . . There's also a kind of initiation. You have to remember what Bayreuth meant to me for years! Because really, when I first began to listen to Wagner, Bayreuth seemed very far away, an impossible place, and the first time I went there, it was something! It was truly the greatest moment of my life! Which wasn't the case for you when you went there. The greatest moment of my life, I haven't gotten over it, I still haven't. That being said, I fully admit that I'm a victim of the Wagner machine, I'm quite aware of it.

Claude: As a person, Wagner holds no fascination whatsoever for me.

Guy: To shake Friedelind Wagner's hand—that does something to me!

Anne: And you're not embarrassed?

Guy: Yes, it's embarrassing, I know, I know. Friedelind is the grand-daughter—Wolfgang Wagner's[94] sister—and she looks, she looks like Wagner.

Claude: Give her a beret and it's Wagner!

Guy: It's really him, it's incredible, incredible! But you see, it's not the fetish aspect. It's—it's like coming home, finding something that belongs to me in my own right! I remember, I remember arriving by train at Bayreuth, I remember . . . I remember . . .

"I remember, I remember . . ." The cassette breaks off on these words. A coincidence, naturally, but one that points up the nostalgia that runs through so much of the discussion that night, like an evoca-

[93]Richard Wagner's residence at Bayreuth, now the Richard Wagner Museum.
[94]Richard Wagner's grandson and currently the festival director.

tion of the lost thing the endless and painful quest is always supposed to recover. And of that original Thing, may it not be said that those rare and fleeting moments of jouissance evoked throughout these pages signal the instant in which it is possible to experience its impossible recovery?

Selected Bibliography

Adorno, Theodor W. *In Search of Wagner.* Trans. Rodney Livingstone. London: New Left Books, 1981.

Andreossi, Victor. *L'Esprit du chant.* Geneva: Perret-Gentil, 1949. Rpt. Les Introuvables. Plan de la Tour: Éditions d'Aujourd'hui, 1979.

Azouri, François. "Le Plaisir d'une révolution." *L'Avant-scène Opéra* 23 (September–October 1979), 59–62.

Barilier, Étienne. *Alban Berg.* Lausanne: L'Age d'Homme, 1978.

Barraud, Henri. *Les Cinq Grands Opéras.* Paris: Seuil, 1972.

———. Musical and textual notes to *Die Zauberflöte.* *L'Avant-scène Opéra* 1 (January–February 1976).

———. Musical and textual notes to *Orfeo.* *L'Avant-scène Opéra* 5 (September–October 1976), 23–61.

Bedier, Joseph. *Le Roman de Tristan et Iseut.* Paris: Union Générale d'Éditions, 1981.

Bégin, Marc. "Kundry, l'anti-diva." *Musique en jeu* 31 (n.d.).

Berg, Alban. *Écrits.* Paris: Christian Bourgois, 1985.

Berlioz, Hector. *A travers chants.* Édition du Centenaire. Paris: Gründ, 1971.

———. *Les Soirées de l'orchestre.* Paris: Michel Levy-Frères, 1854. Rpt. Paris: Stock, 1980.

Bertau, Karl. "Tristan and Narcissus." *Bayreuth Festival Program,* 1982, 78–91.

Boucourechliev, A. Musical and textual notes to *Das Rheingold.* *L'Avant-scène Opéra* 6/7 (November–December 1976), 55–137.

Bouju, Caroline. "Rosalie Levasseur, la créatrice d'Alceste à Paris." *L'Avant-scène Opéra* 73 (March 1985), 92–93.

Boulez, Pierre. "Approaches to Wagner." Trans. John Bell. Brochure notes to *Parsifal,* Pierre Boulez, conductor (Bayreuth, 1970).

Bourgeois, Jacques. *L'Opéra des origines à demain.* Paris: Julliard, 1983.

Brunschwig, Jacques. "L'Hymen de Suzanne." *L'Avant-scène Opéra* 21 (May–June 1979), 126–30.

Burney, Charles. *The Present State of Music in France and Italy.* 1773. Facsimile rpt. New York: Broude Bros., 1969.

Chailley, Jacques. *La Flûte Enchantée, opéra maçonnique.* Paris: Laffont, 1975. Rpt. Les Introuvables. Plan de la Tour: Éditions d'Aujourd'hui, 1985.

——. *40,000 ans de musique.* Rpt. Les Introuvables. Plan de la Tour: Éditions d'Aujourd'hui, 1976.

Chrétien de Troyes. *Perceval ou Le Roman du Graal.* Paris: Gallimard, 1974.

Clément, Catherine. *Opera, or The Undoing of Women.* Trans. Betsy Wing. Minneapolis: University of Minnesota Press, 1988.

Corbin, Henry. *L'Homme et son ange.* Paris: Fayard, 1983.

Didier-Weill, Alain. "Quatre Temps subjectivants de la musique." *Ornicar?* 8 (1976–1977).

Felman, Shoshana. *The Literary Speech Act: Don Juan with J. L. Austin, or Seduction in Two Languages.* Trans. Catherine Porter. Ithaca: Cornell University Press, 1983.

Fernandez, Dominique. *Porporino, or The Secrets of Naples.* Trans. Eileen Finletter. New York: Morrow, 1976.

Fourquet, Jean. *Wolfram d'Eschenbach et le conte del Graal.* Paris: Belles Lettres, 1938.

Frappier, Jean. *Chrétien de Troyes et le mythe du Graal.* Paris: Société d'Édition d'Enseignement Supérieur, 1979.

Freud, Sigmund. *Totem and Taboo.* Trans. A. A. Brill. New York: Vintage, 1946.

——. *Three Essays on the Theory of Sexuality.* Trans. James Strachey. New York: Basic Books, 1962.

——. "Esquisse d'une psychologie scientifique." In *La Naissance de la psychanalyse.* Paris: Presses Universitaires de France, 1979.

Gaumy, Christian. "Le Chant des castrats." *Opera International,* December 1984–January 1985.

Goldet, Stéphane. Musical and textual commentary to *Wozzeck. L'Avant-scène Opéra* 36 (September–October 1981), 19–85.

Gregor-Dellin, Martin. *Richard Wagner.* Paris: Fayard, 1981.

Guilain, Elisabeth. "Rousseau analyste de Gluck." *L'Avant-scène Opéra* 73 (March 1985), 85–91.

Hocquard, Jean-Victor. *La Pensée de Mozart.* Paris: Seuil, 1958.

——. Musical and textual notes to *Don Giovanni. L'Avant-scène Opéra* 24 (November–December 1979); 35–125.

Jameux, Dominique. Musical and textual notes to *Tristan und Isolde. L'Avant-scène Opéra* 34/35 (July–August 1981), 41–146.

Jankélevitch, Vladimir. *La Musique et l'ineffable.* Paris: Seuil, 1983.

Jouve, Pierre-Jean, and Michel Fano. *Wozzeck, d'Alban Berg.* Paris: 10/18, 1964.

Juranville, Alain. *Lacan et la philosophie.* Paris: Presses Universitaires de France, 1984.

Kierkegaard, Søren. *Either/Or.* Ed. and trans. Howard V. Hong and Edna H. Hong. Princeton: Princeton University Press, 1987.

Kintzler, Catherine. *Jean-Philippe Rameau: Splendeur et naufrage de l'esthétique du plaisir à l'âge classique.* Paris: Sycomore, 1983.

Kobbé, Gustave. *Kobbé's Complete Opera Book.* 9th ed. New York: Putnam, 1976.

Krop, J.-P. "Le Sillon de Gottfried." *L'Avant-scène Opéra* 34/35 (July–August 1981), 13–17.

Lacan, Jacques. *Le Séminaire, Livre VII: L'Éthique de la psychanalyse.* Paris: Seuil, 1986.

——. *Le Séminaire, Livre XI: Les Quatre Concepts fondamentaux de la psychanalyse.* Paris: Seuil, 1973.

——. *Le Séminaire, Livre XX: Encore.* Paris: Seuil, 1975.

Lévi-Strauss, Claude. "De Crétien de Troyes à Richard Wagner." *Bayreuth Festival Programme,* 1975. Rpt. in *L'Avant-scène Opéra* 38/39 (January–February 1982), 8–15.

Maehder, Jürgen. "A Mantle of Sound for the Night—On the Score of *Tristan and Isolde.*" *Bayreuth Festival Program,* 1982, 92–100.

Massin, Jean, and Brigitte Massin. *Wolfgang Amadeus Mozart.* Paris: Fayard, 1970.

——, eds. *Histoire de la musique occidentale.* Paris: Messidor/Temps Actuels, 1983.

Millot, Catherine. *Horsexe: Essai sur le transsexualisme.* Paris: Point Hors Ligne, 1983.

Milner, Jean-Claude. *L'Amour de la langue.* Paris: Seuil, 1978.

Nietzsche, Friedrich. *The Birth of Tragedy.* In *The Basic Writings of Nietzsche,* trans. and ed. Walter Kaufmann. New York: Modern Library, 1968.

——. *Nietzsche contra Wagner.* In *The Portable Nietzsche,* trans. Walter Kaufmann. New York: Penguin, 1982 .

Noiray, Michel. "Les Éléments d'une réforme." *L'Avant-scène Opéra* 73 (March 1985), 20–25.

——. Musical and textual notes to *Alceste.* *L'Avant-scène Opéra* 73 (March 1985), 31–91.

Partch, Harry. *Genesis of a Music.* New York: Da Capo, 1974.

Pommier, Gérard. *D'une logique de la psychose.* Paris: Point Hors Ligne, 1982.

Pucher, Georges. Musical and textual commentary to *Salome.* *L'Avant-scène Opéra* 29 (January–February 1983), 53–108.

Reik, Theodor. *Ritual Psycho-analytic Studies.* Trans. Douglas Bryan. London: Hogarth, 1931.

Rey-Flaud, Henri. *La Névrose courtoise.* Paris: Navarin, 1983.

Richard, Jean-Vincent. "L'Homme qui n'existait pas." *L'Avant-scène Opéra* 38/39 (January–February 1982), 117–119.

Rilke, Rainer Maria. *Les Élégies de Duino.* Paris: Aubier-Montaigne, 1943.

Roland-Manuel, Claude, ed. *Histoire de la musique.* Paris: Gallimard, 1960.

Rouget, Gilbert. *La Musique et la transe.* Paris: Gallimard, 1980

Rousseau, Jean-Jacques. *Essay on the Origin of Language.* Trans. John H. Moran. In *On the Origin of Language.* Chicago: University of Chicago Press, 1966.

———. *Écrits sur la musique.* Paris: Stock, 1979.

Sans, Edward. "L'Amour dans *Tristan,* ou Le Romantisme surdimensionné." *L'Avant-scène Opéra* 34/35 (July–August 1981), 18–27.

Schopenhauer, Arthur. *The World as Will and Representation.* Trans. E. F. J. Payne. New York: Dover, 1969.

Stratz, Claude, cond. *Le "Lucio Silla" de Mozart.* Brussels: Beba, 1984.

Syberberg, Hans-Jürgen. *Parsifal: Notes sur un film.* Paris: Cahiers du Cinéma/Gallimard, 1982.

Tosi, Pierfrancesco. *Observations on the Florid Song.* Trans. J. E. Gaillard. 1743. Rpt. London: William Reeves, 1926.

Tranchefort, François-René. *L'Opéra.* Vol. 1, *D' "Orféo" à "Tristan";* vol. 2, *De "Tristan" à nos jours.* Paris: Seuil, 1978.

Vernant, Jean-Pierre, and Pierre Vidal-Naquet. *Myth and Tragedy in Ancient Greece.* Trans. Janet Lloyd. Atlantic Highlands, N. J.: Humanities Press, 1981.

Wagner, Richard. *Richard Wagner's Prose Works.* 9 vols. Trans. William Ashton Ellis. 1893. Rpt. St. Clair Shores, Mich.: Scholarly Press, 1972.

———. *Ma Vie.* Paris: Buchet-Chastel, 1978.

Wedekind, Frank. *Lulu.* French adaptation by P.-J. Jouve. Lausanne: L'Age d'Homme, 1983.

Wolfram von Eschenbach. *Parzival (Perceval le Gallois).* Trans. Ernest Tonnelat. Paris: Aubier-Montaigne, 1977.

See also the monthly magazine *L'Avant-scène Opéra,* each issue of which analyzes one opera; and the magazine *Opera International.*

Index

Library of Congress Cataloging-in-Publication Data

Poizat, Michel, 1947–
    [Opéra, ou, Le cri de l'ange. English]
    The angel's cry : beyond the pleasure principle in opera / Michel Poizat ; translated
by Arthur Denner.
        p. cm.
    Translation of: L'Opéra, ou, Le cri de l'ange.
    Includes bibliographical references and index.
    ISBN 0–8014–2388–0 (acid-free paper).
    1. Opera. I. Title.
ML1700.P6513   1992
782.1—dc20   91–55532